Using Tradesmen in France

A Practical Guide and Glossary for
English-Speaking Homeowners

Using Tradesmen in France

A Practical Guide and Glossary for
English-Speaking Homeowners

Duncan and Lesley Webster

THE CROWOOD PRESS

First published in 2009 by
The Crowood Press Ltd
Ramsbury, Marlborough
Wiltshire SN8 2HR

www.crowood.com

© Duncan and Lesley Webster 2009

All rights reserved. No part of this publication may be reproduced or transmitted in any form or by any means, electronic or mechanical, including photocopy, recording, or any information storage and retrieval system, without permission in writing from the publishers.

British Library Cataloguing-in-Publication Data
A catalogue record for this book is available from the British Library.

ISBN 978 1 84797 129 6

Disclaimer
The authors and the publisher do not accept any responsibility in any manner whatsoever for any error or omission, or any loss, damage, injury, adverse outcome, or liability of any kind incurred as a result of the use of any of the information contained in this book, or reliance upon it. If in doubt about any aspect of using tradesmen and women in France readers are advised to seek professional advice.

Photograph credits
AFCD – supplier and installer of automatic gates and doors
CHAUVINEAU Olivier – electrician
Habitat Naturel – a bimonthly publication devoted to eco-friendly housing and the use of renewable energy sources
Sarl Ma-Sy – plasterer
Sarl THERAUD Patrick – heating engineer and plumber

All other photographs were taken by the authors.

Frontispiece: A *menuisier*. (*Habitat Naturel*)

Typeset by Manila Typesetting Company

Printed and bound in Singapore by Craft Print International Ltd.

Contents

1 Introduction	7
2 What Is an *Artisan*?	12
3 Getting an Estimate	35
4 Checking an *Artisan*'s Credentials	51
5 Accepting an Estimate	61
6 Obtaining Planning Permission	67
7 Meeting Legal Obligations	83
8 Understanding VAT and Other Financial Issues	91
9 What Are My Rights?	100
10 French Language Skills – Or Lack of Them!	115
Appendix I: Useful Websites	125
Appendix II: Conversion Tables for Imperial and Metric Measures	130
Glossary	
How to Use the Glossary	134
French–English: Arranged by Category	135
English–French: Arranged Alphabetically	163
Index	191

Dedication

To Gordon and Reg

Acknowledgements/Remerciements

Our heartfelt thanks go to all our neighbours and other friends we have made locally, not only for their warm welcome to our new life here, but also for their practical help and encouragement with this book – and with our on-going building projects: Jean-Louis and Liliane, Jean-François, Marcel and Thérèse, Henry and Michelle, Jean-Pierre and Annie, André and Marie-France, Jacqueline and the late Gilles, Gérard and Jacqueline, and Patrick and Gaëlle. Thanks also to Ian and Penny for their input, and to all our family and friends on both sides of the Channel for their support.

Introduction

How and Why This Book Was Written

It was snowing heavily early that October morning in 2003 as we drove off the overnight ferry to begin our new lives in France. The roads were treacherous and our previously high spirits slumped considerably as we crawled at a snail's pace southwards to our new home.

We had decided to rent an unfurnished house at first so that we could test the water, before taking the plunge and buying a property. We chanced upon an eighteenth-century winemaker's house in a small hamlet which appeared to meet all our requirements. Because of the complicated French inheritance laws, it was jointly owned by some ten descendants of the original owners, who could not agree to sell the house outright and so had decided to let it. Having viewed the property with an estate agent and, more importantly, having been interviewed and approved by the head of the owning family, we duly signed the lease. We returned to our house in England and started to pack up our belongings ready for the move. Then we received an email from the landlord enclosing instructions for the upkeep of the house and its gardens – a closely-typed, twelve-page document full of technical vocabulary – totally in French, of course.

Although, between us, we were reasonably fluent in French (in other words, Lesley had studied the language to degree level and Duncan was capable of ordering a beer at the bar!), we soon discovered that we had a lot to learn about owning and running a house in France. It took a full day's work with our 'best friend' (a French-English dictionary) to translate enough of our landlord's document to understand what was expected of us, from maintaining the parquet floors in tip-top condition to having the chimney swept annually.

We eventually arrived at the house in time for a site meeting with the estate agent and the landlord. After we had been painstakingly shown every nook and cranny, every idiosyncratic feature (including practical demonstrations of how to use all the door keys), and agreed a detailed inventory under the watchful eye of the local *huissier* (a legal officer, without a real English equivalent), the removal men arrived and started to unload our belongings.

The following day, when we were finally alone and able to explore our new home at liberty, we realized that there were many opportunities for things to go

Our first home in France, a rented property that looked idyllic but was to need a lot of maintenance.

wrong – and, of course, they did. Fortunately, our landlord, although somewhat pedantic, was fiercely proud of his family home and had made it very clear that, should we have any problems, we were to contact him immediately – we can still recite his telephone number by heart.

It was only then that we fully realized the extent of what we had done – closed down our British business, sold our house and said goodbye to England – an awful lot to reflect upon (although a bottle of Champagne did help somewhat).

After such a stressful forty-eight hours, Lesley felt in need of a relaxing soak in the massive, nineteenth-century bath. Half an hour later, Duncan, who was reading quietly downstairs, was perturbed to hear the sound of running water in the next room. He rushed into the hall to see water cascading through the ceiling straight on to the immaculate parquet floor. Although not a DIY expert, Duncan knows enough about basic plumbing to understand that the water is meant to go down the plug-hole, via a hidden network of pipes, to wherever it is meant to drain, so he shouted to Lesley to put the plug back in – quickly. Both of us were quite surprised to see in the hall just how much water a bath can hold.

When we telephoned the landlord with some apprehension the following morning he did not seem unduly surprised. Obviously, we were not the first to experience this problem, even though it had not been noted in our instructions. The landlord said that he would contact a plumber and arrange for the necessary repairs. And so we met our first French *artisan*.

We had always associated the word *artisan* with craftsmen (and women) who make things by hand, such as potters, needlewomen and wood turners. In France, however, *les artisans du bâtiment* refers to skilled tradesmen, such as bricklayers, electricians, joiners, plasterers . . . and plumbers. Like many of his calling, M. Robinet was a cheerful, friendly fellow who knew the property well and soon had the problem solved. Fortunately, he required little help from us, as he spoke not a word of English and, despite Lesley's fluency in French, a plumbing vocabulary had not been included on the syllabus either at school or college.

We stayed in that first house for nine months, during which we became quite friendly with the plumber. We also became acquainted with the roofer, the locksmith and the joiner, and realized that our communication difficulties with M. Robinet were not unique.

Our months in rented accommodation had proved to us that we did not want to buy an old property in need of extensive renovation, and so we purchased a house that was only thirty years old but, sadly, had been poorly maintained for the last ten. After an informal survey conducted by an English friend (surveys are not a normal procedure in France), we saw that it needed quite a lot of work. We drew up a list of priorities, an ambitious, but, we felt, achievable blueprint to transform our rather sad little house into a happy home. This formidable list formed the basis of a 'five-year plan', structured so that we would not have to live on a permanent building site.

The first task was a complete overhaul of the unsafe electrical wiring and the replacement of the thirty-year-old fuse-boxes with a properly-protected distribution board. As mains gas is available in our town, we decided to have it installed so that we could update the somewhat unreliable, oil-fired, central heating boiler with a more efficient (and cost-effective), gas-fired condensing model. At the same time, it seemed sensible, as the house is in a very chalky area (good for the vines but not for the kettle), also to have a water softener installed.

All this was achieved in year one. The following years saw the installation of a completely new kitchen, bathroom and cloakroom, along with several other smaller projects. During this time, not only did we learn much more French vocabulary related to houses and the building trade, but also realized that construction techniques and working practices are often radically different from those in Britain. Indeed, they can even vary between the different regions of France due to such factors as the climate and the availability of local materials. In addition, we were sadly lacking in DIY skills. As a result, we soon became dependent on the services of our local *artisans*, very few of whom spoke any English whatsoever. They included cabinet-makers, electricians, heating engineers, joiners, locksmiths, masons, plasterers, roofers and tilers, not to mention gate-installers, gardeners, tree surgeons – and even a professional musician. The idea of any form of privacy soon went out of the *fenêtre*.

This book is the result of our experiences. As each project progressed, we kept notes and photographs. One day, while chatting to some expat friends, it became clear that we were sitting on a treasure trove of knowledge, and so the first seed that led to the publication of this book was sown. As it began to germinate, we spoke to more and more homeowners, all of whom seemed to have at least one anecdote of praise or horror regarding their *artisanal* experience. This demonstrates that, first, it isn't just us, and, secondly, it isn't just our region – the contents to a greater or lesser degree hold true throughout France.

The book is designed to provide practical help to fellow English-speaking homeowners in France – people like you, we hope.

Our Sources of Information

As well as illustrating our and other expats' experiences anecdotally the book contains a wealth of factual, legal and commercial information relating to having all aspects of building work carried out to your property in France, and how, if the system is used correctly, it can be of great advantage to you. Of course, we also describe how trying to side-step the regulations can be a recipe for disaster. We use the word 'factual' deliberately, as our research in the twelve months leading up to the publication of the book has revealed significant areas of publicly available misinformation – not necessarily, we hasten to add, spread maliciously but rather through lack of knowledge. The main culprit for this is, perhaps not surprisingly, the Internet. Duncan, on one of his strolls down memory lane to his Boy Scout days remembers the adage that an axe is a good servant, but a bad master – and so, we feel, is the Internet. There is no doubt that there is a wealth of valuable information to be gleaned online, as long as you sort the wheat from the chaff. We have found, however, that a number of sites, and particularly those targeting expats, seem to transform opinions and second-hand stories into hard fact, and a chain of Chinese whispers can often be identified when attempting to get to the truth-based reality. For this reason, the factual content of the book has been taken, translated and interpreted from its root source in French, whether it be the currently applicable legislation or commercially accepted practices.

Anyone who has been through the process of purchasing land or property in France will know that the French are world champions when it comes to bureaucracy (after all they did invent the word). Ever since Napoleon established his *Code* to record the laws relating to virtually every aspect of French life, so everything has been and, as you will have probably noticed, still is, recorded in writing. This can at times be frustrating, but the big advantage for us is that, if you know where to look, you can establish the true state of affairs without having to rely on rumour. We love and constantly use the Internet, but merely advise that where French law is concerned it should be treated with some caution.

What's In the Book?

We start by examining the roles of the various types of *artisan* and the rules under which they operate legally – and why it is inadvisable to utilize the thriving black economy. You will find advice on who to use for what, how to find them and then approach them for an estimate. Having agreed a price and terms for your project, we tell you what to expect before, during and after the work is carried out, and how to deal with any problems. The chapter on the various financial incentives that are available for house projects could help you to save money. At the very least, we hope we can help you to avoid what could be expensive mistakes.

Chapter 10 gives some tips and advice regarding the use of the French language and the level of linguistic skills you may find necessary when dealing with non-English-speaking tradesmen. This is followed by two appendices. First, there is a directory of some websites which we have found useful, including those that have provided us with much of the factual information for the book. Inevitably, rules and regulations are constantly evolving and there may well have been changes since it went to press. By consulting the official websites listed you can verify the latest information. Secondly, a series of conversion tables shows the multiplication factors necessary to convert from imperial measures to metric and vice versa.

The second part of the book consists of a comprehensive cross-referenced glossary of many of the technical terms that you may encounter, along with a selection of useful 'SOS' phrases that can easily be referred to in times of domestic crisis. If you lend or rent your property, the book could prove invaluable to short-term tenants who experience unforeseen problems (plumbing or otherwise).

You may also find the book helpful when trying to explain to the friendly, but bewildered, local *artisan* that your super new kitchen should include a waste disposal unit but your French pronunciation isn't up to *broyeur d'ordures* – just point to the entry in the book. And, if you are a DIY enthusiast, the book will provide an extensive and easy to use household lexicon, for example when you need to visit the *quincaillier* for *un clou de cent cinquante millimètres* (to buy a six-inch nail from the ironmonger).

2
What Is an *Artisan*?

> ### *Artisan* or *Artisane*?
> The use of the masculine gender throughout the book should not be taken to imply that there are no female *artisanes*. Although there are not yet great numbers of them, more and more women are entering many of the traditionally male trades. We use the masculine form simply for the sake of convenience and to avoid confusion.

In its most general meaning, the word *artisan* is used to describe a worker skilled in a particular trade or craft. In France, being the home of bureaucracy, there is, of course, an official listing of trades in which *artisans* may work, covering many diverse industry sectors. Its 250 entries range from an ambulance driver to a taxidermist, and include such eclectic trades as butchers, cobblers, hairdressers, jewellers, and tailors, to name but a few. This book is, however, devoted to those in the building trade, and so we will confine ourselves to this particular sector.

The legal definition of an *entreprise artisanale* is, quite simply, a company employing fewer than ten people, whose business is devoted to one of the defined 250 trades. By law, any such companies are obliged to register in the trades directory (*Répertoire des Métiers*) administered by the local Chamber of Trade (*Chambre des Métiers*).

The term *artisan*, however, not only indicates that a person works in a particular trade, but also that he has a certain level of skills and/or practical experience. It should be used only by individual tradesmen or by the directors of a company, who have either been registered in the Chamber of Trade's directory for at least six years or who have a recognized vocational qualification. They are entitled to use a distinctive blue logo.

An *artisan* becomes a *maître artisan* (master tradesman) after two years' practical experience if he has a superior vocational qualification in his trade or when he has been registered with the Chamber of Trade for ten years. The logo then changes to a red one.

> ### A Brief Description of Vocational Qualifications
>
> The entry-level qualifications for an *artisan* are the CAP (*Certificat d'Aptitude Professionnelle*) or the BEP (*Brevet d'Études Professionnelles*) in a specified trade. These can be acquired either at a vocational training school or through an apprenticeship contract and qualify the recipient as a skilled worker. He may then choose to study further for a BAC PRO (*Baccalauréat Professionnel*), or combine study with on-the-job training for a BP (*Brevet Professionnel*) or a BTS (*Brevet de Technicien Supérieur*). The French building industry offers some 75,000 apprenticeship contracts each year. These take the form of practical training working with an experienced tradesman, alternating with a theory course at a centre run under the auspices of the Chamber of Trade.

It is illegal for anyone who does not meet the preceding criteria to describe himself as an *artisan*. The punishment for the offence is a fine of up to €7,500. It should be noted that individuals registered with the Chamber of Trade are not automatically recognized as *artisans*, even though they work for *entreprises artisanales*. Larger building companies, with ten or more employees, must register with their local RCS or *Registre du Commerce et des Sociétés*.

The Different Trades and What They Do

It is not common in France to simply employ a 'builder' to carry out your project and to rely on him to sub-contract specialist work where necessary. Instead, the French tend to choose each tradesman individually. This is a practical solution when you are on-site to oversee and coordinate the work, but may be a problem if you are trying to control the project from a distance, especially when several different tradesmen are involved.

Unless you have appointed an architect or some other project manager, it is essential that you leave clear, detailed instructions of the work to be carried out (with drawings, if appropriate), and that both you and the *artisans* have the same understanding of your expectations. You should be aware, however, that any timescales and costs quoted are likely to be more flexible if you are not there in person to keep a close eye on a day-to-day basis. Moreover, any unforeseen problems that come to light during the progress of the project in your absence will be much more difficult to resolve by telephone or email.

When we were having a new kitchen fitted, we asked a local specialist company to carry out the work. Having approved the design, chosen units, taps and tiles, and selected the kitchen appliances, we left them to get on with the job. The planner had specified that the built-in, eye-level oven was to go in a corner at a 45° angle, and that the separate hob would be positioned in the adjoining work surface. Fortunately, we were at home on the day that the joiner was building the carcass for the oven. As he was checking that the oven fitted correctly, but before the electrician installed it permanently, we noticed that the oven door opened direct over a corner of the hob, effectively making the front ring unusable. We pointed out the impracticality – and danger – of such an arrangement and, after the designer (a man, of course!) had been called in to inspect the problem, the angle of the oven was changed. What was a fairly easy adjustment at that stage would have been a nightmare had it not been spotted until after the tiles had been fixed and the kitchen completed.

Although most *artisans* specialize in a particular trade, it is not unusual for them to carry out more than one type of work; these are generally connected in some way. For example, a plumber may also be a central heating engineer, a chimney sweep and a zinc roofing worker. This sort of grouping is particularly noticeable in rural areas, where registered *artisans* are more thinly spread. Overall, the trades are not dissimilar to their British counterparts. The main differences are to be found in the materials, systems and regulations that tradesmen are qualified to work with.

The main categories of *artisan* are as follows:

Carreleur – Tiler
The *carreleur* specializes in floor and wall tiling, but not roof tiles, although some other areas of exterior work may well be within his remit, for example, terraces, patios and swimming pools. As in Britain, the tiler's role is constantly developing as new materials and techniques emerge. So, in addition to traditional ceramic, natural stone and marble tiles, he must now be adept in using, for example, glass, plastics and porcelain.

Whether the tiler you select prefers to work from drawings, written or even verbal instructions, it is, of course, essential to make sure that there is clear understanding down to the smallest detail on both sides – it is not so easy to pull tiles off once they have been properly fixed and grouted. Nor is it particularly practicable to change the brilliant white grout that he has used for the more subdued shade of grey that you feel would look better with the tiles that you have painstakingly selected – believe us, we've been there!

When our new bathroom was being installed, all the surfaces apart from the ceiling were to be tiled; it seemed a good idea at the time to ask M. Carré if he could put a coat of paint on the ceiling to finish the job off. The result could have come straight from a cartoon comic strip as he and his two labourers fell silent and stared at us with mouths wide open. Eventually, after swallowing hard and taking a deep breath, he said indignantly, 'But *Monsieur*, I am a tiler, *not* a painter', and clearly, in his opinion, never the two should be confused.

Chauffagiste – Heating engineer
In many enterprises, the role of the *chauffagiste* (sometimes known as an *installateur thermique*) is often combined with that of the *plombier* (or *installateur sanitaire*), although, of course, specialist companies can also be found, especially in larger towns.

The *chauffagiste* installs and maintains an ever-increasing variety of heating, ventilation and air-conditioning products and systems. The traditional fuel sources – electricity, gas (town and bottled), oil and wood – continue to dominate, but there is a strong ecological push towards the use of renewable energy sources such as solar power. These are becoming increasingly popular as they attract substantial financial incentives from the government (*see* Chapter 8). It should be noted that electrical heating systems are often the domain of the *électricien* rather than of the *chauffagiste*.

Another important service usually provided by the *chauffagiste* is *ramonage* – cleaning chimneys and boiler flues. This is extremely important as annual sweeping is both a requirement of household insurance policies and a legal obligation (*see* Chapter 7).

Our first encounter with a *chauffagiste* was when our not particularly efficient central heating boiler decided to stop producing any hot water. We asked M. Chaudet to have a look at it and tell us what needed to be done. We naturally expected the obvious reply of, 'A new boiler, *Monsieur*'. We took him down into the basement where this antique contraption was housed. He looked at it for a couple of minutes, and nodded his head sagely, '*Mais oui*' is all that he said. Then, with a level of concentration and accuracy that would have put any self-respecting fly-half to shame, he gave the thing an almighty kick with his well-booted right foot, and the boiler immediately sprang back into life. Indeed, it continued to work perfectly for the next six months until we had it replaced. He said nothing more, but with a rueful smile looked down at our slipper-shod feet, and shook his head sadly. He obviously decided that we would be a good source of future business since he didn't charge us for this service.

Couvreur – Roofer
The job of the *couvreur* involves the preparation and application of protective coatings to roof surfaces. On new projects his work follows on from that of the *charpentier* (carpenter) who will have created the timber framework. The *couvreur* will

cover the new roof structure and install the necessary weather proofing materials. On existing buildings he is primarily responsible for repairs and maintenance, inspecting the roof for defects, evaluating repair requirements and, where necessary, stripping the structure and checking the underlying roof timbers.

Depending on the roofing styles of the region that he works in, he will be adept in using a variety of materials that may include terracotta, schist or slate tiles, thatch, zinc or timber. In addition, he will fit rainwater pipes, gutters, skylights and ornamental accessories such as chimney stack filters, ensure that chimney bases are properly sealed and will also check that your loft space thermal insulation is adequate.

Ebéniste – Cabinet maker
The *ébéniste* is a skilled woodworker. As well as designing and producing original items of furniture, in either antique or contemporary styles, he will create doors, staircases, fitted cupboards and other wooden structures in your home. He will also be capable of repairing, restoring and conserving such items.

As the *ébéniste* is a highly skilled specialist, his charges are likely to reflect the fact. When we purchased our house, we agreed that the seller could take with her a pair of antique, built-in cupboard doors that had belonged to her grandparents and so had some sentimental value to her. This left us with an unsightly hole in the wall in the middle of our entrance hall, which clearly needed replacement doors to be fitted. The size was not standard and so ready-made doors were not an option. We called in the local *ébéniste* for a quotation. M. Lebois viewed the space, took the appropriate measurements, established our 'exact' requirements, and went away to think about it. His quotation, accompanied by an impressive drawing of his proposed creation, duly arrived. We read it, reread it, and then picked ourselves up from the floor. The price was €8,500 (at that time, just over £5,000). Perhaps not surprisingly, we decided to have the hole bricked up and the wall replastered – it was an awful lot cheaper.

Electricien – Electrician
In addition to domestic wiring, the *électricien* installs and maintains electric central heating systems, air conditioning and ventilation apparatus, and automatic gates and garage doors. He may also supply and install TV aerials and satellite dishes. As in the rest of Europe, electrical work is best left to the professional. The official regulations and specifications for domestic wiring in France are very complicated and registered tradesmen are regularly updated with the latest amendments.

Unlike Britain, the French electrical system does not use a ring main, but is based on a network of spurs, with a limited number of sockets being permitted for each spur. The more energy-hungry major appliances (such as washing machines and

What Is an Artisan? 17

The ébéniste's ornate design for hand-crafted cupboard doors came with an ornate price tag.

dishwashers) must have their own individual spur – regulations that a registered *électricien* will be conversant with, but clearly not a subject for the faint-hearted.

You should be aware that you are able to choose the wattage of electricity EDF (*Electricité de France*) supplies to your house – the current choices range from 6 to 36kW. If, like us, you buy a relatively recent property, then it will probably not be necessary to change the level already being supplied. If, however, yours is an older property, you may find that the supply could be as low as 3kW, which will support only a very limited range of modern electrical appliances. In this case, an upgrade

18   *What Is an* Artisan?

It only takes one Frenchman to change a light bulb – and to check the safety of an outside light fitting.

may well be essential, although it will inevitably bring with it an increase in the annual standing charge.

You should also make sure that you know exactly where to find the fuse-box(es) or distribution board – and the circuit breaker, especially if you live in an area prone to electrical storms. Be aware that in France it is the responsibility of the householder, and not the power supplier, to ensure that the property is properly earthed. A quick check by an *électricien* will soon establish whether this has been done satisfactorily.

It should be noted that the use of certain British-approved materials (for example, some types of cable) may invalidate your French household insurance. It is extremely important therefore that only materials specifically complying with French specifications are used. In this respect, for example, the useful British/French converter plug that you bought at the airport should be used only as a temporary measure.

With the best intentions in the world, there are always, of course, unforeseen difficulties. We still chuckle when we remember an *électricien* we called to our new home. The job was small and, we thought, quite straightforward – connecting a new ceiling light fitting in our sitting room. This was a necessity rather than an aesthetic whim as the previous owner had taken not only the existing fitting but also the bulb, bulb-holder and ceiling rose with her (not an uncommon practice in France) leaving an uninsulated wire dangling in mid-air. The room in question is very high and the ceiling is supported by sturdy, antique oak beams – the fitting was to be fixed to one of these beams. The *électricien* looked up, and looked worried. Would the beam support the weight of his ladder, would the terracotta floor tiles provide a safe base for the ladder, he asked? We assured him that both the beam and the tiles were perfectly safe, but our man was still clearly very concerned, and continued to prevaricate as he came out with every conceivable objection to doing the job. Then suddenly the *centime* dropped – he was afraid of heights and didn't want to go up the ladder. Not the best possible qualification, one would think, for an *électricien*.

Maçon – Bricklayer

The English term 'bricklayer' is an understatement of the role of the *maçon*. Although not strictly accurate, the word builder might be a more appropriate translation in many cases. Trained to work with concrete, bricks, breeze blocks and stone, the *maçon* is responsible for laying the foundations and then constructing the walls, supports and floors of a new building or renovation, whether internal or external.

He should not be confused with a *tailleur des pierres*, who is an ornamental stone mason, nor with a *marbrier* who is a monumental mason, and certainly not with a *franc-maçon*, who is a freemason.

Menuisier/charpentier – Joiner/carpenter

The *menuisier* is a specialist in the manufacture, assembly and installation of doors, windows, shutters, floors, panelling, stairs and fitted cupboards. Working both in his own workshop and on-site, he uses a wide variety of materials including wood,

A charpentier *builds the structure for a new roof (Habitat Naturel).*

glass, Perspex, aluminium and plastic. Increasingly, the *menuisier* is becoming involved with the installation of double glazing, laminate flooring and other non-traditional products, making him a versatile generalist.

The *charpentier*, on the other hand, could be described as a traditional carpenter. Indeed, both words derive from *charpente*, meaning framework, as he is the tradesman who builds the structure (for example, a roof) for other *artisans* to develop into the finished product.

Peintre — Painter/decorator
Perhaps more commonly known in Britain as a painter and decorator, the main role of the *peintre* is obviously to apply paint, wall coverings and other materials to the interior and the exterior of buildings. He is also responsible for the surface preparation before painting or decorating, including the removal of any previous finishes, surface repairs, sanding and cleaning. As well as carrying out the usual decorating functions, many *peintres* are talented artists, skilled in more specialized areas such as decorating furniture, *trompe-l'œil* or fresco work.

Although home decoration normally comes within our limited sphere of DIY expertise, we have on occasion employed a *peintre* for some of our bigger projects.

One thing we noticed was that he mixed his own paints to obtain the exact shade we wanted rather than rely on the ready-mixed variety. The problem with this is that it is virtually impossible to replicate the same mix, which can prove somewhat annoying if future 'touch-ups' are needed. We soon learnt to ask for the remains of the paint to be left with us.

Plâtrier – Plasterer
The *plâtrier* applies different kinds of plaster to internal surfaces such as walls, floors and ceilings. He either uses the traditional 'float and trowel' techniques or, increasingly, mechanical methods. His work can involve new buildings or the repair and restoration of existing plasterwork. If necessary, he will demolish walls and make good the surface. He will also construct internal dividing walls. Outside the building he may apply finishes using sand, stone, cement or stone-effect materials.

Most *plâtriers* are involved in the provision of solid plasterwork, but some choose to provide other services such as fibrous plastering (which focuses on ornate plasterwork), installing thermal insulation or soundproofing.

Plombier – Plumber
The work of the *plombier* embraces a wide variety of operations involving, for example, water supply pipework, sanitary fittings, drainage and gas installation. As with electrical work, there is an extensive range of statutory regulations that affect water and gas supply and their associated connections, and which all homeowners in France must adhere to. This is why the services of a registered plumber should be engaged for all but the simplest of tasks. In any event, a registered *plombier* **must** be employed to make connections from the house to the main drain, and is strongly recommended for work related to the connection of septic tanks, where the regulations are even stricter and more complex. Similar rules apply for making the gas connection between the meter, supplied and installed by GDF (*Gaz de France*) and your house. Indeed, the gas supply will not be turned on until the completed installation has been inspected and approved by the independent certification body, Qualigaz.

Although the materials commonly used in plumbing work tend to be the same throughout Europe, there are significant differences in the diameters and hardness of copper piping. This means that the methods of bending it differ, as do the joining techniques, where the French braze rather than solder (which is why any pipe joints you buy will be made of untinned copper). The golden rule should be that, when in France, use French-sourced materials (even if it does on the surface appear cheaper to import them from your favourite British DIY store). Remember, too, that the pressure of the French mains water supply is higher than that in Britain, and, although reduced for domestic usage, equipment sourced in France will be designed to accommodate this higher pressure.

22 *What Is an Artisan?*

A plâtrier *preparing to finish work on a loft conversion.*

Serrurier/métallier – Locksmith/metal worker
In a nutshell, the *serrurier-métallier* works on all types of metal construction, focusing both on household security and artistic design (such as wrought ironwork). The range of possible projects that he can carry out for you is, therefore, extensive, and

> ### Some Industry Statistics
>
> The building trade describes itself as the *première entreprise de France* – the leading business sector in the country – and it employs a total of almost 950,000. The official statistics (SIRENE) for the end of 2007 reveal that there are more than 360,000 building companies throughout France. Of these, 55 per cent employ between one and nine people, and a further 40 per cent are one-man bands. The vast majority, therefore, are registered with the Chamber of Trade as *entreprises artisanales*. Of course, many of the larger building companies are involved with public works, but those employing fewer than twenty get most of their business (80 per cent) from private individuals. What is more, 70 per cent of their business, in terms of turnover, is represented by the maintenance and renovation of existing properties.

includes manufacturing, installing and maintaining locks, making new and replacement keys, door furniture, balconies, staircases and security products, utilizing an ever-growing range of materials such as iron, steel, aluminium, copper, brass and numerous alloys.

Much of his creative work will necessarily be carried out in his workshop (or forge). It should be noted that, although their trades are in many respects similar, he has not completely replaced the traditional blacksmith (*forgeron*) and certainly not the farrier (*maréchal-ferrant*), should you have a horse in your paddock that needs a new shoe.

Using a General Building Company

When your project entails the use of a number of different specialists, you may feel more comfortable dealing with a general building company, or *entreprise générale de bâtiment*. Such companies employ a range of tradesmen and will subcontract any work for which they do not have their own skilled *artisans*. The company will assume responsibility for the whole project, coordinating and overseeing all aspects of the work.

Employing an Architect

If you are having extensive work done to your house, you may well decide to have an architect design and draw up plans in accordance with your requirements. Indeed, the use of an architect is obligatory when applying for planning permission where the total floor area of your property is 170sq.m or more, or if it will reach this size once the building work has been completed. (*See* Chapter 6 for more information on building and planning regulations.) It is also advisable to use an architect when you are contemplating any project that may impinge on the underlying structure of the property. Having examined the current state of the building, he can provide you with valuable advice and suggestions on how to overcome any potential problems and give you an estimate of the likely costs, as well as drawing up the necessary plans.

Incidentally, even if you choose not to employ an architect you can obtain free architectural, technical and regulatory advice from one by consulting your local department's CAUE (*Conseils d'Architecture, d'Urbanisme et de l'Environnement*); see www.fncaue.asso.fr for contact details.

The exact scope of the architect's involvement in your project needs to be agreed in advance. It is up to you whether he just works on the initial concept, establishing the necessary plans and specifying the work to be carried out, or oversees the whole project as a *maître d'œuvre* up until its satisfactory completion. In the latter case, as well as ensuring that all the formalities are complied with, he will select and liaise with the various *artisans* as necessary, and generally supervise the progress of the project from start to finish.

Finding A Good Tradesman

Although the statistics appear to indicate that there are plenty of tradesmen about, why is it often so difficult to find one for your project? First, most good, reliable *artisans* will already have as much work as they can handle. There is a shortage of qualified labour as young people are increasingly opting for further education

---

Maître d'œuvre and *Maître d'ouvrage* – What's the Difference?

A *maître d'œuvre* is essentially a manager, employed on a contractual basis to oversee and coordinate a specified project. The *maître d'ouvrage* is the person (or company) who specifies what work he wants done and signs off the job once it is completed. In practice, you will normally be the *maître d'ouvrage* and, unless you appoint an architect, general building company or some other project manager, you will also be the *maître d'œuvre*.

rather than vocational training. The tradition of skills being handed down from father to son is now an exception rather than the rule. At the same time, the demand for building work has increased, partly due to the attractive financial incentives available (*see* Chapter 8) – not to mention the influx of British and other immigrants restoring dilapidated properties.

There are considerable variations in the numbers of *artisans* located in the different regions of France, and among different trades. If you can find one, you may be tempted to use a locally-based British builder (*see* Chapter 4 for the legal implications of using a British-registered company). This does, of course, help to overcome any communication barriers, but there may be disadvantages. Unless well established in the area, a British builder will not necessarily have a wide network of equipment suppliers, contacts with specialized tradesmen, knowledge of French rules and regulations or experience of local building materials and techniques.

Another option is to do the work yourself, particularly if you are a keen and experienced handyman. You will have to familiarize yourself with French building methods and materials and you will need at least a rudimentary understanding of the language in order to purchase the necessary supplies – for which we hope this book will prove an invaluable aid. The two big disadvantages of DIY are that you will not be able to profit from the reduced rate of VAT on your purchases (*see* Chapter 8), and that the work will not be covered by a ten-year guarantee (*see* Chapter 9), which might become an issue when you come to sell your house. And there will undoubtedly be some occasions when you will need to call in a professional – perhaps because the work falls outside your range of expertise or there may be a legal requirement (for example, new gas installations) or, if you are like us, you need someone to repair the mess you've made!

So, in a situation where the demand for qualified tradesmen often exceeds supply, how do you find the right *artisan* or *entreprise générale de bâtiment* to work on your house? Here, in order of preference, is our list of suggestions:

1. Word-of-mouth

This is by far the safest and most efficient method and, particularly in areas or trades where there is little or no competition, it may be the only way to find the best tradesman for the job. If an *artisan* has a full schedule he does not need to pay for advertising, but can find enough business solely through recommendations from his existing, satisfied customers. So, if you are planning a project, talk about it – to your neighbours, the people in the bar, local shopkeepers and fellow expats – and ask whether they know of a suitable *artisan*.

We did just that when we were looking into replacing our central heating boiler. Our neighbour, Jean-Louis, recommended the heating engineer he had used a couple of years previously. Not only did he give us the man's phone number but he also showed us his new installation and a copy of the invoice as an indication of the costs.

Word-of-mouth can also come from the *artisan* himself. When we casually asked a local *menuisier* whom we met socially why we should ever employ him rather than one of his competitors, his reply was simple: he was born in the town, he had worked all his life in the town, his reputation had been built in this town and he wished to carry on living and working and being respected here. Good enough for us.

Other sources of recommendation are:

a. The *Répertoire des Métiers* listing all the registered *entreprises artisanales* in your area can be consulted at your local *Chambre des Métiers*. In some departments this can be accessed on the Internet – find the address by visiting www.artisanat.fr and click on the map of France.
b. Your local *Mairie* (Town Hall) will know the tradesmen they use for public contracts.
c. The estate agent through whom you purchased your house will have a list of contacts, although he may be paid a commission and so his advice will not necessarily be impartial.
d. Your household insurance agent should also be able to suggest the names of tradesmen used for repairs in the case of insurance claims. Some insurance companies even have lists of approved *artisans* on their websites.

But you should also bear in mind that word-of-mouth may be negative, so listen out for names of tradesmen with a poor reputation.

2. Other Artisans

Where a project requires the involvement of more than one trade then you should be willing, where appropriate, to follow any recommendations given by the 'lead' or principal *artisan*. He will know all the other local specialists and, more importantly, know which of them he prefers to work with. The *plombier*, for example, is likely to have a preferred *carreleur* and the *menuisier* a preferred *électricien*. This principle worked to excellent effect when we were having our new bathroom and cloakroom built. On the recommendation of the *plombier* four out of the six *artisans* employed were people whom he worked with regularly and equally were used to working with each other. It was also a bonus that they all knew the other two, and happily endorsed our decision to include them in the team. After all, a group of men that can enjoy each other's company for a quick beer in the local bar on their way home from work are likely to give you the benefits of team-working that, with the best will in the world, a group of strangers could not.

3. Outdoor Advertising

Often tradesmen will erect a sign outside sites where they are working, or you may see their van(s) parked with the contact details displayed. If the project is an external one, you can keep an eye on progress yourself, seeing how long the job takes, how tidily the site is kept and what the finished result looks like. If you know the owners of the property – or if you are feeling particularly bold – you can approach them and ask whether they are satisfied with the work that has been carried out. At the very least, you will know that someone else has been through the process of finding an *artisan* and has, presumably, selected this one for good reasons.

It may also be the case that the *artisan* has erected an advertising board outside his home (or other place of business). This is a useful source for compiling a list of local tradesmen and, as well as giving information about the services that he offers and contact details, it will also show you how close he is located to you (useful if things were to go wrong) and what state his own property is in. After all, you wouldn't go to a hairdresser with terrible hair or a dentist with bad teeth.

Satisfied customers display the supplier/installer's details beside their new automatic gates.

4. Exhibitions

It is likely that the principal town(s) in your *département* will have an annual show devoted to home improvements. Look out for advertisements in the local press or on roadside posters for events such as '*Salon de l'Habitat*', '*Foire Expo Maison*', and the like. Visiting such a show will give you the opportunity to meet prospective tradesmen on neutral territory, to discuss your project with them and to arrange for them to visit your house in order to provide an estimate. As an added bonus, sometimes special show discounts are available on certain products or services.

5. Equipment Suppliers

If you know the names of the manufacturers of any of the equipment your project will require, look at their websites to see whether they have a list of recommended installers. If you are buying your own materials, ask the supplier if he can arrange the fitting. You may be able to benefit from a reduced rate of VAT on both the supply and the installation (*see* Chapter 8). Some DIY stores have notice boards where local tradesmen advertise their services.

Utilities providers such as EDF and GDF offer advisory services for any project concerning energy efficiency. You can find the latest information on their websites or by contacting your local branch (details will appear on your utility bill). Note that some of these services will incur a charge.

6. Local Press

Look in regional newspapers and free publications for advertisements by tradesmen in your local area. Also look out for editorials in the press and in your *commune*'s newsletter announcing details of new businesses starting up. Although they sometimes may not have much experience, they are more likely to be available to carry out the work.

7. Internet

There are numerous websites where you can register and define your project online. These details will be circulated to a number of 'selected' *artisans* within your area, who will then provide you with an estimate. You should, however, bear in mind that these may not always be the best *artisans*, but those who have paid to be registered on the site. As such, they will represent only a relatively small proportion of the total number of tradesmen.

Many organizations which award professional accreditations provide members' details on their websites. See the section at the end of this chapter for their addresses.

A number of trade associations, such as CAPEB (*Confédération de l'Artisanat et des Petites Entreprises du Bâtiment*), FFB (*Fédération Française du Bâtiment*) and Qualibat, have searchable directories on their websites (many of them listed in Appendix I).

Note, however, that the results will include only tradesmen who are members of these associations.

8. Yellow Pages

Perhaps the most extensive listing of all tradesmen is to be found in the *Pages Jaunes*. As well as the printed directory which covers your *département*, it is sometimes useful to consult the online version at www.pagesjaunes.fr. This will not only allow you to search neighbouring *départements* but also provide links to individual *artisans*' websites where these are available.

9. Using an Intermediary

In the last few years, a number of franchised businesses known as *courtiers en travaux* have been set up to provide an introductory service between property owners and tradesmen. Two of the best established, with virtually nationwide coverage, are *Activ Travaux* (www.activ-travaux.com) and *Illico Travaux* (www.illico-travaux.com).

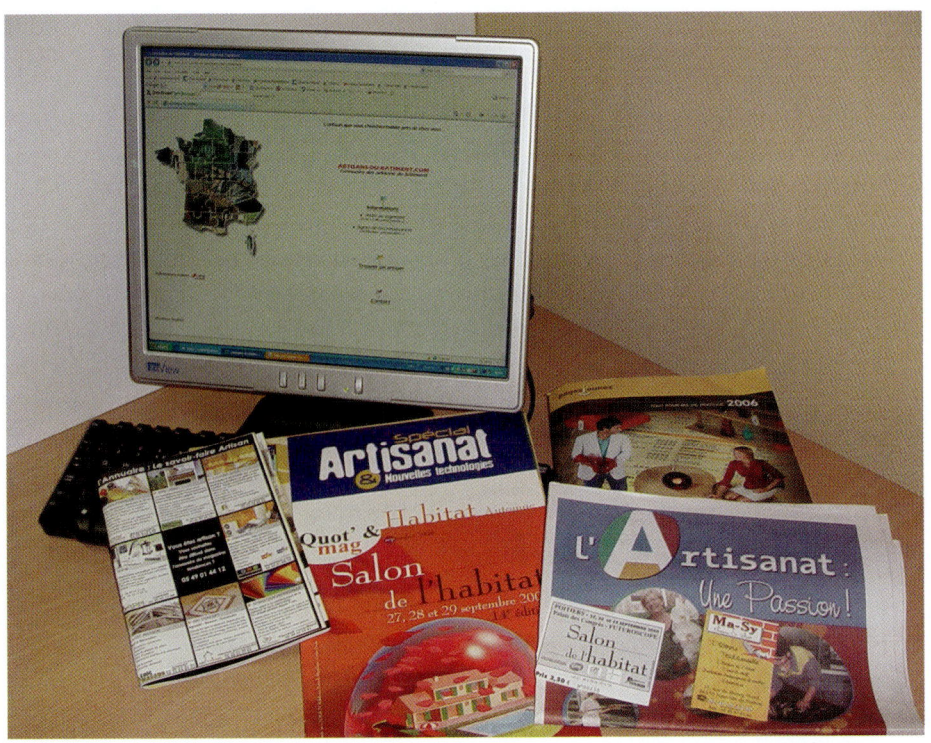

Doing your homework to find the right artisan using a variety of different sources.

You can contact them, via their websites or by telephone, with a brief description of your project. The local representative will then arrange to visit you to find out more details, before contacting his network of tradesmen for estimates. He will then present these to you, and explain any points that require clarification. It is up to you to select which you wish to accept.

The franchisee acts merely as a broker between you and the tradesman. He assumes no responsibility regarding the quality of the work, nor the competitiveness of its cost. The main advantage of using such a service is that it is relatively quick and easy and so may be worth considering if you do not have much time. On the other hand, be aware that the broker will recommend only those tradesmen who are members of his network, and not necessarily those who are best qualified for the job. Also, although there is no charge made for this service, the franchisee being paid a commission by the tradesmen he recommends, this may well result in inflated costs being quoted to you.

10. Cold Calling

Telephone calls from companies (or call centres working on their behalf) trying to sell their services are becoming increasingly common. Duncan finds that it is usually a good opportunity for him to remember that he does not speak a word of French.

You may also encounter people coming to your door prospecting for business. On the whole, in our experience, they are quite open and honest about what they are selling. We did, however, encounter one pair who claimed to be carrying out an official survey into energy-saving on behalf of the local *Mairie*. Having agreed to answer their questions, we quickly realized that they were, in fact, trying to find out whether we might be in the market for roof insulation. Our advice for dealing with cold callers of any kind is to be cautious, and on no account to permit them to enter your home. You may possibly make an exception when a tradesman has done some work for a neighbour and then introduces himself to you.

Ex-directory Options

If you subscribe to France Telecom, you can restrict the publication of your telephone number by registering on one of their *Listes* — *Orange* not to appear in direct marketing files, *Chamois* not to appear in the printed or the electronic version of the phone directory, or *Rouge* not to appear anywhere at all.

As previously mentioned, if you employ an architect to supervise your project then he is likely to have a local network of skilled tradesmen whose services he uses regularly. And to find an architect in the first place, we advise you to follow many of the same recommendations we make when you are trying to find an *artisan*. In addition, since all the 29,000 architects practising in France must register with their professional association, the *Ordre des Architectes*, you can locate those in your area from the website www.architectes.org.

Professional Accreditations

There is a plethora of acronyms, qualifications and logos that can be used by tradesmen to provide assurances of the quality of their services. None of them, however, are obligatory and there are many excellent *artisans* who are not accredited by any of these organizations. We dealt with two of the most significant – *Artisan* and *Maître Artisan* – at the beginning of this chapter. Here we list some of the other important ones that you may encounter.

Qualibat

This is an independent organization which assesses the quality of companies in the building industry (excluding those in the electrical/electronic sector – see Qualifelec below). It provides a guarantee of the professionalism of the directors of the business and of their financial resources, and evaluates the personnel and the technical skills they possess. It also checks that the company is legally registered and has the necessary insurance cover. Operating within strict guidelines and regularly updated, Qualibat's database consists of some 40,000 businesses throughout France. It can be searched online at www.qualibat.com. Certificates are issued on an annual basis and entitle the holder to use a distinctive blue logo.

Qualifelec

Operating in a similar way to Qualibat, the Qualifelec certificate not only assures the quality of building work in the electrical/electronic sector, but also gives a guarantee that the installers comply with all the latest safety regulations. Its database of 8,000 companies can be accessed at www.qualifelec.fr.

AB5

In an attempt to remove some of the confusion surrounding the multitude of different accreditations and logos, the organization representing small builders, CAPEB, introduced yet a further qualification. AB5 is a voluntary charter relating to the quality of service provided to clients. Its adherents, who must be registered in the

An électricien *displays his accreditations on his van.*

Répertoire des Métiers and have to undertake a special two-day training course, agree to five commitments:

- to clearly demonstrate their skills in their particular trade;
- to respond promptly to the client, from the initial contact onwards;
- to provide a detailed estimate within two weeks (unless otherwise agreed with the client);
- to adhere to all the conditions contained in the estimate without any modifications (unless otherwise agreed with the client);
- to ensure that the client is fully satisfied with the work undertaken by means of a customer questionnaire.

PG, PMG

PG (*Professionnel du Gaz*) and PMG (*Professionnel Maintenance Gaz*) were introduced by the major gas suppliers to guarantee the quality and safety of gas installations in the home. Tradesmen holding this accreditation (there are more than 20,000 of them) have to demonstrate a high standard of technical skills and have a thorough understanding of all the relevant rules and regulations. Any materials and equipment they supply must comply with the standards that are currently in force. They must also offer an after-sales service (although you are not obliged to subscribe to an on-going maintenance contract with the same enterprise that installed the equipment). You may still see some references to PGN and PGP, which were replaced by PG in 2007. You can search for registered gas installers on the website www.pgn-pgp.com.

Quali'sol / Quali'bois / Quali'Pv

These are accreditations for installers of heating systems using renewable energy sources – solar, wood and photovoltaic, respectively. All three are administered by Qualit'EnR and lists of accredited installers can be found via the website www.qualit-enr.org.

An accredited chauffagiste *with the appropriate logos outside his premises.*

34 *What Is an* Artisan?

Qualifioul

To find installers/maintainers of domestic fuel heating systems, consult the website www.chaleurfioul.com.

Quali'Eau

Instituted by the building trade and recognized by the Ministry of Health, this is an accreditation for plumbers, denoting that they follow all the necessary health and safety procedures when installing domestic drinking water networks.

3
Getting an Estimate

What Is a *Devis*?

In France, an estimate is known as a *devis*, and failure to obtain and understand this important document can be the cause of many problems. Whether you are embarking on a full restoration, a home extension, a new kitchen, a boiler replacement or the decoration of your sitting room, if you are going to employ one or more *artisan(s)* the *devis* is an extremely important ingredient in your project recipe. Once signed by both parties, the *devis* forms a legally-binding contract, and so it is essential that you fully understand its contents, requirements and implications.

The Legalities

A law of 1990 sets out in detail the rules concerning many aspects related to work carried out on property. It specifically covers all work related to breakdowns, repair and maintenance of a house and its equipment in the following areas:

- masonry;
- heating, ventilation and air conditioning;
- chimney and flue sweeping;
- insulation;
- carpentry and joinery;
- locks and security equipment;
- roofing;
- plumbing;
- waterproofing;
- plastering;
- painting and decorating;
- glazing;
- the fitting of wall and floor coverings in any material;
- electrical installations.

The same law also extends to the replacement or the addition of equipment or parts following the connection, installation, repair, maintenance or adjustment of any electric or electronic equipment. It does not, however, apply to interventions covered by a maintenance contract or under guarantee where no additional payment is required. Nor is the law relevant for connections to a public service such as mains gas or the telephone network, where the tariffs are fixed and available to the general public.

The decree states that before any work is carried out the provider must inform the customer of the following points:

- the hourly labour rate, including tax;
- a breakdown of how his or his company's time will be spent;
- the prices, including tax, of the different fixed services offered;
- his travel costs, if applicable;
- whether the estimate is free of charge or must be paid for and, if the latter, what the price is;
- the terms of payment.

If you visit the provider's premises, such information should be clearly displayed where all customers can see it. In the more likely event of receiving a tradesman on-site, he must present you with a written document containing this information. In practice, this information is usually combined with that required in the *devis*.

In addition to these requirements, the law stipulates that an *artisan* must provide a detailed written estimate or *devis* of the work to be carried out where it meets either or both of the following criteria:

- the total cost of the work, including tax, is estimated to be above €150;
- the customer requests an estimate.

The only exceptions where a *devis* is not required are in cases of extreme emergency and/or where people's safety or that of the building could be endangered.

The *devis* must be supplied before the work is carried out and must include the following:

- the date of the *devis*;
- the name and address of the *artisan* or business, and his SIREN/SIRET number (*see* Chapter 4);
- the customer's details – name, company name (if applicable) and address, and the address where the work is to be carried out;
- full details of the work to be carried out, including a description of all the services and materials to be supplied, their unit price, quantity required (for

example, *9m tube inox 125 @ €12.53 = €112.77*), the labour costs and, if appropriate, travelling costs;
- the total cost to be paid, both excluding tax (*hors taxes* or *HT*) and including it (*toutes taxes comprises* or *TTC*), with an indication of the rate of VAT (*TVA*) that is applicable;
- the length of time for which the *devis* will remain valid (this normally ranges from two months to six);
- whether the *devis* is free of charge or must be paid for and, if the latter, what the price is.

While most *artisans* will supply a *devis* free of charge, this is a commercial gesture rather than a legal obligation. Some may ask for payment, but the cost should be established and agreed beforehand. The cost may be deducted from the total amount if the *devis* is subsequently accepted.

Although not stipulated by law, the *devis* may also include:

- the heading *Devis* or, more rarely, *Proposition de prix*;
- sales conditions giving added protection to the *artisan* and/or the customer;
- conditions under which the prices may be revised, for example, if the cost of raw materials should rise during the course of the project;
- the conditions for carrying out the work or of delivery.

From our experience, it is advisable to ask the *artisan* to include a written starting date for the work and an indication of how long it will take to complete. Indeed, this is obligatory if the total value of the *devis* exceeds €500.

You will receive two copies of the *devis*. Should you wish to accept it, you should sign and date it and add the words *Devis reçu avant l'exécution des travaux* (Estimate received before work carried out). In practice, it is usual simply to sign the *devis* under the words *Bon pour accord* or *Bon pour exécution* to indicate that you accept the estimate and that the *artisan* can go ahead with the work. You should keep one copy of the *devis* and return the other to the *artisan*. Once signed, the *devis* becomes a legally-binding contract between you and will serve as a reference document in the case of a dispute. This is why it is critical that you specify all the aspects of the work you wish to be carried out and ensure that all are detailed in the *devis*. It is not obligatory for the *artisan* to have signed the *devis*; simply presenting it to you is deemed to be a definite commitment on his part. If any of the conditions in the *devis* (relating to timescales, extent of the work or costs, for example) are not respected, you can seek redress from the defaulting *artisan*. Obviously, if you change the specifications of the job while it is in progress you should expect to pay extra for any additional materials or labour costs. If such changes are significant you should ask the

38 *Getting an Estimate*

Les Toits de l'Ouest

DEVIS

Couverture, Zinguerie, Isolation, Demoussage, Traitement de charpente, Ramonage

Date :	04/01/2005
Devis n° :	cx04012005

Mr Mme WEBSTER Duncan
(Customer address)

DÉSIGNATION DES TRAVAUX	Qu	val	prix unit	Total HT
Application d un demoussant alcalin sur l ensemble de la toiture et enlever les blocs de mousse	144	m2	20,00 €	2 880,00 €
Lavage demoussage hudrofugation de la façade avec MURSAM + HYDROCYM	55	m2	15,00 €	825,00 €
Démontage et remplacement du débord de toit partie haute	3,5	ml	35,00 €	122,50 €
Pose dune gouttière demi ronde de 25 cm de dev en zinc	3,5	ml	25,00 €	87,50 €
Pose dune naissance	1	unit	12,00 €	12,00 €
Pose de 2 talons gouttière	2	unit	7,00 €	14,00 €
Pose d un tuyau de descente finissant sur toiture	2	ml	21,20 €	42,40 €
Pose d un zinc sous chevron	6,5	ml	26,00 €	169,00 €
			TOTAL H.T	4 152,40 €
			TVA 5,5%	228,38 €
			TOTAL T.T.C	4 380,78 €

Les travaux débuterons, des que le devis sera signé et retourné par le client,
Bon pour accord, date et signature:

Le client:

Modalités de paiement:
30% a la signature du devis
Le solde a la fin des travaux, comptant sans escompte sur présentation de la facture

L.T.D.O : rcs 482443603-POITIERS-ape 201B
Siége Social : 35 rue Paché 86170 AVANTON
Tel / Fax : 05.49.51.53.14 PORT : 06.99.66.18.19

A typical devis *containing all the legally required elements.*

artisan to revise his *devis* to reflect the higher price. On the other hand, the *artisan* himself does not have the right to modify the *devis* of his own accord once you have signed it. He cannot carry out any additional work and invoice you for a higher sum than that of the *devis*, unless he has agreed it with you beforehand.

It is a legal requirement that all contracts in France are written in French. Should you decide to contact an English *artisan* and receive a *devis* written in English it will not be binding. You should request it to be written in French, accompanied by an English translation, if you wish. Otherwise, there could be complications if anything goes wrong and you find yourself trying to sort things out in a French court (*tribunal*), as they will insist on dealing only with French documentation.

If you decide to accept a *devis* and then later change your mind you should be aware that the *artisan* has the right to insist on carrying out the work or to charge you a penalty payment equivalent to the total value of the *devis*. The only exception to this is if the *artisan* writes out a *devis* on your premises. In this case, the law on door-to-door selling applies and, having signed the *devis*, you have a cooling-off period of seven days.

Larger Building Projects

If you are undertaking large-scale reconstruction or renovation work, you may choose to use a general building company or *entreprise générale du bâtiment*. If this is the case, you will be required to sign a contract (*contrat d'entreprise*) with them. Such contracts are not standard documents, and the terms will need to be carefully negotiated and agreed by both parties in advance. It is recommended that the contract should include a full description of the project, *devis* and detailed work plans from each of the tradesmen concerned and a statement that the company is insured for its professional responsibility. A breakdown of the costs should be given, along with the payment terms. If payment is to be made in stages, make sure that you leave a balance of at least 5 per cent to the end as a *retenue de garantie* or sum that can be withheld if you are not satisfied with the work carried out. Finally, you are advised to specify the date by which the work should begin and the deadline for its completion. You may include an automatic penalty of a fixed number of euros per day for any delays incurred beyond this date.

Contacting the *Artisan(s)* You Have Shortlisted

It is always advisable, whenever possible, to contact a number of tradesmen before deciding on the one you wish to carry out the work. Depending on the scale of the project, in general a minimum of three estimates will allow you to compare the different services offered and to receive a competitive range of prices.

> **Use of Email**
>
> Generally speaking, the French are far less likely to use email than we are and, even if your *artisan* has an email address, he probably checks for messages infrequently – and responds even less frequently.

But, having made a shortlist of *artisans,* how should you contact them? The most direct method is to telephone. As most *artisans* are either one-man bands or members of very small enterprises, few have commercial premises or secretarial staff, and most tend to work from their own homes. For most of the day the *artisan* will be busy working on-site, so the best time to call is either at lunch-time (between 12.15pm and 1.45pm) or in the evening. Even then, it is quite possible that the *artisan* will not be available and you may have to leave a message, either with a member of his family (often wives act as 'secretaries') or on his answering machine. Keep your message short and simple, speak clearly, be prepared to spell out your name and know how to give your telephone number in French (*see* Chapter 10).

When you first speak to the *artisan* you should give him a brief description of the project so that he can advise you whether it is the sort of work that he can do. If so, you should make an appointment to meet him at the site where the work is to be carried out and where you will be able to explain your requirements in greater detail. Be prepared to give directions on how to find your property, especially if it is off the beaten track (*see* Chapter 10). If you live in a town, remember that your departmental telephone directory contains street maps of all the communes, and you can advise the *artisan* to refer to this. Also remember that the French often use the twenty-four-hour clock when making appointments. We have to admit that we have been caught out on more than one occasion, confusing, for example, *seize heures* (four p.m.) with *six heures* (six o'clock). We now always double-check the time in both formats.

We mentioned in Chapter 2 that when we asked our neighbour Jean-Louis for advice about finding a *chauffagiste* to supply us with a new central heating boiler he gave us the telephone number of the *artisan* that he had employed. That evening Lesley decided to ring the man and, having spent some time trawling through dictionaries and trade brochures to prepare the right vocabulary (unfortunately this book wasn't available to us!), made the call. It sounded as though he was expecting her to ring, and indeed he was. Not only had Jean-Louis given us the number, he had himself contacted the chap to explain that his new English neighbours wanted a *devis* for a replacement heating system, and he would be very grateful if M. et

Mme Webster could be given priority treatment. We were, and true to Jean-Louis's word, M. Chaudet did an excellent job for us.

Meeting the *Artisan*

Before your first meeting with the *artisan* you should prepare fully. Make sure that you have thought about all the aspects of your project and be ready to give as much

Duncan meets and greets an artisan *at our home.*

detail as possible. Where applicable, you can use photographs, brochures and drawings, to complement your explanations, particularly if your French language skills are not up to scratch (and don't forget to keep this book to hand).

It is then up to you to let him know exactly what you want done – remembering all the while that, although a qualified professional he is not a mind-reader. Take your time and do not feel flustered if there is a language problem. Having made the effort to visit you he will generally make allowances for your being foreign – after all your euros are as good as the next man's – and it is often assumed (in our case incorrectly) that British expats have lots of them.

Ask questions to make sure you – and the *artisan* – have a clear mutual understanding of exactly what you expect. Tell him what timescales you have for the work to be carried out – thus if you are expecting a house full of guests for Christmas, you will want the bathroom to be functional before the end of December. If timing really is critical this should be made known to the *artisan* before he prepares the *devis*, although you are unlikely to get cast-iron guaranteed dates. Sometimes, however, it is necessary to be insistent. When our new bathroom and cloakroom were being built, for example, we decided to escape the worst of the demolition by planning a two-week trip to Britain. We explained that we would be back on a certain date and, as we handed over the house keys to the *artisan* in charge, we made it very clear that when we returned late at night on that date, we would be less than happy if at least one of the new lavatories was not installed. To be on the safe side, Lesley rang the *plombier*'s wife from Britain the day before our return to ensure that her husband had understood and acted on our instructions. Mme Robinet assured us that we had no need to worry as we would definitely have a fully functional loo. Much to our relief, she had instructed her husband accordingly – although when we got home the sealant and cement were still damp as it had clearly been done at the very last minute.

Be prepared to be flexible in your requirements, and listen to any suggestions the *artisan* may have. Remember that he has much more experience of working on French buildings than you do, and he will have practical knowledge of complying with any legal or other operational requirements. If, however, you are particularly keen to include – or not to include – a certain feature in your plans, stand your ground.

This was certainly the case with our new bathroom, when we had to 'convince' the team of *artisans* we had selected that, despite their initial misgivings, two elements we had specified should be included.

The first was the shower enclosure. We had decided at the planning stage that we did not want a standard, cabinet-style installation, but rather something a little more individual, practical and eye-catching. Situated in a corner between two walls covered from floor to ceiling in ceramic tiles, we wanted a third side to be formed

What a relief! Returning home from the UK to find a very newly installed, functioning, loo.

from glass blocks. There was to be no shower tray as such, but a walk-in shower which would be covered in non-slip, ceramic floor tiles. We explained this at an early site meeting with all the *artisans* concerned. The *carreleur* liked the idea, especially as the glass blocks were something of a novelty to him; the *plombier* was very happy with our shower suggestion, and approved our positioning of the taps and shower unit; the *électricien* could see no problems; which left the *peintre* who, although not directly involved at this stage, felt that he should make a contribution to the discussion. He duly enquired about the style and fitting of the shower door. Knowing smiles all round, '*Mais oui, Monsieur et Madame Webster, la porte?*'. To us the answer was quite straightforward – there wasn't going to be one, the door space would be left open so that we could simply walk in and out. Now this might not sound earth-shattering, the 'wet room' concept has, after all, been around for some time, but not in a small market town in rural France. To a man they looked at us in amazement, a shower must have a door to keep the rest of the room dry! Their disbelief turned into bemused incredulity, but, having all individually dealt with us previously, they were convinced that, like all English folk, we were slightly eccentric. Our heels, however, were firmly dug in deep, and we countered each objection (in a friendly atmosphere) until we got our own way, having promised

Zut alors, *a shower with no door! It was worth digging our heels in – and the shower remains door-less to this day.*

that we would call in the *plombier* at a later date to fit a door should the need arise. Interestingly, about six months later, one of our neighbours mentioned to us that she was having a new bathroom fitted and M. Robinet, our *plombier,* was doing the job. She really liked his design especially, she explained, as it included a shower area with no door ...

Having won the Battle of the Shower, our next engagement concerned the bath. As we wanted a whirlpool model, we took M. Robinet's (very healthy) advice and chose a *balnéo* (short for *balnéothérapie,* a therapeutic combination of air and water jets). With his obvious approval, as well as that of all the other team members, surely this would be plain sailing. And so it was until we mentioned that we would, *bien sûr,* want the matching bath panel. How could this possibly be controversial – but it was. Nobody, apart from us, was in favour of such a large expanse of white plastic in 'their' bathroom! Our argument that the manufacturer of this somewhat expensive piece of equipment recommended and, indeed, supplied such a solution fell on deaf ears. We were, however, getting slightly worn down by this time and so we agreed to listen to an alternative idea – tile it, said the *carreleur* (well, he would, wouldn't he?), a suggestion that certainly got the French vote. We agreed, albeit reluctantly, and the project was duly started. It was only some weeks later that the *carreleur* felt that he should inform us that, due to the oversize dimensions of the bath, a tiled panel would be too heavy – in spite of the fact that this had been his suggestion in the first place. A further meeting with the *plombier* and the *menuisier* was rapidly convened. This time, it was suggested that a wooden panel should be custom-made for the bath. We agreed to call in an *ébéniste* for a *devis,* and so it was that M. Lebois came round to measure up the job. We explained what was wanted, a wooden panel to match the bathroom furniture and which could be easily re- moved for maintenance purposes. Fortunately we had explained that this was not our idea, which was somewhat pleasing as he told us that, not only would it be almost impossible for him to find wood to match our other fittings, but also it would be very expensive. We are pleased to be able to report that, in our opinion, the white plastic panel looks really good.

Points to Check During Your First Meeting

Obviously, you should ensure that the *artisan* is qualified to carry out the work. Just as you would not visit a dentist for problems with your eyesight, so do not ex- pect a *maçon* to do the work of a *menuisier.* Does he have any accreditations and/or qualifications and can he provide proof of them? Ask if he has worked on any similar projects and if he can supply references or pictures. It may also be sensible to ask to see his Chamber of Trade identity card (*Carte d'Identification* – see Chapter 4), and his insurance certificate (Chapter 9).

In some cases you will find that it is not the *artisan* himself who does the work, but his employees. Take this opportunity to ask about his workforce. You should satisfy yourself that he has enough manpower, with the necessary skills, to complete the project in the timescales you expect. Find out whether any of the work will need to be sub-contracted, perhaps because the *artisan* does not have adequate technical means and equipment. If so, you will need to ensure that the work is carried out to the required standard.

If appropriate, for example with a new central heating boiler, establish whether the *artisan* provides any form of after-sales service, and, if so, under what terms. It may be the case that he is willing to offer you a service contract, but, as with all such documents, make sure that you fully understand exactly what it includes or, perhaps more importantly, what it excludes. Such an arrangement should, of course, be considered only in the light of the terms of the manufacturer's guarantee/warranty (*see* Chapter 9) – and always ensure that all the documentation for this has been left with you, along with the instruction manual for the equipment. Of course, any such documentation is likely to be written in French but, if you look at the manufacturer's website, you may be able to download an English version from the Internet.

If an inclusive, after-sales contract is not available, then establish the *artisan*'s call-out terms and conditions – for example, for what hours will he be available in an emergency, and does he have a standard call-out charge?

Check whether he can supply all the materials required. Make sure that he has a good network of suppliers so that you can select the equipment you want and benefit from the lower rate of VAT. This again can be illustrated by our bathroom project. In his initial *devis*, M. Robinet, the plumber, included just guideline prices for the supply of items such as the WC, bath, washbasin, taps and shower fittings. He gave us the names of four local bathroom stockists with whom he had trade accounts and instructed us to visit them in order to make our choices. Unlike the UK, the concept of a 'bathroom suite' does not exist in France and each element is chosen individually. And believe us, the choice available is bewilderingly extensive. In addition to the items displayed in the showrooms, the stockists are also able to supply equipment from a large number of other manufacturers. Fortunately, the advice and help given to us by the showroom staff proved to be invaluable and eventually, after several visits and many hours spent poring over brochures, we succeeded in compiling our definitive list of requirements. We then visited each store again and established a detailed list with them of the items that each would supply. We were given one copy, the store retained a second and the third was sent to M. Robinet, enabling him to finalise his *devis*. A similar procedure was followed for the selection of the wall and floor tiles.

Normally, having noted all the relevant details of the project and measured up, where appropriate, the *artisan* will take his leave, promising to let you have a *devis* once he has calculated the costs. In some situations where there is a lot of competition, such as roof treatments, double glazing and insulation, it is a common practice to complete a preprinted *devis* form on the spot. You will be encouraged to sign your acceptance of the *devis* there and then. Of course, you do not have to but, if you do, you should remember that the law relating to door-to-door selling allows you a seven-day cooling off period. Indeed, the *devis* often contains a detachable form (*bordereau de retractation*) you can complete in order to cancel the contract. If you change your mind, you should notify the *artisan* by registered post (*lettre recommandée avec avis de réception*) within a week.

Less occasionally, the tradesman may simply leave you with a price scribbled on the back of his business card. If you are tempted to use his services, you should insist on receiving a proper *devis* before agreeing to proceed. Any reputable *artisan* will readily comply; those who do not should be avoided.

Understanding the *Devis*

You should not need to make assumptions about what the *devis* does or does not include, it should be comprehensive and transparent, and, if you are in any doubt, discuss it with the *artisan*. First of all, you should read the *devis* carefully to ensure that it contains everything that you require. For example, will light bulbs be supplied with the new fitting? If any demolition work is to be carried out before reconstruction, check what will happen to the rubble – you do not want a huge pile of it left in the middle of your garden. If you are having a room redecorated, how many coats of paint will be applied, and will the floor be protected? If the *artisan* provides you with alternative options, make sure you understand what the differences are.

The list is endless, so make sure that you are very clear about what you will be paying for. Remember, if it is not specified on the *devis*, you can and will be legitimately charged for the item(s) as 'extras'. As well as being needed for your budget planning, this is essential when comparing *devis* from different *artisans*. Unless they are like for like, you will not necessarily be able to select the best quotation. Unlike Britain, where builders tend to give a price for the entire project without detailed breakdowns of materials, the French *artisan* will not – so let the buyer beware.

There is, of course, no reason why you should not attempt to negotiate the price with the *artisan* before finally signing the *devis* – especially if you have two or more apparently similarly specified offers at different prices. On the whole, however, you will find that most genuine *artisans* prepare their *devis* diligently and fairly, leaving little leeway as far as the bottom line is concerned. The only opportunity for bargaining may arise in the selection of the materials and equipment to be supplied, provided that you are prepared to be flexible.

There is little point in trying to insert so-called 'penalty clauses' into a *devis*. For a start, the *artisan* is unlikely to accept one, and in any case it would be very difficult to enforce. If something were to go badly wrong, you would be able to seek redress without any such clauses, so why start off a project with a negative attitude by implying to the *artisan* that you do not trust him?

It is, of course, possible, if not likely, that some changes to specifications will occur as the job progresses. If you want to make any modifications, then obviously you must first discuss them with the *artisan* and, depending on the extent of the changes, obtain a new *devis*. Having a double rather than single electric plug socket can easily be informally agreed, whereas a request to knock down a wall or switch from basic hypermarket own-brand tiles to Italian hand-made marble is a different kettle of *poissons*. Similarly, if the *artisan* finds that the job entails more work than he originally expected, he should inform you of any additional expenses that could result. This often requires you to make a quick decision – for which you will have to rely on the advice of the *artisan* – and which may not always be the best one. One of our very first projects involved the replacement of the original, antiquated electrical fuse-box with a modern distribution panel, complete with circuit-breakers. We accepted a *devis* from a local *électricien*. After a morning's work, he appeared to have completed the job. At lunch-time, however, he approached us with some 'bad news'. Having wired up the new panel, he had discovered that we had not one but two fuse-boxes at opposite ends of the basement. He would be able to replace the newly discovered box with a new panel but, of course, it would mean double the work – and double the cost. We reluctantly agreed, as this seemed to be the only option, but took the decision not to use this particular *artisan*'s services again in the future. It was only some months later, when another *électricien* was working in the house, that the suggestion was made to combine the two distribution panels – a much more efficient solution.

A visit from a tradesman does not automatically imply that he wants the work. We have already explained that many *artisans* will either currently or potentially have all the work that they can handle, and so are able to cherry-pick the jobs that they are willing to take on. It will not necessarily be the size of the job that is critical. Indeed, a half-day 'filler' may fit well into an already busy schedule. We received a call from our *chauffagiste* one October morning, telling us that one of his men was sweeping chimneys in our area that day and that they had just had a cancellation for an afternoon visit. Would we like to take the slot for our annual *ramonage*? The answer was an immediate acceptance. It acted as a reminder to us that our chimney needed sweeping before the winter log fires were lit, saved us a telephone call and helped him out – so everybody was happy. In that instance we did not, of course, ask for a written *devis*, the cost being less than €150. He simply quoted the price over the telephone, and we happily accepted it verbally, knowing that a formal invoice (*facture*) would be forthcoming.

There are many reasons why an *artisan* may not want to work for you, including, of course, his understanding of your exact requirements. With the best will in the world, if there is a poor level of communication between you, the *artisan* cannot be blamed for shying away from your project.

You should not, therefore, assume that just because the *artisan* has visited you he will automatically send you a *devis*. He will decide after the visit not only if he wants the job but also whether he wants to work for you, whether there is likely to be sufficient profit and how it would fit into his schedule. He also realizes that, if you accept a *devis*, he is committed, and so he will always veer to the side of caution.

Similarly, you should not expect the *artisan* to drop everything in order to prepare your *devis* – indeed, a delay of two to three weeks is not exceptional. Note, however, that *artisans* with AB5 accreditation (*see* Chapter 2) are committed to supplying a *devis* within two weeks. The more complex the job, the more difficult the detailed preparation of a *devis* becomes, and an *artisan* with plenty of work will not be inclined to give it top priority; here, as in many aspects of life in France, patience should be your watchword.

It may also sound obvious, but it is extremely important, when you are employing two or more tradesmen for your project, that they each know exactly what, where and when the others are doing. For example, the *carreleur* will want to know exactly where the *électricien* is fixing sockets and switches, just as the *menuisier* may well need to know the *plombier's* routing plan for new piping.

After being in our new home for several weeks and having formulated our five-year plan – which consisted largely of what we considered to be the more pressing projects – we then went through the house room by room, making a detailed list of all the jobs that needed to be done. Although many required a level of DIY that was not beyond even our limited capabilities, there were several items that we felt necessitated the employment of a professional (or, in Duncan's native Yorkshire *patois*, 'a proper bloody man'). We therefore bundled the jobs into what we felt was a varied and substantial package for a *menuisier*. In total, we contacted seven local tradesmen, five of whom agreed to come round and discuss our requirements. All five appeared interested and on average each spent at least half an hour with us, leaving with smiles and handshakes. In the event, we received only a single *devis*, which is not an unusual experience. Coincidentally, one of them came round the morning that a bedroom door lock had somehow managed to jam itself from the inside (to this day we have no idea how). We, therefore, asked the *menuisier* if he could have a look at it for us while he was there. He willingly agreed and spent the best part of an hour trying to free the door, resulting in his having to force off the old lock, replace it with a brand new one and make good the damage that he had done to the frame – it was a really neat and professional piece of work, a good man to have around we thought. Not only did he fail to submit a *devis*, but neither did he send us a bill (*facture*) for the time and materials required to repair the door. It was then that we realized that we should not expect a *devis* from everyone who views the job, nor indeed an invoice from everyone who does any work.

In this respect, we always think of our favourite *électricien*, an extremely pleasant, competent and generally helpful young man. Nothing is ever too much trouble, and he will pop round at the drop of a hat if we have a problem. On one occasion we went out and bought a combined light and fan fitting for our bedroom in the anticipation of a long hot summer. On getting it home and reading the instructions, however, it was painfully clear that installing the thing was well beyond our level of competence – hence a call to M. Lumière for assistance. Although he is always willing to prepare a *devis*, he is also the first to admit that his administration skills are pretty hopeless, and we have come to know him well enough to trust and accept verbal quotes from him for smaller jobs. On the agreed day he turned up with his two assistants. He stayed for about half an hour and then left after having explained carefully to the two lads exactly what they had to do. He returned a couple of hours later to inspect the job, which had only just been completed, and, once he was satisfied that all was well, off they went to lunch. As it happened, it was several months before we had need of his services again, but then after we called him we realized in horror that we had not paid him for the previous job – simply because he had not sent us a *facture*, and in the hustle and bustle of life it had slipped our minds. When he arrived, we apologized profusely and asked how much we owed for the earlier morning's work. He looked first confused and then bemused. 'Hadn't he sent us a *facture*? Well, administration wasn't his strong point. *Mais c'est pas vrai,* we were asking him for a bill, we were actually volunteering to pay? What strange people these *anglais* are! The French would never chase a *facture* – *jamais!*' Yes, we persisted, but how much did we owe him? 'Well, it's such a long time ago, let's forget it, shall we?', he replied, and meant it. We have noticed that for many *artisans* it is their wife that looks after the business's administration and accounts. M. Lumière is, needless to say, a bachelor – our advice to him, find yourself a good *femme*!

4
Checking an *Artisan*'s Credentials

The Black Economy – and Why You Should Not Use It

In France, it is a legal requirement that all businesses are officially registered, have the appropriate insurance cover and pay business taxes and social charges. Many would-be entrepreneurs are, however, deterred by the extensive formalities they must go through in order to set up a business. Not only is there a complex web of administrative paperwork to complete, but there are also significant, up-front investments to be made in the form of social security charges before the company even starts to make any money. Those British tradesmen who relocate to France expecting to be able to set up a business as easily as they did at home are in for a nasty shock. With the lifting of restrictions on employment across the European Union you may encounter tradesmen of many different nationalities, either working as sub-contractors or in their own right. Some will have made an effort to follow the rules, but others have either chosen not to do so or perhaps just do not understand the regulations. For all these reasons, it is not unusual to find tradesmen operating illegally in France, which is commonly referred to as *sur le noir* or 'on the black'. And it is not only foreigners who break the law. In fact, these businesses are just as likely to be run by native French citizens, even though there is no direct French translation of the term 'cowboy builder'.

Many French people find it normal and acceptable to employ tradesmen illegally, especially if they think they can save money by doing so. So be careful when you ask for recommendations from your French acquaintances. When we were chatting to the owner of a local bar about our forthcoming bathroom project he told us of a very good plumber who lived in the neighbourhood. When, however, he went on to say that the man would be happy to carry out the work in the evenings and at weekends, it became obvious that he would be moonlighting. We politely but firmly refused to take his telephone number. Similarly, you should be suspicious of any tradesman who refuses to give you a written estimate or who asks for payment in cash.

It is understandable that if you are having difficulties finding an *artisan* for your project, you may be tempted to employ someone 'on the black'. Our response to this is very simple and definitive – *don't!*

The main reason for this advice is that it is illegal and that both you and the workman could be prosecuted. It is your responsibility as the client to ensure that any tradesman you use is working legally. If you knowingly call on the services of someone who is not registered, whose registration application has been refused or who has been struck off the register, then you could be fined as much as €45,000 and even face a three-year prison sentence. You could also be financially liable if you do not request a written *devis* (or any other document which provides proof that the tradesman is legally registered) for work costing €3,000 or more. If it turns out that the tradesman you use is not registered you could be asked to pay all the taxes and social security charges that he should have paid if he had been trading legitimately, and even his workers' salaries if he had been paying them below the statutory minimum wage. And if he is not an EU national but is working in France without the necessary work and residence permits, the sanctions could be even greater.

Another reason for not using unregistered builders is that when you come to sell your property you will not be able to offset the costs of the work they have carried out against any capital gains tax for which you might be liable (*see* Chapter 8).

If these arguments are not enough to convince you, remember that you will be totally responsible should anything go wrong. The work will not be covered by any sort of guarantee or insurance, and you will be liable for any claims resulting from damage to property and/or injuries to people, including third parties. If a worker falls from a ladder and needs hospital treatment, you will have to pay the bill. He may even sue you for compensation or loss of earnings. If the work is substandard you will have little chance of either having it repaired or getting your money back. If the work is not completed you will have absolutely no legal redress, as there is no valid contract between you. And, finally, in many instances, people working in the black economy charge as much as, if not more than, legitimate tradesmen.

How Can You Tell Whether a Tradesman Is Legally Registered?

As stated in Chapter 2, all *artisans* must register with the *Répertoire des Métiers* of their local Chamber of Trade before starting to do business. This procedure automatically triggers their registration with the appropriate tax and social security offices. Once the formalities have been completed, the *artisan* will receive an identity card (*Carte d'Identification*) from the Chamber of Trade, which acts as the official proof that he is registered. Any genuine *artisan* will be quite happy to show you a copy of his card.

In addition, all businesses, from sole traders to multinational corporations, registered in France are allocated a unique, nine-digit identification number, known as the SIREN. A further five-digit reference is suffixed to identify individual sites of each enterprise. Together, the two parts of the number form the SIRET. Even if a business has only one address it will have a fourteen-digit SIRET number. A company with two trading locations, however, will have one SIREN and two SIRET numbers. When a business ceases to trade its SIREN/SIRET numbers are immediately withdrawn. The numbers cannot be transferred to anyone else; if the company is taken over a new SIREN/SIRET number is issued.

How the SIREN/SIRET numbers are displayed depends on the official status of the business. For example, an *artisan* registered at the Chamber of Trade can use the format *321 654 987 RM 012*, where the first nine digits represent the SIREN, RM stands for *Répertoire des Métiers* and 012 identifies the Chamber of Trade concerned. If a business is set up as a registered company the format will be *RCS PARIS 321 654 987*, where RCS stands for *Registre du Commerce et des Sociétés*, followed by the town in which registration has taken place and then the SIREN number. Although it is only legally necessary to use the full SIRET number in limited circumstances, many businesses choose to display it in preference to the SIREN number, for example, *RCS PARIS 321 654 987 12315*, where 12315 indicates the individual establishment of the enterprise. Incidentally, the SIREN number is also used as the last nine digits of a company's VAT (*TVA*) number, which should appear on its invoices.

The SIREN/SIRET numbering system, known as SIRENE (*Système Informatique pour le Répertoire des Entreprises et de leurs Etablissements*), is administered by the national statistical service INSEE (*Institut National de la Statistique et des Etudes Economiques*). The database can be searched at http://avis-situation-sirene.insee.fr/ provided that you know the enterprise's SIREN/SIRET number. In addition to the basic company details, the database contains the date when the company was first registered, its legal status, the number of employees and the main activity it undertakes. This information is also available from commercial organizations which, usually for a fee, offer additional information about the companies on the database, such as financial reports. You can check that a tradesman is legally registered by using the search facilities at the following websites:

www.cofacerating.fr
www.euridile.com
www.infogreffe.fr
www.manageo.fr
www.societe.com

54 *Checking an Artisan's Credentials*

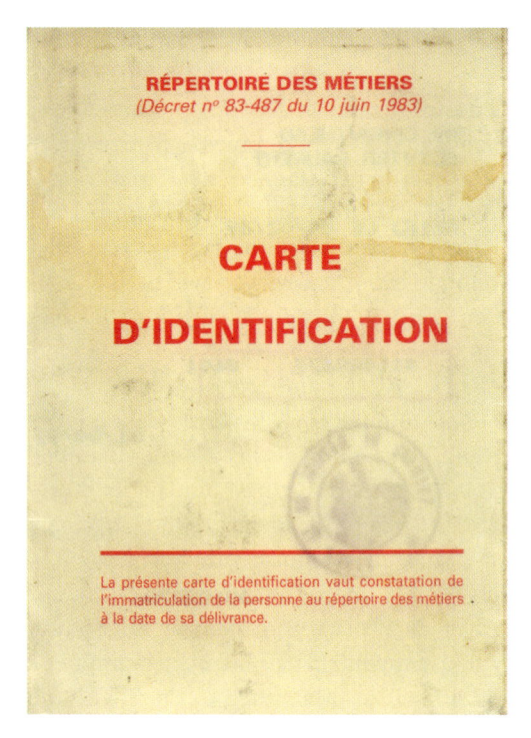

The Carte d'Identification, *an* artisan's *"passport"...*

In most cases, you can enter either the SIREN/SIRET number or the name under which the business is registered (*raison sociale*). Sometimes, just the *artisan*'s name (*nom du dirigeant*) or telephone number will suffice. Entering the department number will reduce the number of results if it is a very common name. Although all the websites listed use the same official source for their information, it is not unusual to find an *artisan* listed on one but not on another. We therefore recommend that you consult at least two of the websites when you are trying to confirm that a business is a legitimate one.

It should be noted that, although businesses are not legally required to display their SIREN/SIRET number on advertisements (although some do), it is obligatory on headed paper, price lists and printed publicity materials, as well as on legal documents, such as estimates and invoices. There have been instances of tradesmen using false or fake registration numbers. If you have any doubts, you should ask the *artisan* for his number and check it on one of the websites listed above. Sometimes the words *SIRET en cours* are used to show that the business is currently awaiting allocation of its number. You can ask the *artisan* to show you a copy of

CHAMBRE DE MÉTIERS	CDM DE LA VIENNE	PERSONNE PHYSIQUE
Mr CHAUVINEAU OLIVIER LAURENT NE(E) LE N° d'immatriculation au Répertoire des Métiers 4114896677 R.M. 8601 Délivrée le : 01/04/97 Numéro de gestion 0010029786	Domiciliation de l'entreprise : 2 CHE DE CHAMP LOUP Nombre d'établissements : 1 Activités artisanales : ELECTRICITE BATIMENT, VENTILATION MECANIQUE CONTROLEE Nom commercial : Néant ACTIVITE : Permanente Sedentaire Non ambulante DEBUT D'ACTIVITE : 07/04/97	CONJOINT COLLABORATEUR : NEANT ARTISAN

… and its content, showing his contact details and the trade(s) for which he is registered.

his application form. You may also wish to ask him for evidence of his insurance, both for public liability (*responsabilité civile*) and for the ten-year guarantee (*garantie décennale*).

As well as the SIRENE, INSEE administers the NAF (*Nomenclature des Activités Française*). Regularly updated, this is a database of industrial classifications similar to the SIC (Standard Industrial Classification) used in the United Kingdom. When setting up, all businesses have to declare their principal activity which is given an APE (*Activité Principale Exercée*) code, consisting of four numbers followed by a single letter. They can also register their secondary activities, which normally have an obvious link with the primary one, although these are not always publicly listed. Here is an extract of the principal codes relating to property construction and renovation, along with an explanation of the areas they cover:

- 41.20A *Construction de maisons individuelles* Construction of houses;
- 43.11Z *Travaux de démolition* Demolition work;
- 43.12A *Travaux de terrassement courants et travaux préparatoires* Standard excavation work and other preparatory work to clear and level a building site, and the digging of trenches ready for cables and pipework;
- 43.21A *Travaux d'installation électrique dans tous locaux* Electrical installation work in any premises, including cabling and installation of electrical appliances, lighting, telephone and computer networks, aerials and satellite dishes, burglar and fire alarms, and solar panels;
- 43.22A *Travaux d'installation d'eau et de gaz en tous locaux* Water and gas installation work in any premises, including the installation of pipework, plumbing and sanitary equipment, and automated lawn-watering systems;
- 43.22B *Travaux d'installation d'équipements thermiques et de climatisation* Installation and maintenance of heating and ventilation equipment, including electric, gas and oil-fired boilers, and air conditioning systems;
- 43.29A *Travaux d'isolation* Insulation work – thermal (including double glazing), soundproofing and anti-vibration;
- 43.29B *Autres travaux d'installation n.c.a.* Other installation work not listed elsewhere, including window blinds and canopies, fences and gates, lifts and central vacuum cleaning systems;
- 43.31Z *Travaux de plâtrerie* All types of plasterwork, including its supporting structures, the fixing of plasterboard and erection of plaster-based partition walls;
- 43.32A *Travaux de menuiserie bois et PVC* Carpentry and joinery in wood and PVC, including doors, windows, shutters, built-in cupboards and kitchen units, wood panelling, staircases, partition walls, conservatories and loft conversions;

Checking an Artisan's Credentials 57

On the level, a legally registered and insured artisan *at work (Habitat Naturel – Chantier Christophe Sabourin (86)).*

43.32B *Travaux de menuiserie métallique et serrurerie* Metalwork and locks, including shutters, garage doors, staircases and conservatories;

43.33Z *Travaux de revêtement des sols et des murs* Wall and floor covering work, including tiling, wooden floors, fitting of carpets, lino, vinyl and other floor coverings, and wall-papering and associated preparatory work;

43.34Z *Travaux de peinture et vitrerie* Painting and glazing, including application of decorative and/or protective coatings, paints and varnishes, installation of plate glass doors and dividing walls;

43.39Z *Autres travaux de finition* Other final finishing work, including clearing up a site after building work (exterior only), and ornamental ironwork;

43.91A *Travaux de charpente* Construction of roof framework;

43.91B *Travaux de couverture par éléments* Roof tiling, corrugated roofing, installation of gutters, and other roofing work including cleaning;

43.99A *Travaux d'étanchéification* Waterproofing work – specialist treatment to seal, for example, roof terraces, basements and swimming pools, and other dampness treatments;

43.99B *Travaux de montage de structures métalliques* Erection of metallic structures, including scaffolding and work platforms;

43.99C *Travaux de maçonnerie générale et gros œuvre de bâtiment* General building and structural work, often using concrete and cement, including applying a roughcast finish to walls using mortar;

43.99D *Autres travaux spécialisés de construction* Other specialist construction work, including building foundations, chimneys, fireplaces and outdoor swimming pools.

As well as checking that an *artisan* is legally registered, you should also ascertain that his principal activity is relevant for the work you wish to be carried out. It should be noted, however, that the APE codes are used by INSEE purely for statistical analysis and carry no legal rights or obligations. When our roof developed a leak we called in a number of *artisans* to quote for its repair. One of them was a young man who had apparently just set up a roofing business in a local village and was keen to obtain work. After an impressively thorough inspection of our roof, he gravely descended the ladder and told us that the only option was to have it completely re-tiled. We were rather taken aback as he was the only *artisan* to offer such an opinion, but we nonetheless asked him to prepare an estimate. When we received it we duly checked his SIRET number. Although the number was indeed correct, we discovered that he was registered as a property-letting agent. Needless to say, we chose to use a genuine, experienced roofer, who discovered a hairline crack in one of the roof tiles, replaced it and charged us some €17,000 less than the property-letting agent.

The full range of trades for which an *artisan* is registered will appear on his Chamber of Trade identity card. Similarly, his insurance company will have supplied him with a certificate listing the activities for which he is covered.

It should be noted that while a general building company (*entreprise générale du bâtiment*) will probably show only its principal APE code on its official documents, it may in fact be registered under several other secondary categories.

Using British-Based Builders

It may be tempting to pay a British-based builder to come and work on your property in France, if only to avoid any communication problems. While British-registered companies are permitted to work in France, it is a legal requirement that they have the appropriate French insurance cover. It is possible (but not always so) that their public liability insurance may be valid in France, depending on the specific terms of their policy, but they are unlikely to have the necessary insurance to provide you with the compulsory ten-year guarantee (*assurance décennale*) on any work they carry out. Needless to say, obtaining such insurance is virtually impossible unless the company is registered in France. It is, therefore, extremely unusual for a builder registered in Britain but not in France to be able to work legally in France. Even if family and friends help you with any work on your house for no payment you could be liable should anything go wrong.

It should be noted, however, that in some areas of France, there are increasing numbers of British expats who have set up building businesses. Many of them are properly registered, insured and operate correctly within the framework of French legal requirements. Others, however, either deliberately or through ignorance (which is no defence in the eyes of the law), work 'on the black' and should be avoided at all costs. If in any doubt, ask to see proof of their credentials and check them carefully as the use of falsified documents is not unknown.

Reporting Illegal Working

By cheating the system and not paying their proper dues, people who operate 'on the black' present unfair competition to all those genuine workers who follow the rules. It also means that people who pay direct and/or indirect taxes in France (that is to say, anyone who owns property in France) effectively subsidize those who defraud the system. The French government is increasingly, therefore, taking active measures to control the situation. Random checks, for example, are frequently carried out on French building sites and other locations where illegal working may be found.

Being British we have, perhaps, been brought up to 'play the game' and 'do the decent thing', which, ironically, exclude 'sneaking', 'snitching' or 'grassing' on known offenders (that's simply not cricket). Having said this, it should be remembered that the attitude in France is often quite different. If you so wish, it is not considered bad form to report any instances you come across of illegal working to the local *Préfecture*, tax office or social security contributions (URSSAF) office. Indeed, the latter has a special section dedicated to this. You can contact them anonymously with all the details you have regarding the business working illegally and they will follow up the matter.

Having read this chapter, you may still be considering employing someone 'on the black'. Apart from suggesting that you reread the advice we gave at the very start, we should point out that it is quite possible that one of your neighbours or one of the other genuine *artisans* you contacted for an estimate may feel that it is their duty as good French citizens to report the case of illegal working to the authorities. *Artisans* tend to stick together in informal local networks and bitterly resent non-registered workers taking work that they consider to be rightfully theirs. They will not, therefore, hesitate to take whatever action they consider appropriate to protect their livelihoods. They will soon notice the unmarked white van outside your house that is clearly commercial but which does not belong to any of the locally registered tradesmen and will know exactly what to do about it. As we said before, it is not only the illegal worker that the authorities may take action against, it is also the householder that is foolish enough to employ him. Need we say more?

5
Accepting an Estimate

Selecting a *Devis*

Having located your *artisans* and received a number of estimates, how do you decide which to accept?

First, use your instinct. Did the *artisan* turn up for your first meeting on time? Was he friendly? Did you establish a rapport with him? Do you trust him to work, perhaps in your absence, in your home? Are you sure that he is legally registered and insured to carry out the work you require? Are you confident that he has the necessary experience and resources to do a good job? On a practical level, did he make notes and take measurements so that he can provide you with the necessary detail on the *devis*?

If, after answering these questions, you still have a number of *devis* to choose from, here are our suggestions, in order of preference, to help you to make the final choice:

- By recommendation – if an *artisan* has been personally recommended to you, you will have the assurance that his work has met with the approval of at least one other customer. Indeed, most people will only make a recommendation if they are particularly satisfied with the work carried out. Be careful, though, that it is a genuine recommendation and not one from a member of the *artisan*'s family or one of his friends. If you choose a local, well-established *artisan*, he will be keen to maintain his good reputation.
- By price – but remember that the most expensive is not necessarily the best and vice versa. Make sure that you are comparing like with like. Are all the materials and equipment to be supplied of the same quality? Are all facets of the job identical, or does one of them include something extra?
- By professional accreditation (*see* Chapter 2) – but be aware that, although these give some, varying, indications of the quality and reliability of an *artisan*, they can never provide an absolute guarantee that the work will be carried out to your satisfaction.
- By availability – the first, or perhaps the only one, to respond to your request for an estimate. The difficulty of finding an *artisan* may mean that you are forced to select the first (or only) one who is available, particularly if you need

an emergency repair. You do not want to be without any heating in the midst of winter or have a leaking roof during the April showers (which, incidentally, as they arrive early in France, are known as the *gibboulées de mars*). Bear in mind, however, that the best *artisans* are often those with the fullest schedules, and it may be worth waiting a few months if you can.
- By language – he speaks English – or maybe he is English. Do not, however, rely on a Frenchman's apparent ability to speak English for the intricate technical details of a project.
- By chance – for instance, the one with the biggest display advertisement, the first listed in Yellow Pages or one who has popped a leaflet into your letterbox.

If you are using an architect or project manager to oversee the work he is likely to have a network of tradesmen who he recommends and uses on a regular basis. You are, of course, able to specify that you wish to employ a particular *artisan* if you so wish, perhaps if he has already done some work to your property and is familiar with it.

Deposits and Stage Payments

There are no hard and fast rules regarding deposits and stage payments, although you should *never* pay the whole cost up-front. The *devis* should clearly specify what the *artisan* in question expects, and so you should be fully aware of your obligations before signing it.

In an attempt to prevent fraud, French law limits cash payment for goods and services to a maximum of €3,000. If the invoice (including tax) exceeds this sum, you are allowed to pay a cash deposit of up to €460. You should, of course, make sure that you get a receipt as proof of payment. In practice, it is common to pay a deposit (*acompte*) of 30 per cent, but this can be up to 50 per cent if the *artisan* has to spend a significant sum on equipment and materials before starting the work. For small jobs or those where the work is to be carried out within a short timescale the deposit is often overlooked, and the full amount becomes payable on completion. Occasionally, an *artisan* will not cash your deposit cheque until the job has been started, but do not bank on this for your cash-flow purposes. Remember, it is illegal to draw a cheque on a French bank if there are insufficient funds in your account to support it. And there is no point in post-dating a cheque, since it becomes payable as soon as it is deposited in the payee's account regardless of the date written on it.

Depending on the scope of the project, you may be asked to make stage payments. These should be clearly specified in the *devis* and should be paid only on the satisfactory completion of the agreed extent of the work. Obviously, if you are not happy with the work done to date you should inform the *artisan*, and allow him the opportunity to put it right, before you pay him. (For advice on what to do if the matter cannot be resolved between you *see* Chapter 9.) The final payment (*solde*) should be made only when you receive the *artisan*'s final invoice and you are satisfied with the work he has done. An invoice must be issued for any work charged at €15.24 (100 Francs in old money) or above. A cheque can be stopped in only very limited circumstances, for example, if it has been lost or stolen, or used fraudulently, or if the payee has gone into liquidation. It is illegal to stop a cheque if you are simply not satisfied with the work carried out by the payee. If the amount invoiced exceeds that stated on the *devis*, and provided there have been no subsequent changes to the details agreed, you can contest the invoice by sending the *artisan* a letter by registered post.

The *artisan* will not, and should not have to, wait ages for payment for a job well done. In any case getting a local reputation as a bad payer will hardly endear you when trying to get future *devis*. If you do not pay his bill on time the *artisan* is

Sample Letter 1

Objet: Contestation de facture

J'ai accepté votre devis du [date] *pour les travaux de* [give brief details of the work agreed]. *Le montant indiqué sur la facture que vous m'avez envoyée est supérieur à celui fixé dans le devis, bien que je n'aie pas demandé de travaux supplémentaires.*

Je vous rappelle que, selon l'article 1134 du Code civil, vous êtes tenu de respecter les informations indiquées sur le contrat.

Je vous demande donc de revoir votre facture et de vous en tenir à la somme prévue dans le devis initial.

Translation

Re: Contesting an invoice

I accepted your estimate of [date] for [give brief details of the work agreed]. The total sum on the invoice you have sent me is higher than that stated in the estimate, even though I did not request any additional work.

May I remind you that, under article 1134 of the civil code, you are required to respect the details indicated in the contract.

I request, therefore, that you revise your invoice to reflect the sum stated in your initial estimate.

entitled to charge interest on the outstanding amount. If you still fail to pay, he can impose a penalty charge, having first given you written notice. These points may well appear in the small print of the conditions on the back of his *devis*. Note that any equipment supplied remains the property of the *artisan* until it is paid for.

An *artisan* is not obliged to give you a receipt for a payment by cheque. Once he has paid it into his account and the money has been transferred then legally the debt is discharged.

Remember to keep all the paperwork safely, even though it may by now have started to look like a bureaucratic nightmare. It may well be worth its weight in gold if you have problems later on. For example, two years after our roof space had been re-insulated and we had applied for, and benefited from, the available tax credit (*see* Chapter 8), we received a letter from the tax office asking for documentary evidence that this work had been carried out legitimately. We were able to provide the *facture* easily and the matter ended without further investigation. If, on the other hand, we had been tempted by the *artisan* to accept a price reduction in return for a cash payment and did not have the correct paperwork, we could well have found ourselves in serious trouble. If you use the French system properly, more often than not it works in your favour, but if you try to cheat, it can be merciless.

Once You Have Accepted a *Devis* – What Can You Expect?

They say that it is bad news that sells newspapers, and similarly horror stories about French workmen seem more prevalent than good news. The truth, of course, is that the vast majority of projects carried out by *artisans* are completed to a high standard, and so the nightmare tales, although often perfectly true, should be viewed in the correct perspective.

In our experience, and from that of the many other expats we have spoken to during our research for this book, the workmanship of registered *artisans* is excellent and that should not be surprising. They have served a long and often demanding apprenticeship to achieve a status of which they are proud, and which they are not going to spoil by sloppy workmanship. They are small business people who rely for their livelihoods on mainly local people, and would be given short shrift by the French if they were not up to scratch.

The typical *artisan* is hard working and conscientious and, arriving usually between 7.30 and 8.00 in the morning, will hit the ground running. Assuming that there are no unforeseen problems, he will work through until midday when, like the rest of France, it is down tools for lunch. In our early days here we caused some not inconsiderable amusement when offering to make cups of tea or coffee half way through the morning. Such breaks are not the French way – although the occasional cigarette break in the garden is regarded as quite normal. We have only once experienced a worker lighting up inside the house and that was when we were having our new kitchen built. On this particular day, M. Carré, the tiler, was at work with his young assistant. We happened to be in the adjoining salon and noticed through the window that the older man had gone out to his van for some reason. We then smelt cigarette smoke, which is very noticeable in a non-smoking household. Duncan was about to pop into the kitchen to speak to the lad when the boss returned and hit the roof. We actually felt quite sorry for the young man as M. Carré explained in no uncertain terms, and with a voice that could probably have been heard several houses away, that smoking inside a client's house was completely unacceptable, and that if he ever did it again it would be a swift *au revoir*. The *artisan* then stuck his head round the salon door and apologized profusely on his assistant's behalf.

On returning from lunch at 2.00, work resumes non-stop until about 5.30, then a quick clean up and off home to the paperwork. If for any reason the job starts to fall behind, and this can quite legitimately happen, then it is certainly not unknown for the *artisan* to ask your permission to work on into the evening in order to catch up. After all, it is in his interest as much as yours for him to get the job finished on time, for until it is he will not be paid, and cash-flow is as critical to an *artisan* as it is to any other small business. As we say, there are perfectly acceptable reasons why a job may fall behind: the *artisan* may be let down by his suppliers, by another *artisan* on the project, because of illness in his family or because he has been called out to an emergency. If the last should happen, do not be too harsh on the man. Remember that next time *you* might be the emergency in the middle of somebody else's job.

The reality is that unforeseeable problems are not uncommon and annoying (but unavoidable) delays are a fact of life. We can recall several occasions when we have been affected in this way. The first happened at the final stage of our kitchen project, when the room had been completely gutted and rebuilt and was finished apart from the decorating. We had chosen and ordered the wallpaper in good time, as there was a three-week delivery period, but had bought and taken home the matching frieze, which happened to be in stock. On schedule, M. Pinceau completed the paintwork and prepared the walls for papering, telling us that he would collect the wallpaper the following day and the job would be finished by the end of the week. That evening we received a telephone call from his wife, informing us that she had checked with the shop but the wallpaper had not yet arrived. She was *désolée* but the wholesaler was out of stock and there would be a further two weeks' delay. Unfortunate, but these things happen. Our patience and attitude, however, hardened somewhat a fortnight later when we were informed that there was a strike at the wallpaper manufacturers and no one knew when it would be resolved. As a month had now passed, we decided to cut our losses and selected another paper – one that was in stock and matched our frieze. The result was a long delay that was in no way preventable by either the *peintre* or us.

Smaller Projects

For some small jobs you may choose to use an odd-job man (*homme toutes mains*) rather than a fully qualified *artisan*. Payment can then be made using a *Chèque emploi service universel* (CESU). This system was introduced for personal services provided in your home by, for example, cleaners, babysitters and gardeners. It also includes small household maintenance jobs or *petit bricolage*. The advantage is that you can employ someone in your home without having to declare it to the authorities. By paying with a CESU (which you can obtain from your bank) all the social security contributions are automatically paid, giving the service provider the same protection and benefits as a salaried worker. From your point of view, you can receive an income tax credit of 50 per cent of the sum paid, provided that the total annual amount does not exceed €500 and that each job takes no longer than 2hr. (*See* Chapter 8 for information on other tax credits.)

6
Obtaining Planning Permission

Needless to say, a Frenchman's home is not always his *château*. Owning a property in France does not give you the automatic right to carry out whatever work you like on it. Any extension you wish to build, or any other modification to the external appearance of the building is subject to the building and planning regulations of the commune in which it is situated. Since October 2007 the planning process has been greatly modified and is now much more straightforward. You may, of course, be using the services of an architect (which in some circumstances is obligatory) or other project manager who will deal with all the planning administration on your behalf. But remember though, that ultimately *you* are responsible for ensuring that your project meets the necessary requirements, and it is you who will pay the price if all the procedures are not followed correctly. It is important, therefore, that you have an understanding of at least the basic principles of the planning process. Note that this chapter concerns only work carried out to residential property. If your project includes an agricultural, commercial or industrial application you should seek specialist, professional advice.

Local Building and Planning Regulations

Nationally, general planning laws which apply throughout France are listed in the RNU (*Règlement nationale d'urbanisme*). These, however, apply only to communes which have not formulated their own specific plans. These local regulations will be contained in a document known as the PLU (*Plan local d'urbanisme*), which has largely superseded the POS (*Plan d'occupation des sols*), although the latter may still be in force in some areas. Smaller communes with fewer regulations may publish them in a *Carte communale*. These are all public documents which you are entitled to consult, free of charge, at the planning department (*service d'urbanisme*) of your local *Mairie*. In small communes it may well be M. le Maire himself who deals with your request. Alternatively, you can apply at the offices of your *département*'s DDE (*Direction départementale de l'équipement*), which also has responsibility for approving planning applications.

In general, the PLU or the POS will state what construction is permitted in the different zones of each commune and the distances to be maintained with respect to public highways and neighbouring buildings. It may also stipulate such aspects as the materials to be used for the outside of the building, the slope of the roof, the colours permitted for the walls and the shutters, and the maximum height of building allowed.

Measuring the Surface Area

For planning purposes there are two different measures that need to be calculated. The first is the SHOB (*surface hors œuvre brute*). This is the total surface area on each floor of your property, including the thickness of the internal and the external walls. It also includes balconies, mezzanine floors and galleries, basements and attics (regardless of whether they are used or not), roof terraces, terraces at ground floor level and garages or other parking spaces when they are integral to, or attached to the building. If you have several buildings on your land, then the surface area of each must be included.

The SHON (*surface hors œuvre nette*) is the SHOB after certain deductions have been made. Unlike the SHOB, the SHON excludes areas of basements and attics that cannot be used for either living or working purposes (or where their height is less than 1.8m), basement cellars that do not have a door or window to the exterior, open external areas such as balconies and terraces, and garages and other parking areas. You may also deduct the area of agricultural buildings on your property, provided that they are not used as housing, an office or a shop. Once this calculation has been made, a further 5 per cent of the resulting figure may be deducted to account for insulation. Two further deductions may be applied in special circumstances – 5sq.m if your project involves improving the sanitation of the building, such as creating a new kitchen or bathroom, where none existed before; and 5sq.m if the work is to improve the building's interior accessibility for disabled people.

There is a form to help you with this calculation, entitled *Fiche d'aide pour le calcul des surfaces hors œuvre brutes et nettes des constructions*. It is available either from the *Mairie* or online at www.urbanisme.equipement.gouv.fr (click on the link *Les nouveaux formulaires* and then on *La déclaration préalable* or *Le permis de construire*). For professional advice on calculating these areas, you should consult either an architect or a surveyor (*géomètre-expert*).

The regulations will also contain the COS (*coefficient d'occupation des sols*), a figure which will allow you to calculate the maximum size of building permitted in relationship to the total surface area of your building plot. This could limit the size of extension you can add to your existing property. If, for example, the area of your land is 1,000sq.m and your commune's COS is 0.25, then the maximum floor area (SHON – *see* page 68) of the building should not total more than 250sq.m (1,000 × 0.25). There are, however, certain circumstances when this figure can be exceeded by up to 20 per cent, notably when the project involves the installation of a heating system using energy produced from renewable resources. For specific advice you should consult an architect or your *département*'s CAUE (*see* Chapter 2).

The *Certificat d'Urbanisme*

Each plot of land in France has certain restrictions imposed on it regarding what it can be used for and what building is allowed on it. All the necessary information is contained in the *Certificat d'urbanisme*, which you can apply for at the *Mairie* of the commune where the land is situated. There are two versions of this certificate. The first is a *Certificat d'urbanisme d'information* which, as its name suggests, is for information purposes only. It contains details from the PLU or POS regarding local regulations applicable to the land, the existence of any public rights of way over the land and a list of taxes and other charges payable. To find out whether or not you can build on the land, and whether your project is feasible, you will need a *Certificat d'urbanisme opérationnel* which will also advise you of any existing or proposed public services available, such as roads, water supply, electricity and gas. Neither certificate, however, gives you any form of authorization; you will still need planning permission if you want to build on the site.

Both forms of the *Certificat d'urbanisme* remain valid for a period of 18 months. During this time it is guaranteed that no new taxes or rights of way will be imposed on the landowner – unless they relate to public health and safety. The certificate may be renewed for a further period of 12 months, by applying to the *Mairie* at least two months before the original expiry date.

Building Work that Does Not Require Authorization

A number of small building projects do not require any official approval, although they must not contravene any of the regulations contained in the PLU or POS. They include:

- new constructions less than 12m high and which add 2sq.m or less to the total surface area (SHOB), for example, a small shed, patio or built-in barbecue;
- conversion of an attic into a bedroom or other living space, provided that no more than 10sq.m of SHOB is transformed into SHON, and provided that no changes are visible from the exterior, such as the addition of a roof window;
- installation of a small, outside swimming pool, not exceeding 10sq.m in surface area;
- installation of an inside swimming pool, provided that there is no change to the exterior appearance of the building;
- erection of a greenhouse up to 1.8m high;
- construction of a boundary wall or fence (unless local regulations apply or if the land is situated in a conservation area);
- construction of a retaining wall (unless it is in a conservation area);
- renovation of a roof, replacement of existing windows and shutters with identical ones, provided that there is no significant change to the exterior appearance of the building;
- installation of underground cables and pipes.

In general, inside your house you may also carry out work without planning permission, provided that it does nothing to change the exterior appearance of the building, nor changes its use nor creates an additional storey. You may, however, need approval if it is a listed building or is situated within a conservation area.

Finally, the maintenance, replacement and repair of existing structures are not subject to any administrative formalities.

Building Work that Requires a
Déclaration Préalable

We are not aware of a British equivalent to this particular aspect of the French planning procedure. Previously called a *déclaration de travaux* or statement of building work, the direct translation of the new procedure is a 'preliminary statement'. In effect, you apply to your local authority with details of your project, they check that it does not contravene any of the current planning regulations and then issue you with a *déclaration préalable* or permission to proceed. It is applicable to various small to medium-sized projects, as follows:

- creation of a new building, such as a garage, shed, terrace, veranda or built-in barbecue with a surface area (SHOB) of between 2 and 20sq.m;

- extension of an existing building where this will create an additional surface area (SHOB) of 2 to 20sq.m;
- transformation of more than 10sq.m of existing surface area (SHOB) into living space (SHON), for example, when converting a garage or an attic into a bedroom;
- construction of a wall above 2m high;
- construction of a boundary wall or fence of any height when situated within a conservation area;
- installation of an outside open swimming pool of between 10 and 100sq.m in surface area, or a covered pool where the height of the cover does not exceed 1.8m;
- installation of a satellite dish;
- installation of solar panels.

A *déclaration préalable* is used for any work which results in a change to the exterior appearance of the building. Such work includes the addition and replacement of doors, windows, shutters and roof windows, as well as the renovation and restoration of the roof and the exterior walls of the building. A further application of the *déclaration préalable* is where there is a change of use of the building, for example, when offices are converted into a private house. The *déclaration préalable* is necessary even if the change of use does not involve any building work. On the other hand, if the conversion entails, for example, changes to the underlying structure of the building, then full planning permission will be necessary. Any outbuildings your property may have are deemed to have the same usage as the main building. Should you wish to convert one into a room this is not seen as a change of use and, in itself, will not necessitate a *déclaration préalable* – although the latter may be required for other reasons, such as the creation of more than 2sq.m of new SHON.

Building Work that Requires a
Permis de Construire

Full planning permission is obligatory for the construction of all new buildings or extensions to existing buildings which cannot be covered by a *déclaration préalable* – in effect, those larger than 20sq.m (SHOB). It is also necessary when there is a change of use of a property, for example, the conversion of a shop into a private house, which entails modifications to the load-bearing structures or the façade of the existing building.

A further situation where a *permis de construire* is required arises when the work includes a change to the size of the building *and* the installation or enlargement of an

A typical loft conversion requires a déclaration préalable.

opening (door or window, for example) in an external wall of the property. (The creation or modification of an opening by itself requires simply a *déclaration préalable*.)

You will also need a *permis de construire* if you are installing an uncovered swimming pool with a surface area of more than 100sq.m, or a covered pool where the height of the cover exceeds 1.8m.

Building Work that Requires a *Permis de Démolir*

The *permis de démolir* authorizes the partial or complete demolition of a building situated within a conservation area, or in communes where the local council has made it a requirement. It is necessary only when this is not accompanied by a construction project since the application forms for the *déclaration préalable* and the *permis de construire* both contain sections relating to demolition work if required.

The Formalities

Many of the administrative procedures are identical regardless of whether you are applying for a *certificat d'urbanisme*, a *déclaration préalable*, a *permis de construire* or a *permis de démolir*. The steps are detailed below. A summary of the information specific to the individual permissions follows at the end of this section.

Making the Application

To obtain the necessary documentation you can apply in person to the *Mairie* or your local DDE office. Alternatively, you may use the official website at either www.service-public.fr (click on the links for *Logement* and then *Construction* to reach the appropriate page) or www.urbanisme.equipement.gouv.fr (click on the link *Les nouveaux formulaires*). When using the Internet you may either complete the application form online and then print it, or download it and fill it in by hand.

The official forms may at first appear daunting, but do not worry. They have been designed to cover every conceivable eventuality, and not all the sections will be relevant in many cases. But having said that, you should be aware that the authorities will not check the details on the forms but will rely on you to complete them accurately and supply all the necessary supporting material. If it is subsequently found that you have submitted false information, any approvals given will be cancelled and you could face the prospect of having to demolish any building work, as this will have been carried out illegally, and even a penal sanction. If you have any doubts about completing the forms, your first port of call should be the *Mairie* where, in our experience, the staff are always helpful and willing to assist with the paperwork. You could also consider asking the *artisan* you have selected for the project for assistance, but bear in mind that his skills may not run to administrative formalities. Of course, if you have appointed an architect, surveyor or other project manager, then you can authorize him to complete and submit the form on your behalf. He will also deal with any other formalities that are necessary.

Table 1. Summary of Planning Permission Requirements

Project	Details	Permission required
Barn conversion*		PC
Boundary fence, wall or hedge*	In most cases	None
	In conservation areas	DP
Conversion of outbuildings into rooms, gîtes, etc.	With no exterior work	DP
	With changes to exterior or to the underlying structure	PC
Extension of existing building	2sq.m or less	None
	2sq.m–20sq.m	DP
	More than 20sq.m	PC
Garage – construction	2sq.m or less	None
	2sq.m–20sq.m	DP
	More than 20sq.m	PC
Garage – conversion into living space	10sq.m or less, no exterior changes	None
	More than 10sq.m and/or changes to exterior	DP
Garden shed	2sq.m or less	None
	2sq.m–20sq.m	DP
Greenhouse	Up to 1.8m high	None
	1.8m–4m high	DP
Loft conversion	10sq.m or less, no exterior changes	None
	More than 10sq.m and/or changes to exterior	DP
Replacement windows/shutters*	Like for like	None
	Changing the external appearance	DP
Restoration or renovation of exterior house walls*		DP
Satellite dish, solar panels, external air-conditioning unit, etc.		DP
Swimming pool (permanent)	10sq.m or less – uncovered or with a cover up to 1.8m above water level	None
	10sq.m–100sq.m – uncovered or with a cover up to 1.8m above water level	DP
	Any size with a cover more than 1.8m above water level	PC

Table 1. (*Continued*)

Project	Details	Permission required
Swimming pool (inflatable)	10sq.m or less	None
	More than 10sq.m	
	– for up to 3 months	None
	– for more than 3 months	DP
Veranda	2sq.m–20sq.m	DP
	More than 20sq.m	PC
Walls*	Retaining wall	None
	Up to 2m high	None
	More than 2m high or in a conservation area	DP
Wind turbine	Up to 12m high	None
	More than 12m high	PC

Notes * May be subject to additional regulations in the PLU/POS
Permission required: None = no authorization; DP = *déclaration préalable*; PC = *permis de construire*

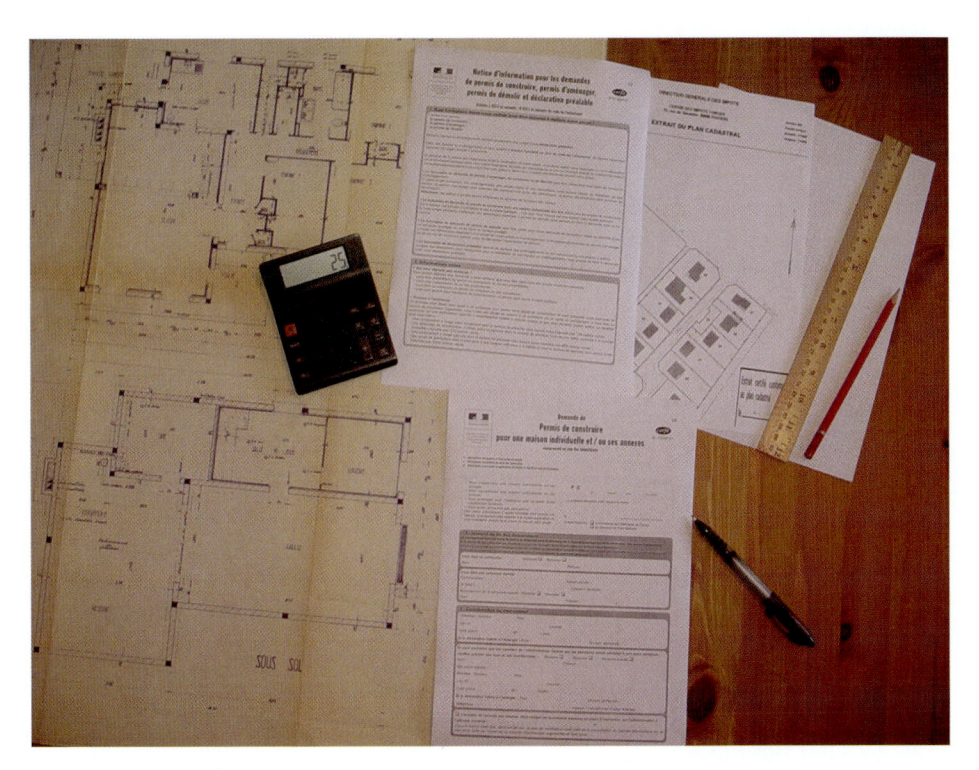

Some of the paperwork required for a planning application.

> **Using an Architect**
>
> The use of a registered architect is obligatory when applying for planning permission where the total floor area (SHON) of your property is 170sq.m or more, or if it will reach this size once the building work has been completed. If, for example, you are planning to add a 25sq.m extension to a 140sq.m house, you are not obliged to use the services of an architect. But, on the other hand, if you are adding the same sized extension to a 150sq.m house then you must use an architect to draw up the plans and complete the other formalities relating to the planning application. You do not, however, have to use the architect to oversee the entire project unless you so wish.

Sections 1 and 2 of each of the forms request your contact details. If you wish, you can add your email address to indicate that you would like to receive any subsequent correspondence electronically. Should you select this option, the official date of notification is that on which you open the email from the *Mairie*, or, at the latest, eight days following the sending of the email, so remember to check your inbox regularly.

Section 3 refers to the address, land registry reference (*référence cadastrale*) and area of the plot where your project is to be carried out. You should refer to the documents you received when you bought the property or land for the details you need. Alternatively, this information is available at your local tax office or can be consulted on the Internet at www.cadastre.gouv.fr. The remaining sections require you to give details of the nature of the project, any changes that there will be to the surface area of the property and what its use will be once the work has been completed. If any demolition work is to be done this may also be noted. Finally, you should sign and date the form. Note that, as with all legal documents, you must also include the name of the town where you signed it. If the land or property is jointly owned, then the application can be made in a single name and signed by just one of the owners.

Along with the application form for the *déclaration préalable*, *permis de construire* or *permis de démolir*, you should have received or downloaded a document entitled *Bordereau de dépôt des pièces jointes*. This refers to the different plans and photographs that should be included with your application, and tells you the number of copies of each that are required. In summary, for all projects you need to provide a plan showing the location of the plot of land where the project is to take place. This should indicate the compass point north and show the scale that is being used (normally 1:20,000 in rural areas and 1:2,000 or 1:5,000 in urban areas). If you are planning a new building or a modification of an existing one, two simple plans with all the necessary dimensions should be prepared, one showing the existing structures and the second the proposed new one(s). If your project modifies any aspect of the exterior of your building you should provide a 'before' and 'after' drawing showing the changes. Note that none of these plans has to be professionally produced, you can prepare them yourself, to scale, of course, either using a computer or with old-fashioned paper, pencil and ruler – and eraser! You should tick the boxes on the *Bordereau* to indicate which plans you are enclosing, and label each plan with the appropriate reference number (DP1 or PC5, for instance).

Once all the paperwork has been completed, you should submit the required number of copies of the application form, plans and the *Bordereau* to the *Mairie* of the commune where the building work is to take place. Remember to keep a copy of all that you submit yourself as the file will not be returned to you once it has been examined. You can either deliver your application by hand or by registered post (*lettre recommandée avec avis de réception*). Your application will be given a reference number and you will subsequently receive an official receipt (*récépissé*) indicating the provisional date on which work can begin. The administration has up to a month in which to request any additional information that was missing from your

---

Property in Conservation Areas

If your property is situated within the perimeter of protection of a historic monument (normally within a radius of 500m), a national park or any other conservation area (*secteur sauvegardé*), building work on it is subject to additional planning approval by the *Architecte des Bâtiments de France* (ABF). Each *département* employs one or more of these professionals in order to protect, restore and conserve protected monuments and other aspects of the area's heritage. They also ensure that any new buildings or modifications to existing ones integrate appropriately with their surroundings. In such circumstances, you will need to supply additional copies of your application to the *Mairie*, who will forward them to the relevant office of your local *département*. (The *Mairie* can also advise you if your project falls into this category, if you are unsure.)

This extra step means that the planning procedure takes a little longer; it is extended by one month for a *déclaration préalable* and by between three and six months for a *permis de construire/démolir*.

initial application. You must supply this within three months, otherwise, the application is considered to be rejected.

Unlike in Britain, you do not have to pay a fee for submitting a planning application. There may, however, be a planning tax (*taxe d'urbanisme*) for the receipt of a *permis de construire* relating to an increase in surface area of your property, but this depends on where you live. It is payable in all communes of more than 10,000 inhabitants, certain communes in the Ile-de-France region and in other communes where the local council has decided that it should be applied.

Within a fortnight of receipt of your application the essential details of your request will be displayed in the *Mairie*. The *Mairie* handles all the administration and remains your point of contact for all planning matters. In small communes (those with fewer than 10,000 inhabitants), however, which do not have their own planning departments, planning applications are usually processed by the DDE. The *Mairie* will also send copies of your documents to any other services it deems necessary for consultation and advice.

By law, a decision must be reached within a fixed timescale and you will be notified, within one month starting from the receipt of your complete application, of the date by which the formalities will be completed (*le délai d'instruction*). If additional time is required, this date may exceed that stated on the *récépissé*.

Table 2. Summary of Planning Application Forms

Type of Application	Cerfa[1] Reference	No. of Copies to Submit[2]	Time for Application to be Processed (months)[3]
Certificat d'urbanisme d'information	13410	2	1
Certificat d'urbanisme opérationnel	13410	4	2
Déclaration préalable	13404	2	1
Permis de construire	13406	4	2
Permis de démolir	13405	4	2

Notes

[1] Cerfa (*Centre d'enregistrement et de revision des formulaires administratifs*) is the national organization responsible for the publication and distribution of all official forms, each of which has a unique reference number.

[2] Additional copies may be required in certain circumstances – check the application form for details.

[3] From the time the *Mairie* receives the complete documentation, including any additional information that is requested. When the plans concern property in a conservation area, planning approval always takes longer. You will be notified of any extension to this timescale, if necessary.

Planning Approval

Approval is usually given tacitly, in other words, 'no news is good news'. If you receive no further communication from the *Mairie* within the time limit that you have been given, you may assume that permission has been granted. In practice, it is a good idea to request a certificate from the *Mairie* stating that the authorities have no objections to your application. If you receive written approval it will usually be accompanied by those forms that you will need to complete as the building work progresses.

Sometimes, the letter will also contain some special instructions or slight modifications to your plans, which should, of course, be respected. If, on the other hand, approval is not granted, you will receive a registered letter from the *Mairie*, along with the reasons for this decision.

Steps that Can Be Taken if Your Plans Are Not Approved

A planning application can be refused only if it does not respect the current planning regulations contained in the PLU or POS. The exact reasons for non-approval should be contained in the letter advising you that permission has not been granted.

Sample Letter 2

Objet: Permis de construire

Je conteste votre décision du [date] *me refusant l'octroi d'un permis de construire à* [address], *en raison de* [state the grounds on which application was refused here].

[Provide your justifications here].

Je vous demande donc de revenir sur votre décision.

Translation

Re: Planning permission

I contest your decision of [date] refusing planning permission at [address], due to [state the grounds for which application refused here].

[Provide your justifications here].

I request, therefore, that you review your decision.

> **Sample Letter 3**
>
> *Objet: Dossier permis de construire*
> Suite à un refus de la Mairie de [name of your commune] *pour l'obtention d'un permis de construire, j'en réfère à votre compétence pour bien vouloir reconsidérer mon dossier.*
> [Provide your justifications here].
>
> *Translation*
> Re: Application for planning permission
> Following a refusal to grant planning permission by the *Mairie* of [name of your commune], I am submitting the application to you for reconsideration.
> [Provide your justifications here].

From receipt of this letter you have a two-month period in which you can send a registered letter to the planning authority (usually the *Mairie*), requesting a review of your application and for the decision to be reconsidered (*see* Sample letter 2).

If you do not receive a reply within two months you may assume that your request has failed. You then have a further two-month period in which you can apply to the administrative tribunal (*tribunal administratif*) for the area in which the building site is located for the refusal of planning permission to be rescinded. This should again take the form of a letter sent by registered post, in which you clearly state the reasons justifying your right to planning permission and enclose copies of all the relevant documentation (*see* Sample letter 3).

It is not obligatory to use a lawyer for this procedure; however, in view of the complexities of French law and language, it is highly recommended. If the court decides in your favour, then the planning authority must reconsider your application.

Procedures to Be Followed Once Approval Is Obtained

To notify third parties of the work to be undertaken, you must display a panel outside the property, clearly visible from the public highway, for the entire duration of the work. Of rectangular format, the panel should measure at least 80cm along its shorter side. The information contained on it must include the name of the person to whom planning approval was granted (normally the owner of the property), the nature of the project and, if applicable, the area of the new building and the address

> ### Modifications to a Building Project
>
> Once in receipt of a *permis de construire*, you may wish to modify aspects of your building project. Any change, however, will require approval, and you will need to complete the Cerfa form reference 13411, entitled *Demande de modification d'un permis délivré en cours de validité*. The form is a little more complicated than that for a *permis de construire*, but you should complete only the sections where there are changes from the original application. You should then submit four copies (additional copies will be required if the property is situated in a conservation area) to the *Mairie*, where it will be processed in the same way and within the same timescales as are applicable to the *permis de construire*.

of the *Mairie* where your plans may be consulted. You can download a model for this panel from the Internet at www.urbanisme.equipement.gouv.fr under the heading *les modèles pour l'affichage*. Similarly, the planning approval will be displayed at the *Mairie*.

Any third party who has objections to the project, either because it will be detrimental to them or because they believe it does not comply with the local planning regulations, then has two months in which to lodge a complaint at the local administrative tribunal. They must also advise both the local authority which granted approval and the property owner. It may, therefore, be wise not to commence the work for two months just in case a complaint is upheld by the court and planning permission is subsequently modified or even withdrawn.

Starting the Work ...

Once granted, the planning approval remains valid for two years. The work must be started within this period and, once started, should not be suspended for more than twelve months – although it may be spread out over the whole of the two-year period. The period is suspended if someone registers an official complaint against the project, but resumes once the court has announced its decision. If necessary, the approval may be extended for an additional year, provided that this is requested no later than two months before the original expiry date.

If the work is subject to a *permis de construire*, the beginning of work must be notified by using the form entitled *Déclaration d'ouverture de chantier* (Cerfa 13407). Three copies of the completed form should be delivered to the *Mairie* in person or by registered post.

> **Transfer of Planning Permission**
>
> During the two-year period in which a *permis de construire* is valid it can be transferred to another person if, for example, the property is sold. The Cerfa form reference 13412, entitled *Demande de transfert d'un permis délivré en cours de validité*, should be completed. Both parties need to sign the form, four copies of which should then be submitted to the *Mairie*. The transfer will be processed within two months.

... and Once the Project Is Completed

Once the building work is completed, a document entitled *Déclaration attestant l'achèvement et la conformité des travaux* (Cerfa 13408) must be submitted to declare officially that the work has been carried out according to the plans for which approval was obtained. It must be signed by the person to whom planning approval was granted, and, if applicable, by the architect who oversaw the work, before being submitted to the *Mairie*.

The local authority has a period of up to three months from receipt of this document in which it can carry out an on-site inspection to check that the work complies with the approved plans. This period is extended to five months if the property is situated within a conservation area. In the latter case, the inspection is obligatory, otherwise, inspections are undertaken only if the authority deems it necessary. If any anomalies are found, the owner may be instructed to carry out remedial work or asked to submit modified plans. If neither of these solutions is possible, then the new building may have to be demolished. Once again, approval is tacit, but we advise you to request a *Certificat de conformité* from the *Mairie*, so that you have proof of the official acceptance of the completed project for when you come to sell your property. Once a year has elapsed after the completion of work has been notified, no legal proceedings to challenge or cancel the planning approval can be instituted.

Within ninety days of the new building becoming usable – even if there is still work to be completed – you should advise your tax office if there are any changes to the surface area or the use of your property, so that the necessary adjustments can be applied to your local taxes (*taxe d'habitation* and *taxes foncières*). This can be done by using form H1 (Cerfa 10867 * 04), which can be downloaded from www.impots.gouv.fr (click on *Particuliers*, then *Rechercher un formulaire*). In certain circumstances, new buildings and extensions may be partially exonerated from *taxes foncières* for a period of two years.

7
Meeting Legal Obligations

Energy-Saving Measures

Since November 2007, in order that France can meet its Kyoto Agreement commitments, several new regulations have been introduced to improve the energy performance of both new and existing buildings. These affect any major renovation, installation and replacement work carried out to heating, hot water, cooling and ventilation systems, and particularly focus on the use of renewable energy sources. For example, when installing replacement windows, the new ones must be at least double-glazed and have a low thermal transmittance value or VIR (*vitrage à isolation thermique renforcée*). When replacing a central heating boiler, the new one must have an output at least equivalent to that of a low-temperature boiler (*chaudière à basse température*). New laws also define the minimum levels of insulation required. When insulating your loft, for example, the thermal resistance (R) value of the insulation must be at least 4.5 or, in other words, have a thickness of between 15 and 20cm depending on the material selected.

Certain buildings are exempt from these measures, including those situated in a conservation area, and houses that were built within the preceding fifteen years. For full details, you should seek advice from your *chauffagiste* or other tradesman, or equipment supplier.

Boiler Maintenance/Chimney Sweeping

It is a legal obligation in France to have your central heating and hot water systems serviced annually. Primarily, this is to lessen the risks of carbon monoxide poisoning, but it should also make their operation more efficient and subsequently result in fuel savings – and economies officially estimated to be between 8 and 12 per cent on your energy bills. An added bonus is that a well-maintained boiler is likely to have a longer lifespan and experience fewer breakdowns, than one that has not been regularly serviced. All types of apparatus are included:

- wood, coal, gas and oil burning boilers;
- water heaters;
- wood-burning stoves;
- wood, coal and gas cookers.

84　*Meeting Legal Obligations*

Meeting legal requirements – installing a new, energy-efficient central heating boiler.

It is not, however, necessary to subscribe to an annual maintenance contract, although this is often advised as the simplest solution. Neither do you have to use the *chauffagiste* who installed the equipment.

At the same time as your annual service, you should have your chimney and other flues swept, as this is also a legal obligation. Not only will this make you a law-abiding citizen, but it too should result in fuel savings. More importantly, it will lessen the risks of a chimney fire or of carbon monoxide poisoning. Failure to comply with the regulation could result in a fine of up to €450 and could invalidate your household insurance in the event of a fire. You should make sure that you receive a certificate confirming that the work has been carried out.

Swimming Pools

In addition to the various planning permissions needed for the installation of a swimming pool (*see* Chapter 6), there are safety regulations which must be observed

Meeting Legal Obligations   85

for all exterior, sunken pools, which also extend to spas and hot tubs. Whichever of the following four measures is chosen, it should prevent access to the pool by an unaccompanied child, less than five years old.

- If safety barriers are erected, they should be at least 1.1m high, with a sliding or pivoted gate opening away from the pool with a childproof lock. They should be capable of resisting a shock equivalent to 50kg and conform to the safety standard NF P90-306.
- Alarm systems that can detect either access around the perimeter of the pool or immersion in it should conform to NF P90-307.
- Safety covers must be capable of supporting a weight of 100kg without deforming or tearing; the relevant standard is NF P90-308.
- Verandas or other shelters surrounding a pool must provide secured access and conform to NF P90-309.

Failure to observe these regulations may result in a fine of up to €45,000. More information is available from swimming pool suppliers and contractors.

Septic Tanks

If, like many properties in rural France, your home is not connected to the mains drainage network (*tout à l'égout*), then it is a legal obligation to have an individual waste collection and treatment system – usually in the form of a septic tank, known as a *fosse septique* or *fosse toutes eaux*. If you are planning to install such a system or if you are modifying or replacing an existing one, you should seek advice either from your *Mairie* or from SPANC (*Service Public d'Assainissement Non Collectif*), a body set up by each commune to ensure that the current regulations are observed.

The first step is to have a survey carried out by a specialist engineer from a *bureau d'études*. He will advise you which of the many possible technical solutions is the most appropriate for your situation, taking into account factors such as the type of soil, the topography of the land, the area available and the presence of any natural water sources, such as streams or wells. Specific requirements include:

- the tank must be situated at least 3m from any neighbouring property and trees;
- the tank must be situated at least 5m from an inhabited building;
- there must be at least 35m between the tank and any natural source of water used for human consumption, such as a well;
- there should be a separate drainage system for rainwater;
- the tank must have a suitable ventilation system.

You should submit a copy of the engineer's survey, along with appropriate plans and the required number of copies of the application form (*Demande d'installation d'un dispositif d'assainissement non-collectif*) to your *Mairie* for approval. If the installation is associated with a new building project, it should be submitted either before or at the same time as the application for planning permission.

After the work has been completed, it will have to be inspected by SPANC to verify that the work has been carried out in accordance with the details given in the application. Thereafter all systems will be inspected every four years by SPANC to check that they are being correctly maintained and that they function efficiently. If there are any problems, you will be given a list of work to be undertaken to bring the system up to standard. The tank must be emptied at least once every four years by an approved contractor. You must obtain a document certifying that this has been done, and produce it at your next SPANC inspection.

Relationships with Your Neighbours

Neighbours' Rights

Whenever you carry out any work on your property, you must ensure that you do not infringe the rights of your neighbours either with regard to their privacy or their access to daylight. There are regulations regarding the distances that must be respected between neighbouring properties – and also between your property and land in the public domain, such as pavements or roads. These are contained in your commune's PLU or POS – or, in the event where this document does not exist, in the national RNU (*see* Chapter 6) – copies of which may be consulted at your local *Mairie*. If there are no regulations to the contrary, then you may build right up to the boundary of your land.

There are also restrictions on the installation of new doors, windows, balconies and terraces. The rules vary depending on whether the view overlooking your neighbours from such new structures is directly ahead or at an angle. In the former case, the new construction should be at least 1.9m from the boundary separating the two properties, while this distance is reduced to 0.6m in situations where it is necessary to turn one's head in order to see the adjoining plot. There are, however, no restrictions on openings towards the sky, on windows facing a solid wall nor on those overlooking a public highway.

Access to Your Property

In some circumstances, it may be difficult, or even impossible, to carry out work to your house without access from a neighbouring property. For example, when your house is situated close to or even on the boundary between the two plots and

Sample Letter 4

Objet: demande de « tour d'échelle »

Je vous demande l'accès à votre terrain pour effectuer des travaux indispensables sur ma propriété.

Je vous informe qu'une jurisprudence constante autorise le propriétaire d'un fonds à passer, à titre temporaire, chez son voisin afin d'effectuer les réparations indispensables (Cour de cassation, 3e chambre civile, 15 avril 1982, Bull. civ. III, no 93).

Les travaux concerneront [give details of work to be carried out]. *Les travaux commenceront le* [date work will begin] *et dureront environ* [length of time].

Bien entendu, je m'engage à prendre à ma charge les dégâts qui pourraient être faits sur votre propriété par les ouvriers. [optional] *Je suis également disposé à vous dédommager pour la gêne occasionnée.*

Je vous propose donc que nous fixions un rendez-vous pour examiner les modalités d'établissement d'un état des lieux pour protéger au mieux vos droits.

A défaut d'accord amiable, je me verrais dans l'obligation de saisir la juridiction compétente.

Translation

Re: request for permission to access neighbour's land

I am writing to request access to your land in order to carry out some essential work to my property.

A judicial precedent has established that a property owner has the right to temporarily access his neighbour's land in order to carry out essential repairs (Court of Appeal, 3rd civil division, 15 April 1982, civil bulletin III, no. 93).

The work involves [give details of work to be carried out]. The work will begin on [date work will begin] and continue for about [length of time].

Of course, I undertake to pay for any damage which may be done to your property by the workers. [optional] I am also willing to pay you compensation for any inconvenience caused.

I suggest therefore that we arrange to meet to discuss carrying out a site inspection in order to protect your rights.

Failing an amicable agreement, I will be forced to take legal action.

you need to carry out repairs to your roof or repaint the exterior walls. In such circumstances you may claim a right, known as *tour d'échelle*, to temporary access from your neighbour's land so that you can position a ladder or erect scaffolding (*échafaudage*). You also need your neighbour's permission if scaffolding situated on your land overhangs his, even though its base is on your land.

Such a right is not conferred by any law, but must be agreed beforehand with your neighbour. Of course, if you are on good terms this should not present any problem. If, however, this is not the case, or perhaps you do not even know your neighbour personally, then you should send him a registered letter giving the necessary details and timings of the proposed work and officially requesting permission for access from his land. You should assure him that you will make good any damage caused to his property. If the work is likely to take a considerable time and/or cause much disruption, then you should offer your neighbour a compensation payment (*dédommagement*) – which may prove to be a good incentive to persuade him to grant permission.

If your neighbour refuses your request for access, then you can take the matter to court – the *tribunal de grande instance* – as an *action en référé*. If you can demonstrate to the judge that the work is essential, and that there is no alternative to access from your neighbour's land, then he will give you the necessary authorization.

Whether you receive permission direct from your neighbour or via the court, before any work takes place you should establish the current state of the land (*état des lieux*) you will be accessing. It is advisable to take photographs of the site where you or your builders will be working in case there is a subsequent dispute over any damage done to it. You could also consider using an independent legal expert (a *huissier de justice*) to carry out a site inspection before and, if necessary, after the work.

Apartments and Other Co-ownership Properties

If you own an apartment or any other property where some of the facilities are jointly owned and shared with others (known in French as *copropriété*), in principle you can carry out whatever work you like to your private accommodation, provided that it does nothing to damage the stability and integrity of the building nor infringe any of the rights of your neighbours. Decoration and electrical work, and even knocking down partition walls, or the installation of an interior staircase, therefore, require no authorization. If, however, your project affects a load-bearing wall or if you want to replace a fitted carpet with a tiled floor, or do any work connected to the heating system that serves the whole of the building, then you must seek permission from all the other residents. Similarly, if the work affects any of the communal areas, or changes the exterior appearance of the building in any way, the details must be added to the agenda for the general meeting (*assemblée générale*), where they will be discussed and voted upon. You should include any information and plans that you think will help your case. Approval will be granted if there is a majority of votes in favour. Note that planning permission will also be necessary for certain projects (*see* Chapter 6).

If your request is refused you can take the case to court (*le tribunal de grande instance*), where you will need to use the services of a lawyer. The *assemblée générale*'s decision may be overturned if you can prove that the project will not infringe the rights of the other owners in any way.

You should check the document entitled *Règlement de copropriété* you received when you purchased your property for the rules and regulations relating to your specific situation.

Property Situated on an Estate

If your house is on an estate or development (*lotissement*) that is less than ten years old, there may well be regulations, supplementary to those in the PLU or POS, regarding the work that can be carried out on it. These will be contained in the *règlement du lotissement*, which may be consulted at your local *Mairie*. After ten years only the rules of the PLU or POS will apply.

On some estates there may be further restrictions and obligations noted in a legal document entitled *cahier des charges*. If applicable, you should have received a copy of this when you purchased your house. These regulations often relate to boundary enclosures, but may also cover the specification of colours and materials to be used on the exterior of your property, the allocation of car parking spaces, and may even place restrictions on hanging out washing. They remain valid indefinitely.

Miscellaneous Local Regulations

In Paris, for example, there is an obligation to keep the façade of your house in good order and to have it repainted or restored at least every ten years. In other communes, and particularly in those of special historical or other interest, similar regulations may apply regarding the external appearance of your property, such as the materials and even the colours that can be used. Once again, the *Mairie* should be your source of information.

Rental Property

If you are living in rented accommodation subject to a lease agreement, you will be responsible for the general upkeep of the property and any minor repairs that are necessary. You are permitted to carry out redecoration and also to install equipment that can be removed without causing any irreparable damage. For more extensive changes, it will be necessary to obtain the approval of your landlord. Preferably, this should be in writing in case of any subsequent dispute.

8
Understanding VAT and Other Financial Issues

Note that all the information contained in this chapter is correct at the time of going to press. Laws and regulations are, however, constantly being changed and you should refer to the official government websites (*see* the list of websites at the end of the book), or take advice from an *artisan* for the latest updates.

Does the Work Qualify for a Reduced Rate of VAT?

For a number of years, certain renovation, maintenance and improvement work carried out on your home has been eligible for a VAT rate of just 5.5 per cent instead of the standard French rate of 19.6 per cent. This measure is currently in force until 31 December 2010, but strong pressure from within the building trade may well result in its being prolonged for a further period – as has happened in the past.

The reduced rate of VAT may be available regardless of whether you are the owner or tenant of the property, it is your main residence or a holiday home or whether the work is on the house or apartment itself or on an outbuilding, provided that the primary use of the property is as a residence. It applies not only to the labour charges but also to the costs of the materials supplied and those of certain items of equipment. Note that such supplies must be provided and invoiced by the tradesman carrying out the work. When you buy equipment yourself and then employ an *artisan* to install it, you will pay the full rate of VAT on your purchase, but the reduced rate on the labour charges. If, however, you buy from a retailer who offers an installation service – either employing his own staff or subcontracting to a third party – you can take full advantage of the lower rate of VAT provided that you meet the other criteria. For example, when we purchased new carpets for our bedrooms, we arranged for them to be delivered and fitted by the store's in-house team and subsequently paid VAT at only 5.5 per cent. This saved us well over €300 (or in Duncan's terms three months' supply of wine). If you are carrying out a major project, the potential savings could potentially keep your wine cellar stocked for years!

> ### *Gros œuvre* and *second œuvre*
>
> Different types of building work are often officially categorized by these two terms. *Gros œuvre* relates to the shell or carcass of the building and its major structural elements, including the foundations, the external walls and internal load-bearing walls, beams, girders, joists and concrete floors. *Second œuvre* refers to the fitting out of the building, and includes all other floors, external door and window frames, internal partition walls, plumbing and sanitary fittings, electrical installations and the heating system.

There are, needless to say, several conditions you need to fulfil in order to be able to take advantage of this beneficial rate. First, your house must be more than two years old, unless the work is related to emergency repairs following weather damage, a water leak or a burglary, for example. Secondly, there are limits to the extent of the work that can be carried out, as detailed below.

To qualify for the reduced rate of VAT the work must not represent the total rebuilding of the house. This is defined as the replacement of more than 50 per cent of the *gros œuvre* or more than two-thirds of each of the elements of the *second œuvre*, within the preceding two-year period. In addition, it does not apply when the total floor space (SHON – see Chapter 6) is increased by more than 10 per cent, nor when the overall height of the building is increased and nor when a totally new construction is added. The table opposite shows some of the most common projects along with the applicable rate of VAT.

In order to take advantage of the reduced rate of VAT you will need to declare that your project meets all the required conditions. This is done by filling in an official tax form entitled either *Attestation normale* or *Attestation simplifiée* (if the work affects none of the *gros œuvre* and no more than five of the six elements of *second œuvre*). Two copies of the appropriate form will normally be given to you by your *artisan*, usually with his *devis* or, more rarely, when he sends you his invoice. You should return one to the *artisan* and keep the other copy yourself, along with copies of the relevant invoices, until at least 31 December of the fifth year following the one in which the work was completed.

What Projects Qualify for an Income Tax Credit?

Provided that your property is your principal home and that you are resident in France for tax purposes you may be eligible for a tax credit when having certain

Table 3. VAT Rates for Building Projects

Work eligible for reduced rate of VAT of 5.5%	Work subject to standard rate of VAT of 19.6%
Re-decoration work including painting and wallpapering, carpet fitting, installation of wooden floors	Any work where the house is less than two years old – unless it relates to emergency repairs
Supply and installation of electrical and security equipment	Work on buildings that are not primarily residential
Plumbing, supply and installation of sanitary ware	New constructions or extensions – for example, a conservatory, garage, terrace – which add more than 10% to the SHON
Supply and installation of central heating, water heating, and fixed air conditioning and ventilation systems	Any equipment bought directly by the house-owner
Supply & installation of equipment using renewable energy sources, such as solar panels, wind turbines, wood-burning stoves, etc.	Supply of free-standing heating and ventilation equipment
Thermal insulation and soundproofing	Supply of non-fitted furniture
Loft, barn and other conversions, provided the total SHON is increased by less than 10%	Supply of kitchen and audiovisual equipment – whether built-in or not
Replacement doors, windows, shutters, etc.	Supply and installation of saunas and spas
Renovation and re-rendering of outside walls, replacement of roof tiles	Installation of swimming pools, tennis courts, and other sports facilities
Supply and installation of television aerials and satellite dishes	Landscaping and maintenance of gardens
Maintenance contracts for central heating boilers, etc.	Architect or project manager's fees

work carried out. For the latest details consult your tax office or visit www.impots. gouv.fr, following the links for *Particuliers – Vos préoccupations – Logement*. Alternatively, your *artisan* or equipment supplier should be able to advise you.

Energy Conservation

The most common tax credit relates to projects that are designed to reduce household energy consumption and protect the environment, and is known as the *Crédit d'impôt developpement durable*.

At the time of writing (2008) the following expenses are included in this scheme:

- tax credit of 15 per cent – purchase of energy-saving, low temperature boilers for properties more than two years old;
- tax credit of 25 per cent – purchase of condensing boilers, heat insulating materials (for instance, roof insulation or double glazing) and heating thermostats, timers and other control systems (provided that the property is more than two years old); the same percentage applies to the purchase of equipment for the collection and treatment of rainwater, in both new and old properties;
- tax credit of 40 per cent – purchase of condensing boilers, heat insulating materials (roof insulation or double glazing, for example) and heating thermostats, timers and other control systems (if your house was built before 1 January 1977 and you have the work carried out by 31 December of the second year following that in which you purchased the property);
- tax credit of 50 per cent – purchase of equipment for the production of energy using renewable energy sources (including wood-burning stoves and other heating systems using wood or biomass fuels, solar panels, wind turbines and water power) and certain heat pumps (where the main objective is the production of heat); this is available regardless of the age of your property.

There are strict criteria for equipment eligible for tax credits, in terms of its performance and technical specifications, and it must conform to all the latest standards. Your installer should be able to advise you on the best solution for your requirements, in terms of both its suitability and its tax-efficiency.

Tax credits originally applicable to expenditure incurred between 1 January 2005 and 31 December 2009, have now been extended until 31 December 2013. They are currently subject to a maximum total claim of €8,000 for a single person and €16,000 for a couple (plus €400 for each dependant), but these figures could be adjusted in future budgets. As energy conservation is high on the French government's agenda, these measures will be kept under review and possibly even enhanced beyond the current deadline.

To be eligible, the installation must be carried out by the same registered enterprise that supplied the equipment, although labour costs are excluded from the calculation of the tax credit. You cannot claim the tax credit if you purchased the equipment direct and then arranged for an *artisan* to install it, nor if you carry out the work yourself.

Installing a solar panel may earn you a tax credit of 50% (Habitat Naturel – Chantier Gérard Nallet – Marc Tricot (86) – Laurent Buisine (41))

Health and Safety Measures

Similarly, tax credits are available if you carry out work to improve your home's accessibility and comfort for elderly or disabled occupants. You can receive a tax credit of 25 per cent for the installation or replacement of special sanitary equipment, such as height-adjustable washbasins, walk-in baths, bath lifts, showers designed for wheelchair access, shower seats and special WCs. The same credit also applies to safety and accessibility aids, such as lifts and stair-lifts, handrails, ramps and various other pieces of equipment designed to help the disabled.

All equipment must be permanently installed, but there are no restrictions on the age of the building. It must, however, be the main residence of the taxpayer claiming the credit, although it is not necessary for an elderly or disabled person to be actually living in the building. The equipment must be supplied and fitted by a professional company and the tax credit is based on both the purchase price and the installation charges.

Tax credits are currently applicable to expenditure incurred between 1 January 2005 and 31 December 2009, subject to a maximum total claim during this period of €5,000 for a single person and €10,000 for a couple (plus €400 for each dependant).

Claiming the Tax Credit

Make sure that the supplier you select is aware that you will be claiming the credit, and that he provides you with the necessary invoice and/or a certificate detailing the specifications of the equipment he has installed.

When you complete your tax return, enter the cost of the equipment, including VAT, in the appropriate box (WF – WQ). Note that if you have received a grant towards its purchase, you should deduct this amount from the total cost of the equipment. Send the invoice with your tax return to your Tax Office. If you submit your return online, make sure you keep the invoice so that you can produce it to the authorities if required. If you cannot do so, any credit you have received will be reclaimed. Your claim should be made against the income received in the same tax

---

Example of a Tax Credit

If you spend €5000, including VAT, on a new condensing boiler, a tax credit of 25 per cent will be applied, equivalent to €1250. Your tax bill in the following year will be reduced by this amount or, if you pay no tax, you will receive a cheque (or a payment direct into your bank account) from the tax authorities for €1250.

year, for example a project carried out in 2009 should be declared along with your 2009 income in 2010. Your Tax Office will deduct the credit from your income tax for that year. If the credit exceeds the amount you are taxed, or even if you have no income to declare, you will receive a payment.

Are Any Other Financial Incentives Available?

Home Improvement Grants

Depending on your financial resources and the size of your household you may be able to obtain a grant from the housing agency ANAH (*Agence Nationale de l'Habitat*) in order to help to finance your home improvements. Although the grant is means-tested, only your income is taken into account, as evidenced by your two most recent tax statements. You do not have to declare any savings. Other conditions are that your house must be at least fifteen years old and you must undertake to occupy it as your main residence for a period of six years following the improvements. In addition, the house must not have benefited from any other state grant or interest-free loan in the preceding ten years. Subsidies are offered for various projects to bring the house up to modern standards of habitation, including energy-saving measures and its adaptation for disabled occupants. Applications should be made before any work is begun and, once approved, the work should be carried out by professional tradesmen within three years.

You can consult the website www.anah.fr to check whether you are eligible and for a complete list of the projects that are applicable, along with an indication of the amounts of subsidy available. You will find the necessary application forms and the address of your local ANAH office (there is one in every *département*) to which your application should be submitted on the website.

Historic Properties

If you live in a listed property the state may pay up to 50 per cent of the cost of essential maintenance work. Other grants towards its upkeep may also be available. Consult your region's DRAC (*Direction Régionale des Affaires Culturelles*) office for more information.

If you live in a house of historic, architectural or some other special interest but one that is not listed, you may be able to obtain help with funding its maintenance from the *Fondation du Patrimoine*. The main stipulation is that the work to be carried out concerns its exterior appearance and that the property is visible from a public highway. *See* www.fondation-patrimoine.com for details.

Grants may also be available from your local commune, *département* or region, especially if you are installing equipment that uses renewable energy sources in your home. They often apply the same criteria as the ANAH. You can find the latest details on the website of ANIL (*Agence Nationale pour l'Information sur le Logement*), the housing advice agency, at www.anil.org/Aides_locales or at the local ADIL (*Agence Départementale pour l'Information sur le Logement*) office in your *département*.

Other Sources of Finance

If you are carrying out work designed to save energy in your home you can apply for a *prêt de développement durable* or sustainable development loan. These 'green' loans are available from a number of banks and financial institutions and generally offer more advantageous terms than conventional loans. Most are limited to the same projects that are eligible for a tax credit, although they may be used for work in a holiday home as well as a main residence. To help you to compare the different offers available, there is an online tool available on the website of the *Agence de l'Environnement et de la Maîtrise de l'Energie* (ADEME) at www.ademe.fr under the heading *EcoPrets*. In addition, both EDF and GDF offer loans with attractive rates of interest for heating and insulation projects, provided that you use tradesmen approved by them. The government is currently considering the introduction of an interest-free loan (*prêt à taux zéro*) to finance homeowners' capital expenditure on energy-saving equipment.

If you receive family allowance from the CAF (*Caisse des Allocations Familiales*) you may be able to arrange a small loan (the maximum is currently €1067) at an interest rate of just 1 per cent. See www.caf.fr for details.

Setting up a *gîte* or *chambres d'hôtes*

In some regions where the promotion of tourism is considered to be a priority, grants of varying amounts are available to help with financing work to convert your home into a *gîte* or *chambres d'hôtes* under the auspices of *Gîtes de France*. If you take advantage of such a grant then you must agree to make the property available through the organization for a period of between three and ten years (depending on your location). For advice and information contact the local office whose address can be found at www.gites-de-france.com.

If you work for a French company you may be able to obtain a loan under preferential rates (*Prêt Pass-Travaux*) from your employer, particularly if you had to relocate for your work.

As in Britain, there is a wide variety of loans and mortgages available from banks and other financial institutions, based either in France or abroad.

Liability for Capital Gains Tax

If your home in France is your principal residence, it will be exempt from capital gains tax (*impôt sur les plus-values*) when you come to sell it. If, however, it is a holiday property or if you are not tax-resident in France, then you will be liable for this tax.

Capital gains tax is calculated on the difference between the purchase and the subsequent sale prices, less the costs of any major renovations. The work must have been carried out by a registered French *artisan* and you should have retained all the relevant invoices that you have paid. If you cannot provide such proof, a fixed reduction of 15 per cent of the purchase price is made, provided that the house is more than five years old. Note that any materials you may have purchased yourself are excluded, as is any work you have carried out yourself.

The amount of capital gains tax you pay diminishes by 10 per cent for each year that you have owned the property after the first five years. If, therefore, you own it for more than fifteen years, there is no tax to be paid.

Once the net capital gain has been calculated, a tax allowance of €1,000 is deducted. The remaining amount is then subject to capital gains tax at 16 per cent and social charges of a further 11 per cent.

It is the duty of the *notaire* handling the property sale to calculate and subsequently pay the tax, which will be withheld from the proceeds you receive from the sale.

9
What Are My Rights?

> **Disclaimer**
> This chapter is for general information purposes only and does not purport to provide comprehensive legal or other advice. The authors and publishers accept no responsibility for any losses that may arise from reliance upon information contained here.

What Happens If Things Go Wrong?

Don't panic! It should be stressed that, for the vast majority of building projects, the work is completed satisfactorily and within budget, and frequently (but not always, since this is France) on time. It is inevitable, however, that now and again things will go wrong in your dealings with *artisans*, but they are often of a minor nature and easily and amicably resolved. Any faults that occur along the way should immediately be pointed out to the tradesman concerned so that he can either rectify them or make any changes that become necessary. Indeed, our beloved bathroom project was plagued by a series of irritating problems – we had selected a vanity unit which included a shelf, a mirror and a built-in lighting plinth above the washbasin. All the components were delivered in good time for their scheduled installation, but, when they were unpacked and checked, it was found that the lighting unit was the wrong size and would have to be replaced. Unfortunately, it was a made-to-measure unit and so a new one would have to be manufactured – and the manufacturers were in Spain, a country not generally known for hurrying. Four weeks later the new unit arrived, the *menuisier* installed it and the *électricien* was able to connect it. They proudly showed us their handiwork, but it was only under full illumination that the flaw in the shelf below was revealed. Once again, a replacement had to be ordered and there was a further delay before the *carreleur* could complete the tiling, and then the *peintre* could finish the decorating. By this time, of course, we were able to use the new bathroom facilities, and it was on cleaning the base of the WC

> ### Other Sources of Help
> Finding an amicable solution to the problem is always the best solution. It can, therefore, be helpful to contact the Chamber of Trade or any other trade association to which your *artisan* belongs since many of them offer a mediation service.

that Lesley discovered that the grey mark we had taken for the plumber's grubby fingerprint was, in fact, a small area which had not been properly glazed. As it was barely visible, we were not too concerned, but, nonetheless, we mentioned it to M. Robinet. Without any hesitation, he said that he would contact the manufacturers and arrange a replacement. So, although the project took almost twice as long as was originally planned, none of the delays were the fault of the *artisans*, and we had absolutely no cause for complaint.

Occasionally, however, more serious problems may be encountered, and we summarize here the steps that can be taken to deal with them. Once again, it is not always the tradesmen who are at fault. Sometimes misunderstandings can occur regarding the work, with each party having a different view of what has been agreed. Before taking legal action against an *artisan*, you should check the contract or *devis* you signed with him very carefully – otherwise you may find that it is *you* who are being sued for wrongly withholding payment for the work.

The *Artisan* Fails to Carry Out the Work

As we have already explained, when you sign a *devis* from an *artisan* or building company a legally binding contract is established between you. If you subsequently find the work has not begun at all or has started and then been abandoned for an abnormally long time or is simply taking too long to complete, your first step should always be to contact the *artisan* direct. There could be a legitimate reason for the delay, such as his awaiting the delivery of goods or adverse weather conditions, although he should have kept you informed. If, however, you are unable to contact him or his response is unsatisfactory, he may have decided to give up on the job. In this case you should send him a registered letter formally demanding that he recommences the work within a reasonable period and completes it by a certain date. If he fails to do so you should notify him that you will take him to court to seek the official cancellation of the contract and claim payment either of damages and interest, or for another company to complete the work at his expense.

Sample Letter 5

Objet: Mise en demeure d'achever les travaux

En date du [date], *j'ai signé avec vous un devis* [or *contrat d'entreprise* if applicable] *pour faire des travaux de réfection / réparation / construction / électricité / plomberie* [delete as necessary]. *Je constate avec inquiétude que, depuis le* [insert date the last work was done], *les travaux n'avancent plus.*

Je vous mets donc en demeure par la présente de reprendre les travaux dans un délai de [insert *huit* or *quinze* to indicate a week or a fortnight] *jours afin de les terminer au plus tard le* [state the deadline date for finishing the work].

A défaut, je me verrai contraint de saisir la justice pour demander la résiliation du contrat et vous réclamer les dommages et intérêts pour non-exécution de vos engagements, en application de l'article 1147 du Code civil.

Or:

A défaut, je me verrai contraint de saisir la justice pour obtenir l'autorisation de faire exécuter les travaux restants par une autre entreprise, à vos frais, en application de l'article 1144 du Code civil.

Translation

Re: Formal notice to complete the work

On [date] I signed a contract with you for some renovation/repair/building/electrical/plumbing [delete as necessary] work. I note with concern that there has been no progress made with the work since [insert date].

I therefore formally give you notice to recommence the work within a week/fortnight [delete as necessary] in order to finish by [date] at the latest.

If you fail to comply, I will be forced to take legal action seeking the termination of the contract and claiming damages and interest from you for not carrying out your obligations, applying article 1147 of the civil code.

Or:

If you fail to comply, I will be forced to take legal action seeking authority to have the remaining work carried out by another company at your expense, applying article 1144 of the civil code.

Needless to say, you should never pay an *artisan* more money in the hope that this will provide him with an incentive to finish the work – on the contrary, you may well never see him, or your money, again.

The *Artisan* Becomes Bankrupt or Goes Into Receivership

Sometimes an *artisan* or building company to whom you have already paid a deposit may go bankrupt or into receivership before being able to complete the work. If this should occur, you should contact the receiver (*administrateur judiciaire*) appointed to handle the liquidation. You can find his contact details from the court (*tribunal de commerce*) or from one of the business registration websites such as www.societe.com (*see* Chapter 4 for other websites).

It will be the receiver's decision whether or not the enterprise's outstanding contracts can be honoured. If you do not receive a response from him within one month, you can assume that the work will not be completed. In such a situation you should contact the creditors' representative (*représentant des créanciers*) within two months in order to register your claim for the reimbursement of your deposit. You can get more information from the receiver or from the clerk's office (*greffe*) at the court.

Taking Delivery of the Work

For small projects, this consists of simply agreeing with the *artisan* that the job has been completed to your satisfaction. Should there be any outstanding faults you should point them out and give him the opportunity to rectify them. There is no requirement for any written document – payment of the invoice in full is proof that you have accepted the work.

When it comes to major projects, such as new buildings and extensions, *la réception des travaux*, as it is known, is very important as it marks the handing over of responsibility for the site from the builders to you, the owner. It also marks the beginning of the various guarantees and insurances that cover any equipment supplied and the quality of the work.

Accompanied by the builder and, if you wish, an architect or other independent expert, you should carry out a close examination of the entire structure to ensure that all the work detailed in the contract has been carried out correctly and according to the plans. Obviously, the checklist varies according to the nature of the project, but here are a few things to look for:

- cracks in plasterwork, tiles, and other imperfections in the finish;
- paintwork that has been missed;
- doors and windows should all open, close and lock correctly;
- appliances should all function – and make sure that you are given any printed instructions for their use;

- electrical switches and sockets should be checked (it is a good idea to have a small appliance that you can plug in to verify the operation of sockets);
- taps should work, toilets flush, and sinks and basins drain properly.

The *réception des travaux* takes the form of a written statement, known as a *procès-verbal*. This should contain your name and address, those of the builder, the address where the work took place and the date. Unless you have used a single building company, you will need a separate document for each *artisan* you have dealt with. If you are happy that the work has been completed to your satisfaction you should simply write that you accept it without any reservations (*J'accepte la réception des travaux sans réserve*). If you have any concerns, however, these should be noted in the *procès-verbal*, along with details of how and when the faults are to be rectified. Both parties should sign the document and each retain a copy. Remember that you are entitled to withhold 5 per cent of the total cost of the building work until any outstanding faults are made good.

If there are numerous faults of a more serious nature you can refuse to take delivery and postpone it until the work is repaired and meets your satisfaction. If, however, the *artisan* refuses to admit that he has not fulfilled his part of the contract you may take legal action against him, via the local court and a judge in chambers (*juge des référés*). It is even possible to take the case to the *tribunal de grande instance* to obtain a ruling that the work must be completed *sous astreinte*, that is to say, with a penalty for each day's delay.

Refusal to take delivery is a serious step to take and you must ensure that you have valid reasons for doing so. If not, the builder has the right to claim damages and interest from you and to seek a judge's pronouncement that the work is complete.

Legal Guarantees

As we mentioned in Chapter 4, you should always inspect the *artisan's* insurance certificate to ensure that he has up-to-date cover for the work he is to do for you. Failure to have such insurance can result in severe penalties for him, and financial hardship for an unwitting client. It is always a good idea to check this before signing the *devis* – if he is playing by the rules then there will be no problem and no embarrassment. If, however, a *devis* seems particularly low, then you should take care that the total value of the work is covered for the whole of the obligatory ten-year period. If you are in any doubt you can always contact the insurer to confirm that the cover is adequate for your project. Note that the ten-year guarantee continues even if an *artisan* retires or becomes bankrupt, or a building company goes into receivership.

All people working in the building trade, such as individual *artisans*, architects and building companies are legally required to have two insurance policies – the *responsabilité civile* and *assurance décennale* – covering, respectively, professional liability and the work carried out.

In giving this brief outline of the interpretation of complex and by no means necessarily clear-cut legal areas, we should point out that we, like the majority of expats in France, have not to date experienced any problems of a legal nature. We provide this information in the hope that you do not become one of the relatively small number that do. Indeed, our only guarantee issue was a few years ago when we had automatic gates installed. There was a two-year guarantee covering all parts and labour but, as fate would have it, we experienced a problem three months after the end of that period when one of the gates refused to close. We contacted the installer and were informed that there was a standard €60 call-out fee. This included the first 30min of labour, and the cost of each subsequent half hour would be €20. We had no choice but to agree and the engineer came straight out and solved the problem in 45min. We duly signed his call sheet and awaited an invoice for €80. Two weeks later a letter arrived from the company, apologizing for the inconvenience that had been caused, hoping we would experience no further problems and informing us that in the circumstances no charge would be made. Needless to say, the choice of supplier for our new automatic garage door has already been decided.

Responsabilité civile

This policy covers liability to third parties that may arise as a result of the work the *artisan* is doing for you. It can be broadly summarized as cover for accidents or damage resulting from:

- fault, error, omission or negligence committed in the completion of the project;
- defective design in planning the project.

Assurance décennale

This is split into three parts as shown in the table overleaf.

1. *Garantie de parfait achèvement*

This is a legal obligation for the *artisan* to repair not only those faults noted during the handover of the project but also any that appear during the twelve months following the *réception des travaux*. It is the only one of the guarantees to include problems related to sound insulation. Claims may be made up to one year following the completion of the work.

Table 4. Summary of *assurance décennale*

Year 1	*La garantie de parfait achèvement*	The *artisan* guarantees the acceptable completion of all aspects of his work
Years 1 and 2	*La garantie de bon fonctionnement*	The *artisan* guarantees that all the fittings (sanitary, heating, electrical, etc.) are in acceptable working order
Years 1 to 10	*La garantie décennale*	The *artisan* guarantees that components concerning the safety, integrity and stability of the work (walls, roofs, floors, foundations, etc.) are acceptable

2. Garantie de bon fonctionnement

Also known as a *garantie biennale*, this covers all the equipment supplied during the building work that could be removed without damaging the fabric of the building, such as central heating boilers and radiators, taps, doors, windows, shutters and false ceilings. The guarantee also extends to decorative work such as tiling, paintwork and wall and floor coverings. It does not include items such as household appliances, which each have a separate manufacturer's warranty. The guarantee does not apply if the equipment has not been used or maintained correctly. Claims may be made up to two years following the completion of the work.

3. Garantie décennale

This insurance covers any major faults affecting the structure of the building, such as large cracks in a load-bearing wall, warped roof timbers or the collapse of a staircase, and those which make it unfit for habitation, such as a roof that is not watertight, poor insulation causing condensation and mould to form, or a defective electrical supply installation. It also covers material that cannot be removed without damaging the fabric of the building, such as ducts and built-in sanitary ware, but excludes any elements that are purely decorative. It relates to faults that are not initially apparent but which appear following the completion of the work. Claims may be made any time during the ten years following the *réception des travaux*. If you sell your house within this period the guarantee is transferred to your purchasers as part of the sale procedure.

Making a Claim

If there is a problem you should immediately notify the *artisan*, who should make the necessary repairs or replace the faulty equipment, as appropriate. If he fails to respond you should put your request in writing, as follows.

Sample Letter 6

Objet: Réparation des malfaçons

En date du [date], *j'ai signé avec vous un devis* [or *contrat d'entreprise* if applicable] *pour faire des travaux de réfection / réparation / construction / électricité / plomberie* [delete as necessary]. *Après la fin des travaux, j'ai constaté une* [or *plusieurs*] *malfaçon[s]* :

[Detail the faults]

Conformément aux articles 1792 et 2270 du Code civil sur la garantie de parfait achèvement, je vous demande de bien vouloir venir constater les malfaçons dans un délai de 15 jours, et fixer un calendrier d'exécution des travaux de réparation.

Or:

Conformément à l'article 1792-3 du Code civil sur la garantie de bon fonctionnement, je vous demande de bien vouloir venir constater les malfaçons, et d'effectuer les travaux de réparation, dans un délai de 15 jours.

Or:

Conformément à l'article 1792-6 du Code civil sur la garantie décennale, je vous demande de bien vouloir venir constater les malfaçons, et d'effectuer les travaux de réparation, dans un délai de 15 jours.

Translation

Re: Repair of faults

On [date] I signed a contract with you for some renovation/repair/building/electrical/plumbing [delete as necessary] work. Since the work has been completed, I have noticed one [or several] fault[s]:

[detail the faults]

In accordance with article 1792-6 of the civil code relating to the guarantee of satisfactory completion, I should be grateful if you would come and inspect the faults within the next fortnight, and agree a timetable for carrying out the necessary repairs.

Or:

In accordance with article 1792-3 of the civil code relating to the guarantee of satisfactory operation, I should be grateful if you would come and inspect the faults, and carry out the necessary repairs, within the next fortnight.

Or:

In accordance with article 1792 of the civil code relating to the ten-year guarantee, I should be grateful if you would come and inspect the faults, and carry out the necessary repairs, within the next fortnight.

> ### *Assurance dommages-ouvrages*
>
> If you are having major structural work carried out to your property or are building from scratch it is obligatory to take out a policy, known as *assurance dommages-ouvrages*, before the work begins. This insurance provides cover for ten years against any damage caused due to poor workmanship that affects the stability and integrity of the building or anything that makes it unfit for habitation.
>
> While this may appear to duplicate the guarantees provided by a tradesman's own insurance policies, it, in fact, supplements them. The main differences are that you do not have to go to court and prove that the *artisan* was responsible for the damage, and that you will receive a settlement allowing you to finance the necessary repairs within a timescale fixed by law.
>
> There can be penal sanctions if you cannot provide proof of having this policy, although it is not obligatory if the work is being carried out by yourself or members of your immediate family. The premium is calculated according to the exact nature and extent of the work to be carried out and can be expensive.
>
> It is worth noting that, if you sell the house within the ten years, the benefits of it are transferred to the new owner. Conversely, of course, if you have not taken it out and sell the house within the period you may find yourself liable to the new owners for any subsequent defects.

If he still fails to respond, you can take him to court, either to seek an order to oblige him to carry out the necessary repairs or to claim the costs of having the work done by another professional.

Contractual Guarantees

All *artisans* are responsible for any damage caused either by faulty workmanship or by negligence. This guarantee includes faults not covered by the legal guarantees previously described, but it is the householder's responsibility to prove that the *artisan* was at fault. Other guarantees may be given, depending on the nature of the project. They should be detailed in the *devis* or contract that you have signed. Finally, if all else fails, it may be possible to make a claim on your household insurance policy.

Consumer Rights and Product Liability

Consumer rights in France, in common with those of other EU member states, are detailed in the European Union Directive 1999/44/EC of 25 May 1999. Briefly, the genesis of this directive is that products purchased throughout the EU must be 'fit for purpose', that is they must do what it says on the tin. Should there be a problem with regard to the manufacture or operation of an item within two years of purchase you are entitled to ask the seller to repair it or refund the price paid. Furthermore, for the first six months of the two-year period it is up to the seller to prove that the goods were up to the correct standard, rather than the buyer having to prove that they were not. The directive also covers manufacturers' and retailers' warranties and guarantees, which must be clear, transparent and understandable to the buyer.

With regard to product liability, France adopted a strict system in 1998 by incorporating the 1985 EC Directive 85/374 into French law. This operates alongside the existing French contract and tort liability systems, and effectively allows the consumer to bring an action relating to a defective product (one that 'does not provide the safety which a person is entitled to expect') without his having to prove that there has been a breach of contract or negligence by the manufacturer. The consumer must, however, be able to prove that the product was defective. If this is not possible, then, provided that there is a formal contractual relationship between the two parties, an action can be brought under the system of contractual liability; if there is no such relationship, the action can be brought under the system of tort liability. In cases where the manufacturer is unknown, the seller or the distributor can be held liable. All product liability actions are subject to time limits, but these vary considerably within the different systems. Clearly, this is a legal minefield that for any serious problem should be left in the hands of a French lawyer.

The French Legal System

Overview

Should you have to use the French legal system for any reason, the first thing to remember is that it bears absolutely no resemblance to the English system. It is derived from the Napoleonic code (*code Napoléon*) which was devised in the eighteenth century. It has three main branches – the *code civil* (civil law), the *code pénal* (criminal law) and the *code fiscal* (tax law) – and is split between cases involving the government (the administrative system) and the bulk of criminal and civil cases (the judiciary). In the civil system, submissions are almost always made in writing (in French, of course), with oral advocacy playing a minor role and cross-examination being virtually non-existent. Unlike the English or the American systems, heavy punitive damages are not given and class actions are not allowed.

It is a slow process, in which it may take over two years before a case is heard; similarly, judgement is rarely immediate but may take months to be given. It can also be very expensive, especially if you use the services of an *avocat*. Indeed, a single consultation with him and the sending of a letter on your behalf to the *artisan* could well cost several hundred euros, with no guarantee of success – and that is before you get anywhere near a *tribunal*.

Which Court to Use?

Your choice of court depends on the value of the contract in dispute.

The first level in the court hierarchy is the lower court of first instance (*Tribunal d'Instance* or *TI*), where you can represent yourself without employing a lawyer (as long as you can do it in French). This is similar to the English district or small claims court and will hear disputes for amounts up to €10,000. If the amount is less than €4,000 the case will be heard by a *juge de proximité* which is similar to a magistrate in England.

This is followed by the higher court of first instance (*Tribunal de Grande Instance* or *TGI*), which is equivalent to the English county court and will hear disputes for amounts above €10,000. Appearance in front of the *TGI*, however, is restricted to French lawyers. The court should have jurisdiction over the geographical area where the property in question is situated. You can find details at www.justice.gouv.fr under the heading *Annuaires et contacts – Annuaire des juridictions*.

Should there be an appeal against a judgement it will be heard by the Court of Appeal (there is one in each of the major administrative regions), after which the final Court of Appeal is the *Cour de Cassation* in Paris, France's supreme civil court, but this gives decisions only on questions of law.

It is unusual for full costs to be awarded to the 'winning' party, which means that the 'loser' is unlikely to be faced with a mammoth bill. This is why the great majority of writs issued result in a court hearing (about 95 per cent). The common English practice of settling out of court before (often immediately before) trial is extremely rare, and, if suggested, may well lead the other side to suspect that you feel that you have a weak case. The French statute of limitations generally puts a ten-year ceiling on the bringing of an action.

The Role of the Notaire

The *notaire* is the publicly-appointed official responsible for notarizing or sealing contracts and other documents, which are then considered to be legally binding. He is responsible to the Minister of Justice (*Ministre de la Justice*) and is appointed by him. His nearest equivalent in England would be a solicitor, although in some areas (for example, preparing leases, conveyances and the formation of companies) he holds a monopoly, in what is effectively a closed shop profession. *Notaires* must be

French citizens, which means that English solicitors cannot currently enter this lucrative market. For most expats the first meeting with a *notaire* will be when buying a house, where it is quite usual (though not legally required) for the *notaire* to act for both the buyer and the purchaser, and to make sure that all taxes are collected on behalf of the government. He will also act in such areas as family law, wills and probate, and administrative and company law. His fees are usually on a fixed scale which he is obliged to tell you if requested.

The Role of the Avocat

While the role of the *notaire* could be compared to that of an English solicitor, that of the *avocat* could be compared to that of a barrister, although the comparisons are far from parallel. Working for either individuals or companies, he will give advice and prepare legal documentation in all areas of law (business, social, tax, family, transport, insurance, property and criminal). He will also advise on whether an issue justifies litigation, or whether it can be satisfactorily settled more quickly (and cheaply) out of court. As the name implies, his main role is advocacy – the presentation of your case in court. Although court proceedings normally take the form of written submissions (prepared by the *avocat*), his presence in court is necessary in order that he can provide oral explanations on points of detail.

The Role of the Huissier

A *huissier de justice* is a law officer responsible, for instance, for acting as an official witness in some circumstances (*constat d'huissier*), *signification* (which in England is called service processing), enforcing court rulings and the execution of such legal decisions as seizure of goods, and even eviction. In Chapter 1 we recalled how we first encountered a *huissier* when an official, legally-binding inventory of the property that we were renting was required. The most common English translation of *huissier de justice* is 'bailiff' (and sometimes 'sheriff's officer' or 'tipstaff'). In France, however, *huissiers* are not government employees. Indeed, the *huissier* is quite dif-

---

Contacting an *Avocat*

Unlike the British system in which a barrister is briefed on your behalf by a solicitor, the same relationship does not exist between a *notaire* and an *avocat*, and you are entitled to make an appointment with either one direct and independently of the other. In disputes with an *artisan* it is the *avocat* rather than the *notaire* who should be contacted.

112   *What Are My Rights?*

ferent from an English bailiff. For example, he will have a law degree and will have served a two-year apprenticeship with a fully qualified *huissier*.

All three of these legal professionals should be addressed as *Maître*, rather than *Monsieur*.

Taking Legal Action

If all attempts to resolve the problem with the *artisan* direct have failed and you are sure that it is not a language or communication problem, you will need to take legal action against him. At this stage, professional help from an *avocat* should be considered. In any case, all communication should be written, in French, and sent by recorded delivery. Having outlined your grievance to the *artisan* and clearly stated what action you expect in restitution, deadlines should be given not only for the completion of the work, but also for a reply to your letter. If you receive a recorded delivery letter from the *artisan* make sure that you respond to it as quickly as possible. If the matter does go to court, non-response may well be viewed as an

The official sign outside a huissier's *office.*

> ## Legal Aid
>
> Legal aid can be given by approval from the *tribunal* subject to certain requirements related to resources, nationality, residence and admissibility. In a nutshell, if you are a French national, an EU citizen or a foreign national lawfully residing in France, then there may be an entitlement to legal aid. It will largely be dependent on your finances, which, in practice, means that your average combined household resources for the preceding calendar year (excluding certain benefits) should not exceed the annual threshold set by the government – although exceptions can be made by the Legal Aid Bureau. It can be given to both claimants and defendants in all courts.
>
> An application form can be obtained from the *tribunal* and includes details of the documentation you are required to provide with the completed form, which should then be sent to the Legal Aid Bureau in the court's area.

indication of liability. If, of course, you have enlisted the services of an *avocat* this will all be dealt with by him.

If you are not satisfied with the *artisan*'s first and subsequent responses then litigation may be necessary, but obviously should be avoided if at all possible. Unless you are supremely confident, you would be well advised to contact an *avocat* at

> ## Sources of Independent Advice
>
> Whether or not you are employing the services of an *avocat*, there are several other sources of independent advice available to you.
>
> - ANIL (*Agence Nationale pour Information sur le Logement*): this is the government national housing information centre with offices throughout France; further information can be found at www.anil.org
> - CDAD (*Conseil Départementale d'Accès au Droit*): these government sponsored centres throughout France give free legal advice and are staffed by volunteer *avocats, notaires* and *huissiers*; see www.annuaires.justice.gouv.fr
> - Huissiers: although a public official, a *huissier* also works on a private basis and his legal training coupled with a high degree of local knowledge make him an excellent source for legal advice on disputes.

this point as you are entering a potential minefield. He will prepare a submission to the *tribunal*, which may include an independent report from either a *huissier* or an accredited building expert. If this is the case, as the party appointing this professional, you will have to pay him up front, which could involve several thousand euros on top of your other legal fees. Provided that your *avocat* advises that your case is strong enough, however, then you should proceed, as you should be awarded this sum as costs when you win.

From now on the problem is out of your hands, and you will have to wait for the *tribunal's* ruling, but do not expect this to be quick. As mentioned earlier, both bringing the case to court and the subsequent deliberations are slow and at times cumbersome. There is no jury system in civil cases, the matter being decided by the judge(s).

As an alternative to the litigation route, it is possible that the matter can be sorted out through mediation, and your local *tribunal d'instance* will be able to supply you with a list of potential mediators.

10
French Language Skills – Or Lack of Them!

Question: What do you call a person who speaks two languages? *Answer*: bi-lingual

Question: What do you call a person who speaks three languages? *Answer*: tri-lingual

Question: What do you call a person who speaks many languages? *Answer*: multi-lingual

Question: What do you call a person who speaks only one language? *Answer*: English!

We said in Chapter 1 that we moved to France with widely differing French language skills, from Lesley's near fluency to Duncan's somewhat more basic level. Six years on and the gap has narrowed, but there is still quite a wide ravine to cross, And so we believe, it will be with our readers. Some of you will be 'Lesleys' and some of you 'Duncans', and many will be somewhere in-between. We have, therefore, decided to target this section at the lowest common denominator, with apologies to those more *au fait* with the language.

This chapter contains tips on various aspects of communicating in French. As noted in Chapter 3, in general, French *artisans* tend not to use email, and you should not rely on this means of communication with them. In most cases, the telephone is the best method to use. There is advice on contacting *artisans* by telephone, leaving messages on an answering machine and giving directions to your house. We show the standard way to lay out a letter in French, into which can be inserted the sample texts that appear in the book. We have listed numbers, dates and times, and included some useful everyday phrases. The final part of the book consists of a comprehensive glossary of French words and phrases that you may well encounter in your dealings with *artisans* and some SOS phrases for use in household emergencies.

Mastering French

Being able to speak the language and converse with our new friends and neighbours has greatly enriched the quality of our new lifestyle. The most important thing to remember is that, whatever your level of fluency, it is always appreciated if you 'have a go'. In our experience, most French people will gladly try to help you as long as you are seen (and heard) to be making an effort to communicate in their language. On the other hand, they have little time for those who studiously refuse to try and insist on speaking only in English.

If you want to improve your French, language classes are widely available, particularly in those areas with extensive numbers of non-French speaking immigrants. They range from informal sessions run by local volunteers, through lessons provided by educational bodies, to courses at private language schools. There are also numerous learning and practice facilities online for all levels of competence, including the BBC website at www.bbc.co.uk/languages/french/ which we particularly recommend.

Pronunciation

One of Duncan's favourite ways of silencing Lesley is by pointing out that we have two ears and one mouth, and that we should use them in that ratio. While she does not often agree with him, she has to admit that, when it comes to speaking French, it is a valuable piece of advice. Listening attentively to native French speakers and trying to imitate their accent, expressions and rhythm (but not necessarily speed) of speaking is one of the best ways to learn and improve in her opinion.

Pronunciation is one of the most important factors in making oneself understood. Although most consonants are sounded in the same way in both English and French (with the notable exception of the letter h at the beginning of words, which is invariably dropped), the vowel sounds are quite different. You can hear examples of these on the Oxford Dictionaries website at www.askoxford.com/languages/fr/ under the heading Pronunciation Guide. The same page also includes the letters of the alphabet, which is useful for when you have to spell out your name, for example.

Telephoning

As a foreigner, one of the most difficult tasks is communicating by telephone. Even though you can prepare your 'script' in advance, you still need to be able to understand the responses – without the help of facial expressions, gestures or any other visual aids. We list here some of the most common telephone expressions to help to simplify the task.

| *French* | *English* |

Note: if you have any difficulty understanding, do not hesitate to use one of the following:

Excusez-moi, je n'ai pas bien compris	I'm sorry, but I don't understand
Vous pouvez répéter, s'il vous plaît?	Could you say that again, please
Vous pouvez parler plus lentement, s'il vous plaît?	Could you speak more slowly, please

Starting the call

Bonjour / Bonsoir	Good morning, afternoon / Good evening
Je suis bien chez Monsieur Dupont?	Is that Mr Dupont's number?
C'est bien l'entreprise Dupont?	Is that the Dupont Company?
Je voudrais parler à Monsieur Dupont, s'il vous plaît	I'd like to speak to Mr Dupont, please
C'est de la part de qui? / Qui est à l'appareil?	Who's calling, please?
Vous êtes monsieur (madame, mademoiselle)... ?	You are Mr (Mrs, Miss) ... ?
Vous vous êtes trompé de numéro	You've got the wrong number
Excusez-moi, je suis désolé(e). Au revoir.	Excuse me, I'm sorry. Goodbye.

Introducing yourself

Je m'appelle Monsieur Webster	My name is Mr Webster
C'est Monsieur Webster à l'appareil	It's Mr Webster speaking
Mon voisin, Monsieur X, m'a recommandé de vous appeler	My neighbour, Mr X, advised me to call you
Je vous appelle pour un devis pour des travaux de ...	I'm calling you for an estimate for some ... work

Giving your contact details

Ça s'écrit W E B S T E R	It is spelt W E B S T E R
Mon adresse est ...	My address is ...
Mon numéro est le ...	My number is ...
Vous pouvez aussi me joindre sur mon portable au ...	You can also contact me on my mobile at ...

Leaving a message

Monsieur Dupont n'est pas là pour l'instant	Mr Dupont isn't here at the moment

118 French Language Skills – Or Lack of Them!

> ### Giving Telephone Numbers
>
> In France, telephone numbers are always pronounced – and usually written – in groups of two numbers, rather than giving each digit individually. For example, the number 01 23 45 67 89 would be pronounced *zéro un* [pause] *vingt-trois* [pause] *quarante-cinq* [pause] *soixante-sept* [pause] *quatre-vingt-neuf*.

Je peux prendre un message?	Can I take a message?
Voulez-vous laisser un message?	Would you like to leave a message?
Je peux laisser un message?	Can I leave a message?
Pourrais-je laisser mon numéro pour qu'il me rappelle?	Can I leave my number for him to call me back?

Answering machines

Vous êtes en communication avec un répondeur automatique	This is a recorded message
Veuillez laisser votre message après le bip sonore	Please speak after the tone
Bonjour, Monsieur Webster à l'appareil. J'ai besoin de travaux dans ma maison à … [name of town]. Pourriez-vous me rappeler, au … [telephone number], s'il vous plaît? Merci. Au revoir.	Hello, this is Mr Webster speaking. I need some work done in my house in … Would you ring me on … please? Thank you. Goodbye.

Ending the call

Bonne journée / bonne soirée / bon weekend	Have a good day / evening / weekend
Au revoir	Goodbye
A mardi / à la semaine prochaine	See you on Tuesday / see you next week
A tout à l'heure / à bientôt	See you later / see you soon

Miscellaneous expressions

Ne quittez pas / ne raccrochez pas	Hold on
Veuillez patienter, s'il vous plaît	One moment, please
Je rappellerai plus tard	I'll call back later
J'essaierai de vous rappeler plus tard	I'll try to call you back later

Giving Directions to Your House

Having arranged to meet the *artisan*, you may need to give him instructions on how to find your house, particularly if it is in a remote area. It is worth preparing directions from the nearest town, main road or other 'landmark' (such as church, supermarket or filling station). Here are some expressions that may be useful.

Notre maison se trouve à X kilomètres de ...	Our house is X kilometres from ...
Au nord/sud/est/ouest de ...	To the north/south/east/west of ...
Du centre ville/de la rue principale	From the town centre/from the main road
Prenez la route de ...	Take the road towards ...
Tournez à gauche/droite (vers ...)	Turn left/right (towards ...)
(Continuez) tout droit	(Carry on) straight ahead
Descendez/montez la rue	Go down/up the road
Allez jusqu'à la station-service/boulangerie	Go as far as the filling station/bakers
Un peu plus loin que le bar/bureau de poste	Just beyond the bar/post office
Passez l'église/la mairie	Go past the church/town hall
Devant/derrière la gendarmerie	In front of/behind the police station
Avant/après la gare	Before/after the station
A côté du cimetière/en face du supermarché	Next to the cemetery/opposite the supermarket
Au coin/bout de la rue	On the corner/at the end of the road
La prochaine/première route à gauche/droite	The next/first road on the left/right
La route fait un virage serré à gauche/droite	The road turns sharp left/right
Au rond-point/carrefour/intersection	At the roundabout/crossroads/junction
Aux feux	At the traffic lights
Traversez l'autoroute/le pont/le passage à niveau	Cross the motorway/bridge/level crossing
La maison avec les volets bleus/le portail vert	The house with blue shutters/the green gate

Writing a Letter in French

Written French tends to be much more formal than English, particularly when it relates to administrative, financial or legal matters. If you need to use one of the sample letters in this book, the following advice on layout and set expressions may help.

It is normal to begin by placing your name and address at the top of the page on the left-hand side. The name and address of the person to whom you are writing should appear below your address on the right-hand side of the page. The full forms (such as *Monsieur*, *Madame*) should be used rather than abbreviations, although the latter are acceptable on the envelope.

Below the addressee's details, you should write the place you are in and the date. Note that the number is always preceded by *le* and that the month is not capitalized, for example, *Paris, le 6 octobre 2009*.

On the left-hand side you should write the subject of the letter, as shown in the sample texts, and on the next line write *Lettre recommandée avec avis de réception* if it is being sent by recorded delivery.

You should open the letter with *Madame* or *Monsieur*, as appropriate. If you do not know whether the addressee is male or female it is acceptable to write *Madame, Monsieur*. The salutation should always be followed by a comma.

The choice of salutation should be repeated in the ending of the letter, for example, *Veuillez agréer, Madame, Monsieur, l'expression de mes salutations distinguées*. This is the equivalent of 'Yours faithfully' in English. You should place your signature immediately below this phrase. The name and address on the envelope should duplicate that used in the letter. Do not put commas at the end of each line. The full street names may be abbreviated, for example, Av. for *Avenue* and Bd. for *Boulevard*. You should include your return address on the back of the envelope after the word Exp. (short for *Expéditeur/-trice* or sender).

Les Nombres		**Numbers**
Zéro	0	Nought
Un(e)	1	One
Deux	2	Two
Trois	3	Three
Quatre	4	Four
Cinq	5	Five
Six	6	Six
Sept	7	Seven
Huit	8	Eight
Neuf	9	Nine
Dix	10	Ten
Onze	11	Eleven
Douze	12	Twelve
Treize	13	Thirteen
Quatorze	14	Fourteen
Quinze	15	Fifteen
Seize	16	Sixteen
Dix-sept	17	Seventeen
Dix-huit	18	Eighteen

French Language Skills – Or Lack of Them! 121

Dix-neuf	19	Nineteen
Vingt	20	Twenty
Vingt et un	21	Twenty-one
Vingt-deux, vingt-trois, etc.	22, 23, etc.	Twenty-two, twenty-three, etc.
Trente	30	Thirty
Trente et un	31	Thirty-one
Quarante	40	Forty
Cinquante	50	Fifty
Soixante	60	Sixty
Soixante-dix	70	Seventy
Soixante-onze	71	Seventy-one
Soixante-douze	72	Seventy-two
Quatre-vingts	80	Eighty
Quatre-vingt-un	81	Eighty-one
Quatre-vingt-deux	82	Eighty-two
Quatre-vingt-dix	90	Ninety
Quatre-vingt-onze	91	Ninety-one
Cent	100	One hundred
Cent un(e)	101	One hundred and one
Cent deux	102	One hundred and two
Deux cents	200	Two hundred
Mille	1 000	One thousand
Mille un	1 001	One thousand and one
Mille deux	1 002	One thousand and two
Mille cent	1 100	One thousand one hundred
Mille cent onze	1 111	One thousand one hundred and eleven

A comma is not used in French after thousands. Instead, a space or, occasionally, a full-stop is inserted. This is not the case when referring to the year.

Mille soixante-six	1066	Ten sixty-six
Deux mille neuf	2009	Two thousand and nine
Premier(ière)	1^{er}(1re)	First
Deuxième	2^e	Second
Troisième	3^e	Third
Quatrième	4^e	Fourth
Cinquième	5^e	Fifth
Sixième	6^e	Sixth
Septième	7^e	Seventh
Huitième	8^e	Eighth

122 French Language Skills – Or Lack of Them!

Neuvième	9^e	Ninth
Dixième	10^e	Tenth
Vingtième	20^e	Twentieth
Centième	100^e	Hundredth
Millième	1000^e	Thousandth
Un demi/une demie	$1/2$	A half
Un tiers	$1/3$	A third
Deux tiers	$2/3$	Two-thirds
Un quart	$1/4$	A quarter
Trois quarts	$3/4$	Three-quarters
Zéro virgule cinq	0,5	Nought point five
Deux virgule six	2,6	Two point six

Note: in decimals, the French use a comma instead of the English point.

Dix pour cent	10%	Ten per cent
Douze virgule cinq pour cent	12,5%	Twelve point five per cent
Cent pour cent	100%	One hundred per cent
Une poignée		A handful
Une dizaine		About ten
Une douzaine		A dozen
Une vingtaine, trentaine, etc.		About twenty, thirty, etc.
Une centaine		About a hundred
Un millier		About a thousand

Les Dates   Dates

Days of the week and months normally start with a small letter in French, not a capital.

lundi	Monday
mardi	Tuesday
mercredi	Wednesday
jeudi	Thursday
vendredi	Friday
samedi	Saturday
dimanche	Sunday
janvier	January
février	February
mars	March
avril	April
mai	May
juin	June

juillet	July
août	August
septembre	September
octobre	October
novembre	November
décembre	December

The general rule in French is that cardinal, and not ordinal, numbers are used to express dates. Like all good French grammatical rules, however, there is an exception, which is the first day of the month, for example:

le quatorze juillet	*le 14 juillet*	The fourteenth of July
le premier juillet	*le 1ᵉʳ juillet*	The first of July
Le printemps		Spring
L'été		Summer
L'automne		Autumn
L'hiver		Winter
Fin septembre		At the end of September
Début juin		At the beginning of June

L'heure / Time

Matin / après-midi / soir / nuit		Morning / afternoon / evening / night
Hier / aujourd'hui / demain		Yesterday / today / tomorrow
Le lendemain / après-demain		The day after / the day after tomorrow
La veille / avant-hier		The day before / the day before yesterday
L'année dernière / l'année prochaine		Last year / next year
La semaine dernière / la semaine prochaine		Last week / next week
Huit jours / quinze jours / une quinzaine		A week / two weeks / a fortnight
A quelle heure?		At what time?
Environ dix heures	10h	About ten o'clock
Avant dix heures quinze / dix heures et quart	10h15	Before ten fifteen / quarter past ten
Après dix heures trente / dix heures et demie	10h30	After ten thirty / half past ten
Dix heures quarante-cinq / onze heures moins le quart	10h45	Ten forty-five / quarter to eleven

Midi	12h	Noon
Midi et demi au plus tard	12h30	Half past twelve at the latest

And don't forget that after midday, the twenty-four hour clock is used:

Treize/quatorze /quinze/seize heures	13h etc.	One/two/three/four o'clock
Dix-sept/dix-huit/dix-neuf/vingt heures	17h etc.	Five/six/seven/eight o'clock

Some Useful Words and Phrases

Parlez-vous anglais?	Do you speak English?
Je ne comprends pas	I don't understand
Excusez-moi	Excuse me
Comment?	What?
Je m'appelle ...	My name is ...
Comment vous appelez vous?	What's your name?
Enchanté(e)	Nice to meet you
Comment allez-vous / Ça va?	How are you?
Ça va très bien, merci	I'm very well, thank you
Combien?	How much/how many?
Quand?	When?
Où?	Where?
Qui?	Who?
Pourquoi?	Why?
Est-il permis?	Is it allowed?
Est-il interdit?	Is it forbidden?
Que faites-vous?	What are you doing?
Qu'est-ce vous allez faire aujourd'hui?	What are you going to do today?
Qu'est que c'est?	What is it?
Ça va mal/bien	Things are going badly/well
Je suis déçu(e)	I am disappointed
Il n'a pas achevé son travail	He left his work unfinished
Je n'accepte pas votre explication	I don't accept your explanation
Je suis d'accord/je ne suis pas d'accord	I agree/I don't agree
Je vous remercie de votre aide	Thank you for your help
Quelle heure est-il?	What time is it?
En avez vous pour longtemps?	Will you be long?
A plus tard/à bientôt	See you later/see you soon

Appendix I
Useful Websites

Government and Other Official Information

ADEME (*Agence de l'Environnement et de la Maîtrise de l'Energie*), www.ademe.fr, information on energy efficiency in buildings (French/English)
Administration Fiscale, www.impots.gouv.fr, access to tax information and on-line administration and payment services (French)
ANAH (*Agence Nationale de l'Habitat*), www.anah.fr, official housing agency with information on various projects and home improvement grants (French)
ANIL (*Agence Nationale pour l'Information sur le Logement*), www.anil.org, government national housing information centre (French)
Cadastre, www.cadastre.gouv.fr, land registry information (French/English)
CAF (*Caisse des Allocations Familiales*), www.caf.fr, family and other social security allowances (French)
CAUE (*Conseils d'Architecture, d'Urbanisme et de l'Environnement*), www.fncaue.asso.fr, departmental network of architectural and planning advice centres (French)
EDF (*Electricité de France*), www.edf-bleuciel.fr, national electricity supply company (mostly French)
France Diplomatie, www.diplomatie.gouv.fr, wide-ranging official French news site (French/English)
French Embassy, www.ambafrance-uk.org/, site of the French Embassy in London (English)
GDF (*Gaz de France*), www.dolcevita.gazdefrance.fr, national gas supply company (French)
Infogreffe, www.infogreffe.fr, service provided by the Clerks' Offices of the Commercial Courts giving information on company registrations (French/English)
Legifrance, www.legifrance.gouv.fr, official information about the French legal system and access to legal texts and codes (mostly French)
Ministère de la Justice, www.annuaires.justice.gouv.fr, Ministry of Justice site with directory of court jurisdictions and links to local CDAD (*Conseil Départementale d'Accés au Droit*) offices for free legal advice (French)
Service Public, www.service-public.fr, portal site providing access to all official documentation and forms (French/English)

SIRENE, www.sirene.tm.fr, information about SIRET registration numbers and NAF business classification codes (French)

Urbanisme Equipement, www.urbanisme.equipement.gouv.fr, information on building regulations and access to planning application forms (French)

Trade Associations

CAPEB (*Confédération de l'Artisanat et des Petites Entreprises du Bâtiment*), www.capeb.fr, national organization representing *artisans* and small building companies (French)

CMA (*Chambres de Métiers et de l'Artisanat*), www.artisanat.fr, national site representing *artisans* and the Chambers of Trade to which they must register (French)

FFB (*Fédération Française du Bâtiment*), www.ffbatiment.fr, site of the French building federation (French)

Finding an *Artisan*

Activ Travaux, www.activ-travaux.com, introductory service between property owners and tradesmen (French)

Artisan Anglais, www.artisan-anglais.com, directory of English-speaking *artisans* throughout France (English)

Artisans de France, www.artisandefrance.fr, directory of *artisans* by region (French/English)

Artisans du Bâtiment, www.artisans-du-batiment.com, classified directory of registered *artisans* throughout France, published by CAPEB (French)

Devispresto, www.devispresto.com, online service for requesting a *devis* for your building project (French)

Find a Trade in France, www.findatradeinfrance.com, finds registered tradesmen throughout France for specified jobs (English)

Illico Travaux, www.illico-travaux.com, introductory service between property owners and tradesmen (French/English)

Ordre des Architectes, www.architectes.org, website of the professional association of architects, including access to its database (French)

PG (*Professionnel du Gaz*), www.pgn-pgp.com, site for finding a qualified gas installer (French)

Qualibat, www.qualibat.com, database of quality-assessed companies in the building industry (French)

QualiDevis, www.qualidevis.com, online service for requesting a *devis* for your building project (French)

Qualifelec, www.qualifelec.fr, database of quality-assessed companies in the electricity industry (French)
Qualit'EnR, www.qualit-enr.org, lists accredited installers of heating systems using renewable energy sources (French)
Qualifioul, www.chaleurfioul.com, lists accredited installers and maintainers of domestic fuel heating systems (French)

Checking *SIRET* Numbers

The following websites offer varying levels of information about legally-registered businesses in France. Currently, all are in French only.

Cofacerating, www.cofacerating.fr
Euridile, www.euridile.com
Manageo, www.manageo.fr
Société, www.societe.com

Home Improvement

Batirenover, www.batirenover.com, wide-ranging home construction and improvement site (French)
Blog-Maison, www.blog-maison.com, comprehensive information on home improvement projects (French)
Bricovideo, www.bricovideo.com, online videos illustrating all the most common DIY tasks, along with a forum (French)
Conseils Infos Bâtiment, www.conseils-infos-batiment.fr, advice and information on home improvements (French)
Fondation du Patrimoine, www.fondation-patrimoine.com, independent organization with funding available for the maintenance of older properties (mostly French)
Habitat Naturel, www.habitatnaturel.fr, website of the publication devoted to eco-friendly housing and use of renewable energy sources (French)
Idées Maison, www.ideesmaison.com, ideas and advice for constructing and renovating your home (French)
Maison Brico, www.maisonbrico.com, wide-ranging advice on using tradesmen and DIY projects (French)
Références Travaux, www.ref-travaux.fr, guide to building and renovating a home (French)
Travaux.com, www.travaux.com, information and a forum on all aspects of house construction and renovation (French)

128 *Useful Websites*

DIY and Other Chain Stores

Most of the big chains have websites giving advice (*Conseils*) on DIY projects as well as details of the products and services they sell. Currently, they are all in French only.

Bâtiland, www.batiland.fr
Bricomarché, www.bricomarche.com
Castorama, www.castorama.fr
CEDEO, www.cedeo.fr
Gedimat, www.gedimat.fr
Lapeyre, www.lapeyre.fr
Leroy Merlin, www.leroymerlin.fr
Mr.Bricolage, www.mr-bricolage.fr
Point.P, www.pointp.fr

French Life

Angloinfo, www.angloinfo.com, information about living abroad with dedicated pages to many regions of France (English)
Complete France, www.completefrance.com, includes an expat forum and links to the sites of *France Magazine*, *Living France* and *French Property News* (English)
Expat Focus, www.expatfocus.com, global relocation advice, services and forum (English)
France Pratique, www.pratique.fr, wealth of practical information about French life (French)
France This Way, www.francethisway.com, aimed at holidaymakers, information about many aspects of visiting France (English)
FrenchEntree, www.frenchentree.com, comprehensive guide to buying property and life in France (English)
Internet French Property, www.french-property.com, covers all aspects of buying and running a property in France (French/English)
Le Particulier, www.leparticulier.fr, practical financial and legal advice site of the monthly magazine of the same name (French)
SOS Net, www.sos-net.eu.org, practical advice about solving legal problems (French)
Total France, www.totalfrance.com, information site and forum for expats (English)

French Language

BBC, www.bbc.co.uk/languages/french, comprehensive French language learning facility

Lexilogos, www.lexilogos.com, French–English/English–French dictionary and translation site
Oxford Dictionaries, www.askoxford.com/languages/fr, French language and pronunciation help
WordReference.com, www.wordreference.com, online translation dictionaries and language forum

Miscellaneous

Alapage, www.alapage.com, online bookshop (French)
Amazon, www.amazon.co.uk (English) or www.amazon.fr (French), online bookshop
Gîtes de France, www.gites-de-france.com, information about self-catering accommodation (French/English)
La Poste, www.laposte.com, website of the French post office (English version)
Pages Jaunes, www.pagesjaunes.fr, France's version of *Yellow Pages* (French)

Appendix II
Conversion Tables for Imperial and Metric Measures

To Convert	From	To	Multiply by
Length			
	Centimetres (cm)	Inches (in)	0.39
	Inches (in)	Centimetres (cm)	2.54
	Metres (m)	Feet (ft)	3.28
	Feet (ft)	Metres (m)	0.03
	Metres (m)	Yards (yd)	1.09
	Yards (yd)	Metres (m)	0.91
	Kilometres (km)	Miles (ml)	0.62
	Miles (ml)	Kilometres (km)	1.61
Area			
	Square centimetres (cm^2)	Square inches (sq.in)	0.15
	Square inches (sq.in)	Square centimetres (cm^2)	6.45
	Square metres (m^2)	Square feet (sq.ft)	10.76
	Square feet (sq.ft)	Square metres (m^2)	0.09
	Square metres (m^2)	Square yards (sq.yd)	1.20
	Square yards (sq.yd)	Square metres (m^2)	0.84
	Square kilometres (km^2)	Square miles (sq.miles)	0.39
	Square miles (sq.miles)	Square kilometres (km^2)	2.59
	Hectares (ha)	Acres	2.47
	Acres	Hectares (ha)	0.40
Weight			
	Grams (g)	Ounces (oz)	0.03
	Ounces (oz)	Grams (g)	28.35

Kilograms (kg)	Pounds (lb)	2.20
Pounds (lb)	Kilograms (kg)	0.45
Kilograms (kg)	Stones (st)	0.16
Stones (st)	Kilograms (kg)	6.35
Kilograms (kg)	Hundredweights (cwt)	0.02
Hundredweights (cwt)	Kilograms (kg)	50.80
Tonnes	Tons	0.98
Tons	Tonnes	1.02

Volume

Cubic centimetres (cm^3)	Cubic inches (cu.in)	0.06
Cubic inches (cu.in)	Cubic centimetres (cm^3)	16.39
Cubic metres (m^3)	Cubic feet (cu.ft)	35.31
Cubic feet (cu.ft)	Cubic metres (m^3)	0.03
Cubic metres (m^3)	Cubic yards (cu.yd)	0.76
Cubic yards (cu.yd)	Cubic metres (m^3)	1.31

Capacity

Litres (l)	Pints (pt)	1.76
Pints (pt)	Litres (l)	0.57
Gallons (gal)	Litres (l)	4.54
Litres (l)	Gallons (gal)	0.22

Temperature

Celsius (°C)	Fahrenheit (°F)
0	32 (freezing point of water)
5	41
10	50
20	68
25	77
30	86
35	95
40	104
100	212 (boiling point of water)

> To convert Celsius to Fahrenheit: multiply by 9, divide by 5 and add 32
> To convert Fahrenheit to Celsius: subtract 32, multiply by 5 and divide by 9

Sheet Glass

Imperial	Metric
18oz	2mm
24oz	3mm
32oz	4mm
3/16 in	5mm
1/4 in	6mm

Paint Brushes

Imperial	Metric
1/2in	13mm
1in	25mm
1 1/2in	38mm
2in	50mm
3in	75mm
4in	100mm
5in	125mm
6in	150mm

Nail Sizes

Imperial	Metric
1/4 in	10mm
1/2 in	15mm
3/4 in	20mm
1in	25mm
1 1/4 in	30mm
1 1/2in	40mm
2in	50mm
2 1/4 in	60mm
2 1/2in	65mm

2¾ in	70mm
3in	75mm
3½in	90mm
4in	100mm
5in	125mm
6in	150mm
7in	180mm
8in	200mm

Metric Prefixes

Mega (m)	×1,000,000
Kilo (k)	×1,000
Hecto (h)	×100
Deca (da)	×10
Deci (d)	10th
Centi (c)	100th
Milli (m)	1,000th
Micro (μ)	1,000,000th

Glossary

How to Use the Glossary

The French–English part of the glossary is arranged alphabetically by trade, and also includes sections covering administration, parts of the house and tools. Each section contains three columns, first, the French word, then its part of speech or gender (French words) and finally the English translation, for example:

Baignoire f Bathtub

The second column consists of masculine nouns (m), feminine nouns (f), plural masculine/feminine nouns (mpl/fpl), verbs (verb), adverbs (adv) and adjectives (adj).

There are inevitably words that are relevant to more than one trade, for example, the word *mur* (wall) could be used by virtually every type of *artisan*, and so rather than duplicate these there is a section headed *Divers* (Miscellaneous) where they can be found.

The English–French glossary is a straight A to Z listing, in the same format (but with the English word in the first column, and the French word in the third). So, if you receive a *devis* for a *baignoire*, your first port of call should be the relevant sections of the French–English part (for this example, look under *Administration* and *Plombier*). On the other hand, if you want to know the French translation of an English word, go straight to the English–French alphabetical section.

Some words are common to both languages, but these have none the less been included, however obvious they may seem (for example, expert, plan, signature, budget and WC!), in order to ensure that the lexicon is as comprehensive as possible, and also for the avoidance of doubt. It should be remembered that our two languages are riddled with *faux amis* (false friends), that is to say, words that look and/or sound the same but which have different meanings, for example, the French word *caution* means a guarantee and *local* can mean premises as well as being an adjective. A further potential pitfall is the incorrect use or understanding of accents, for example, the word *bouche* means mouth, whereas *bouché* means blocked and *chéneau* is a gutter, but *chêneau* is an oak sapling!

French–English: Arranged by Category

Carreleur	m	Tiler
Adhérer	verb	Stick/adhere (to)
Adhésif	m	Adhesive
Adhésion	f	Sticking/adhesion
Adjuvant	m	Additive
Antidérapant	adj	Non-slip
Brique de verre	f	Glass brick
Carreau	m	Tile
Carreau de faïence	m	Ceramic wall tile
Carreau de liège	m	Cork tile
Carrelage	m	Tiling
Carrelage de sol	m	Floor tiles
Carreler	verb	Tile (to)
Carrelette	f	Tile cutters
Céramique	f	Ceramic
Collage	m	Sticking (up)
Colle à carreaux	f	Tile adhesive
Coulis	m	Grout
Coupe-carreaux	m	Tile cutter
Croisillon	m	Tile spacer
Dalle pour plafond	f	Ceiling tile
Eponge	f	Sponge
Faïence	f	Wall tiles/tiling
Finition	f	Finish/finishing
Griffe	f	Tile scorer
Imperméabilisation	f	Waterproofing
Jointoyer	verb	Grout (to)
Liant	m	Binding agent
Liège	m	Cork tile
Lissage	m	Smoothing
Marbre	m	Marble
Mortier clair/liquide	m	Grout(ing)
Mortier-colle	m	Tile adhesive
Mosaïque	f	Mosaic
Mosaïste	f	Worker in mosaic
Pâte	f	Paste
Poudre	f	Powder
Terre cuite	f	Terracotta
Chauffagiste	m/f	Heating Engineer

SOS! — **SOS!**
La chaudière est en panne — The boiler has broken down
Les radiateurs sont tous froids — All the radiators are cold
Il y a une fuite d'eau à un radiateur — A radiator is leaking
Il y a une odeur de gaz; j'ai peur d'une fuite — There is a smell of gas; I'm afraid of a leak
Je pense que le tuyau de fioul est bouché — I think that the oil pipe is blocked
Le conduit de cheminée est bouché — My chimney/flue is blocked

Aérateur	m	Ventilator
Anti-humidité	adj	Anti-humidity
Ballon d'eau chaude	m	Hot water cylinder
Ballon tampon	m	Buffer tank
Brûleur	m	Burner
Bouche d'aération	f	Air vent
Bûche	f	Log
Charbon	m	Coal
Chaudière	f	Boiler
Chaudière à basse température	f	Low-temperature boiler
Chaudière à condensation	f	Condensing boiler
Chaudière à fioul/mazout	f	Oil-fired boiler
Chaudière à gaz	f	Gas boiler
Chaudière au bois	f	Wood-burning boiler
Chaudière de chauffage central	f	Central heating boiler
Chauffage	m	Heating
Chauffage à air chaud	m	Hot air heating
Chauffage à air pulsé	m	Warm air heating
Chauffage au charbon	m	Coal-fired heating
Chauffage au fioul	m	Oil-fired heating
Chauffage au gaz de ville	m	Town gas heating
Chauffage d'appoint	m	Back-up heating
Chauffage central	m	Central heating
Chauffage électrique	m	Electric heating
Chauffage électrique par accumulation	m	Electric storage heating
Chauffage par le sol	m	Underfloor heating

Glossary   135

Glossary

Chauffage solaire	m	Solar heating
Chauffe-eau/ chauffe-bain	m	Water heater
Chauffe-eau à immersion	m	Immersion heater
Chauffe-eau solaire	m	Solar-powered water heater
Chaufferie	f	Boiler room
Cheminée	f	Chimney/fireplace
Chute de température	f	Temperature drop
Circulateur	f	Circulation pump
Citerne à gaz	f	Gas tank
Citerne à mazout	f	Oil tank
Clé de purge	f	Radiator bleed key
Climatisation	f	Air conditioning
Climatiseur	m	Air conditioner
Comptage	m	Counting
Compteur	m	Meter
Condensation	f	Condensation
Conduit	m	Pipe/duct
Conduit d'aération	m	Air vent
Conduit de fumée	m	Chimney/flue
Conduit de ventilation	m	Ventilation shaft
Cuve à mazout	f	Oil tank
Cuve de stockage	f	Storage tank
Energie renouvelable	f	Renewable energy
Energie thermique	f	Thermal energy
Fioul	m	Fuel oil
Foyer	m	Hearth, fireplace
Froid	m	Cold
Fuite d'eau	f	Water leak
Fuite de gaz	f	Gas leak
Gaz	m	Gas
Gaz carbonique	m	Carbon dioxide
Gaz de ville	m	Town gas
Gaz en bouteille	m	Bottled gas
Gaz naturel	m	Natural gas
Gaz propane	m	Propane gas
Gel	m	Frost
Insert de cheminée	m	Built-in, wood-burning stove
Isolation en murs creux	f	Cavity wall insulation
Jauge	f	Gauge
Laine de verre	f	Fibre glass
Manomètre de pression d'eau	m	Water pressure gauge
Marchand de charbon	m	Coal merchant
Mazout	m	Heating oil
Minuterie	f	Timer/time switch
Moisissure	f	Mould/mildew
Pétrole lampant	m	Paraffin
Plancher chauffant	m	Underfloor heating
Poêle à bois	m	Wood-burning stove
Polluant	m	Pollutant
Polluer	verb	Pollute (to)
Pompe	f	Pump
Pompe à chaleur	f	Heat pump
Programmateur	m	Programmer
Purgeur	m	Bleed valve
Raccord	m	Joint/connection
Radiateur	m	Radiator
Radiateur à accumulation	m	Storage heater
Radiateur à ailettes	m	Finned radiator
Radiateur à bain d'huile	m	Oil-filled radiator
Radiateur à eau chaude	m	Hot water radiator
Radiateur électrique	m	Electric fire
Radiateur en nid d'abeilles	m	Honeycomb radiator
Radiateur extraplat	m	Slimline radiator
Radiateur soufflant	m	Fan heater
Radiateur transversal	m	Cross-flow radiator
Radiateur vertical	m	Vertical-flow radiator
Ramonage	m	Chimney sweeping
Ramoner	verb	Sweep the chimney (to)
Ramoneur	m	Chimney sweep
Régulateur	m	Regulator
Rendement	m	Output/yield
Réservoir de fioul	m	Heating oil tank
Robinet	m	Tap
Robinet thermostatique	m	Thermostatic tap/radiator valve
Sèche-serviette	m	Towel radiator
Sonde	f	Sensor
Soupape	f	Valve
Soupape d'admission	f	Inlet valve
Soupape d'échappement	f	Outlet valve

Soupape de purge	f	Bleed valve
Soupape de sûreté	f	Safety valve
Suie	f	Soot
Température	f	Temperature
Température ambiante	f	Room temperature
Thermique	adj	Thermal
Thermostat	m	Thermostat
Thermostat à gel	m	Frost stat
Tuyau	m	Pipe
Tuyau de fuel	m	Oil pipe
Tuyau de gaz	m	Gas pipe
Tuyauterie	f	Piping, pipework
Vanne d'alimentation	f	Supply valve
Vanne de retour d'eau	f	Water return valve
Vase d'expansion	m	Expansion tank
Ventilateur	m	Ventilator
Ventilation	f	Ventilation
Ventouse	f	Flue/air vent
Vis de purge	f	Bleed screw

Couvreur	**m**	**Roofer**

SOS!

La pluie entre par le toit	The roof is leaking
Un coup de vent a emporté plusieurs tuiles cette nuit	Several tiles were blown off last night
La toiture a été emportée par la tempête	The roof was blown away in the storm

Antenne	f	Aerial
Antenne parabolique	f	Satellite dish
Ardoise	f	Slate
Armature à toit	f	Roof truss
Auvent	m	Porch roof/canopy
Avant-toit	m	Eaves
Bâche	f	Tarpaulin
Bande de plomb	f	Lead flashing
Bardage	m	Weather-boarding
Bardeau	m	Shingle
Bitume	m	Bitumen
Chapeau de cheminée	m	Chimney cap
Chaume	m	Thatch
Cheminée	f	Chimney
Chéneau	m	Gutter
Chute	f	Pitch of roof

Conduite d'eau pluviale	f	Rainwater pipe
Couverture	f	Roofing
Cuivre	m	Copper
Débord	m	Overhang
Démoussage	m	Moss treatment
Démoussant	m	Moss removal product
Etanchéité	f	Watertightness
Faîtages (tuiles)	mpl	Ridge tiling
Faîte	m	Ridge
Faîtière	f	Ridge tile
Feutre à toit	m	Roofing felt
Girouette	f	Weather vane
Gouttière	f	Gutter/guttering
Grille anti-volatile	f	Bird guard
Isolation thermique	f	Thermal insulation
Latte	f	Lath
Lauze	f	Schist
Liteau	m	Batten
Lucarne	f	Skylight/dormer window
Mitre	f	Chimney cowl
Noue	f	Gutter tile
Pente	f	Pitch (of roof)
Pignon	m	Gable end
Portée	f	Bearing (load)
Refaire le toit	verb	Re-roof (to)
Revêtement	m	Flashing
Souche	f	Chimney stack
Sous-toiture	f	Under roof covering
Talon gouttière	m	Stop end of a gutter
Tasseau	m	Batten
Terre cuite	f	Terracotta
Toit	m	Roof
Toit d'ardoises	m	Slate roof
Toit de chaume	m	Thatched roof
Toit en auvent	m	Sloping roof
Toit en terrasse	m	Flat roof
Toit de tuiles	m	Tiled roof
Toiture	f	Roofing
Tuile faîtière	f	Ridge tile
Tuile terre cuite	f	Terracotta tile
Tuiles	fpl	Roof tiles
Volige	f	Batten/lath
Voligeage	m	Battening/lathing
Voliger	verb	Batten/lath (to)

Glossary

Ebéniste	m/f	**Cabinet-maker**	*Marqueteur*	m	Inlayer	
			Massif	adj	Solid (wood)	
Abattant	adj	Drop front	*Mélèze*	m	Larch	
Acajou	m	Mahogany	*Meuble à tiroirs*	m	Chest of drawers/ cabinet	
Ancien	adj	Antique				
Antique	m	Antique	*Meubler*	verb	Furnish (to)	
Armoire	f	Cupboard/ wardrobe	*Meubles*	mpl	Furniture	
			Meubles en bois	m	Wooden furniture	
Bambou	m	Bamboo	*Nœud*	m	Knot (in wood)	
Biseau	m	Bevel	*Noyer*	m	Walnut	
Bois	m	Wood	*Orme*	m	Elm	
Bois blanc	m	Deal/whitewood	*Panneau à bois*	m	Wood panel	
Bois contreplaqué	m	Plywood	*Panneaux*	m	Panelling	
Bois de charpente	m	Timber	*Patine*	f	Patina	
Bois de rose	m	Rosewood	*Penderie*	f	Wardrobe	
Bois dur	m	Hardwood	*Peuplier*	m	Poplar	
Bois exotique	m	Hardwood (tropical)	*Peuplier tremble*	m	Aspen	
Bois imprégné	m	Impregnated wood	*Pin*	m	Pine	
Bois tendre	m	Softwood	*Placage*	m	Veneer	
Bois traité	m	Treated wood	*Placard*	m	Cupboard	
Bois vert	m	Unseasoned/green timber	*Plaqué*	m	Veneered	
			Râtelier	m	Rack	
Boiserie	f	Woodwork	*Restauration*	f	Restoration	
Bouleau	m	Birch	*Restaurer*	verb	Restore (to)	
Bureau	m	Desk	*Sapin*	m	Fir	
Capricorne	m	Capricorn beetle	*Séchage*	m	Seasoning	
Cèdre	m	Cedar	*Tablette*	f	Shelf	
Chantier de bois	m	Timber yard	*Teck*	m	Teak	
Châtaigne	f	Chestnut	*Termite*	m	Termite	
Chêne	m	Oak	*Tirette*	f	Pull-out shelf	
Cire	f	Wax polish	*Tiroir*	m	Drawer	
Colle à bois	f	Wood glue	*Travail du bois*	m	Woodwork	
Colorant	m	Pigment	*Ver du bois*	m	Woodworm	
Contre-fil, à	adj	Against the grain	*Vermoulu*	adj	Worm eaten	
Contreplaqué	m	Plywood	*Vernir*	verb	Varnish (to)	
Ebène	f	Ebony	*Vernir au tampon*	verb	French-polish (to)	
Encastré	adj	Built-in	*Vernis*	m	Varnish	
Entaille	f	Notch/groove	*Vrillette*	f	Death-watch beetle	
Epicéa	m	Spruce	*Xylophène®*	m	Wood preservative	
Erable	m	Maple				
Essence	f	Species of wood	*Electricien*	m	**Electrician**	
Fait sur commande	adj	Custom-made				
Fraise	f	Countersink				
Grain	m	Grain				
Hêtre	m	Beech				
Huile de lin	m	Linseed oil				
Marqueterie	f	Marquetry				

SOS!
La maison est sans électricité
Ça sent le brûlé dans la boîte à fusibles

SOS!
There is no power in the house
I can smell burning from the fuse-box

Glossary

Je n'arrive pas à réarmer le disjoncteur		I can't reset the trip switch

Abat-jour	m	Lampshade
Alarme lumineuse	f	Warning light
Alimentation en électricité	f	Power supply
Allumage	m	Lighting
Ampèremètre	m	Ammeter
Ampoule	f	Light bulb
Ampoule à baïonnette	f	Bayonet-fitting bulb
Ampoule à vis	f	Screw-fitting bulb
Antenne	f	Aerial/antenna
Antenne de télévision	f	Television aerial
Antenne parabolique	f	Satellite dish
Appareil d'éclairage	m	Light fitting
Appareillage électrique	m	Electrical equipment
Applique	f	Wall lamp
Bloc d'alimentation	f	Power supply
Boîte à fusibles	f	Fuse-box
Boîte de dérivation	f	Junction box
Borne	f	Terminal
Borne de masse	f	Earth
Bouton	m	Switch
Branchement	m	Connection
Câble	m	Cable/lead
Câble de raccordement	m	Extension cable
Câble de terre	m	Earth cable
Câble enterré	m	Buried cable
Capot	m	Cover
Charger une batterie	verb	Charge a battery (to)
Circuit	m	Circuit
Circuit basse tension	m	Low-tension circuit
Circuit d'induction	m	Inductive circuit
Circuit haute tension	m	High-tension circuit
Circuit intégré	m	Integrated circuit
Circuit ouvert/fermé	m	Open/closed circuit
Circuit de retour à la masse	m	Earth return circuit
Compteur d'électricité	m	Electricity meter
Conducteur	m	Conductor
Conducteur en charge	m	Live conductor
Coupe-circuit	m	Circuit breaker
Couper le circuit	verb	Switch off (to)
Courant alternatif	m	Alternating current (AC)
Courant continu	m	Direct current
Courant diphasé	m	Two-phase current
Courant (électrique)	f	Current (electric)
Courant monophasé	m	Single-phase current
Courant triphasé	m	Three-phase current
Court-circuit	m	Short circuit
Décharge	f	Electric shock
Détecteur (de fumée)	m	Sensor (smoke)
Disjoncteur	m	Circuit breaker
Douille d'une ampoule électrique	f	Lamp socket
Eclairage	m	Lighting
Eclairage au néon	m	Fluorescent lighting
Eclairage extérieur	m	Outside lighting
Electricité	f	Electricity
Electroménager	m	Domestic appliances
Energie solaire	f	Solar power
Eolienne	f	Wind turbine
Faire l'installation électrique	verb	Wire (to)
Fiche	f	Plug
Fil	m	Wire
Fil souple	m	Flex
Fil sous tension	m	Live wire
Fil téléphonique	m	Telephone wire
Fusible	m	Fuse/fuse wire
Gaine	f	Cable sleeving
Génératrice	f	Generator
Griller	verb	Blow – a fuse, light bulb, etc. (to)
Halogène	m	Halogen
Heures creuses	fpl	Off-peak period
Heures pleines	fpl	Peak period
Hotte	f	Extractor hood
Installer l'électricité	verb	Install electricity (to)
Interrupteur	m	Switch (one way)
Interrupteur à bascule	m	Toggle switch
Interrupteur à gradation de lumière	m	Dimmer switch
Interrupteur marche-arrêt	m	On-off switch

140 Glossary

Interrupteur va-et-vient	m	Switch (two way)
Interruption	f	Disconnection
Isolé	adj	Insulated
Isoler	verb	Insulate (to)
Isolant	adj	Insulating
Isolateur	m	Insulator
Isolation	f	Insulation
Lampe	f	Lamp/light
Lampe au néon	f	Neon light
Lampe murale	f	Wall light
Lampe témoin	f	Warning light
Ligne alimentation	f	Power line
Lumière	f	Light
Lumière au néon	f	Neon light
Lumière d'ambiance	f	Subdued lighting
Lumière du jour	f	Daylight
Lumière du soleil	f	Sunlight
Lumière électrique	f	Electric light
Lumière tamisée	f	Soft light
Luminaire	m	Lamp
Luminance	f	Brightness
Mèche	f	Core (of cable)
Mettre en circuit	verb	Connect/switch on (to)
Mettre une lampe hors circuit	verb	Disconnect a lamp (to)
Minuterie	f	Time-switch
Multiprise	f	Socket adaptor
Neutre	adj	Neutral
Panne d'électricité	f	Power cut/failure
Panneau solaire	m	Solar panel
Phase	f	Live
Plafonnier	m	Ceiling light
Plaque chauffante	f	Hotplate
Plinthe	f	Skirting board
Pôle	m	Terminal/pole
Pose de câbles	f	Cable laying
Prise	f	Socket/power point
Prise de terre	f	Earth
Prise pour rasoir électrique	f	Shaver socket
Prise triple	f	Three-way adaptor
Programmateur	m	Automatic timer
Projecteur	m	Flood light
Puissance	f	Power (wattage)
Pylône (de transformateur électrique)	m	Pylon (electricity)
Rallonge	f	Extension lead
Recevoir une décharge	verb	Get an electric shock (to)
Refaire l'installation électrique	verb	Rewire (to)
Réglette étanche	f	Watertight strip-light
Réglette fluorescent	f	Fluorescent strip-light
Relais	m	Relay
Résistance	f	Resistance
Rétablir	verb	Switch on the current again (to)
Rhéostat	m	Rheostat
Rosace de plafond	f	Ceiling rose
Ruban isolant	m	Insulating tape
Saignée	f	Channel in the wall (e.g., for electrical cable)
Socle	m	Base plate
Spot	m	Spotlight
Spot encastré	m	Flush-fitting spotlight
Surtension	f	Electrical surge
Tableau de distribution	m	Distribution board
Tension (basse/haute)	f	Voltage (low/high)
Tension nulle	f	Zero voltage
Terre	f	Earth
Transformateur	m	Transformer
Tube fluorescent	m	Neon tube
Variateur	m	Dimmer switch
VMC (ventilation mécanique contrôlée)	f	Electromechanical ventilation system
Voltmètre	m	Voltmeter
Maçon	**m**	**Bricklayer**
SOS!		**SOS!**
Une partie du mur du jardin s'est effondrée		Part of my garden wall has collapsed
Agrégat	m	Aggregate
Armature	f	Reinforcement

Glossary

Asphalte	m	Asphalt
Assise	f	Course/layer
Béton	m	Concrete
Béton armé	m	Reinforced concrete
Béton prêt à l'emploi	m	Ready-mix concrete
Bétonnage	m	Concreting
Bétonner	verb	Concrete (to)
Bétonnière	f	Concrete/cement mixer
Bloc	m	Block/lump (stone)
Brique	f	Brick
Brique à couteau	f	Arch brick
Brique de ventilation	f	Ventilation brick
Brique perforée	f	Air brick
Brique pleine	f	Solid brick
Brique réfractaire	f	Firebrick
Brique tubulaire/creuse	f	Hollow brick
Briqueter	verb	Brick (to)
Brouette	f	Wheelbarrow
Carrelage en brick	m	Brick paving
Chape	f	Screed
Chaux	f	Lime render
Chaux vive	f	Quicklime
Ciment	m	Cement
Ciment armé	m	Reinforced cement
Ciment à prise rapide	m	Quick-setting cement
Cimenter	verb	Cement (to)
Clef de voûte	f	Keystone
Cloison maçonnée	f	Masonry partition
Contrefort	m	Buttress
Couteau à pierre	m	Stonemason's knife/chisel
Dallage	m	Paving
Dalle	f	Paving/flag stone
Daller	verb	Pave (to)
Damer	verb	Tamp (to)
Déblais	mpl	Rubble
Dresser	verb	Dress stone (to)
Echafaudage	m	Scaffolding
Echelle	f	Ladder
Empierrement	m	Hardcore
Enduit	m	Render
Entreprise de maçonnerie	f	Building firm
Etai	m	Prop
Fissures du mur	fpl	Cracks in the wall
Fondations	fpl	Foundations
Gâchage (de mortier)	m	Mixing (mortar)
Galets	mpl	Pebbles
Glaise	f	Clay
Granit	m	Granite
Granulat	m	Aggregate
Granulats fins	m	Fine aggregate
Gravats	mpl	Rubble
Gravier	m	Gravel
Gravillon	m	Fine gravel/grit
Grès	m	Sandstone
Gros agrégats	m	Coarse aggregate
Gros mur	m	Load-bearing wall
Gros-œuvre (d'un bâtiment)	m	Fabric/basic structure (of a building)
Imperméable	adj	Impermeable
Jointoiement	m	Pointing
Jointoyer	verb	Point (to)
Liaisonner	verb	Bond (to)
Liant	m	Binding agent
Linteau	m	Lintel
Lit de béton	m	Bed of concrete
Maçonnage	m	Bricklaying
Maçonner	verb	Build (to)
Maçonnerie	f	Brickwork/masonry
Marbre	m	Marble
Massette	f	Sledgehammer
Moellon	m	Quarry stone
Mortier	m	Mortar
Mur aveugle	m	Blind wall (no doors or windows)
Mur creux	m	Cavity wall
Mur d'appui	m	Supporting wall
Mur de clôture	m	Surrounding wall
Mur de séparation	m	Dividing wall
Mur de soutènement	m	Retaining wall
Mur mitoyen	m	Party wall
Mur pignon	m	Gable wall
Mur porteur	m	Load-bearing wall
Murage	m	Blocking up
Murer	verb	Wall in (to)
Muret	m	Low wall
Ossature	f	Frame(work)
Parapet	m	Parapet
Parpaing	m	Breeze block

142 Glossary

Pavé	m	Paving stone
Petite maçonnerie	f	Interior building work
Pierre	f	Stone
Pierre à bâtir	f	Building stone
Pierre à chaux	f	Limestone
Pierre angulaire	f	Cornerstone
Pierre apparentes	f	Exposed stonework
Pierre de taille	f	Dressed stone
Pierre du pays	f	Local stone
Pierraille	f	Ballast
Pieu	m	Foundation pile
Pignon	m	Gable
Pilier	m	Pillar/column
Plancher	m	Floor
Portée	f	Span
Poudre à ciment	f	Cement powder
Poutre	f	Beam
Poutrelle	f	Girder
Roche	f	Rock
Sablage	m	Sandblasting
Sable	m	Sand
Sablière	f	Large supporting beam
Sacs de gravats	mpl	Bags for rubble
Soubassement	m	Base, sub-foundation
Truelle	f	Trowel
Trumeau	m	Arch pillar/pier
Tuyau de cheminée	m	Chimney stack
Voûte	f	Arch
Menuisier / Charpentier	**m**	**Joiner / Carpenter**

SOS!

J'ai une vitre cassée qui a besoin d'être remplacée
I have a broken window which needs replacing

Le chambranle est voilé
The door/window frame has warped

Aggloméré	m	Chipboard
Aménager	verb	Fit out (to)
Amiante	m	Asbestos
Appui de fenêtre	m	Window ledge
Arbalétrier	m	Principal rafter
Architrave	f	Architrave
Baguette	f	Beading/moulding
Baie vitrée	f	Picture/bay window
Balcon	m	Balcony
Balustrade	f	Balustrade
Banne	f	Awning/canopy
Biseau	m	Bevel/chamfer
Biseauter	verb	Bevel/chamfer (to)
Bois de charpente	f	Timber framework
Bois pourri	m	Rotten wood
Boîte aux lettres	f	Letter box
Boulon	m	Bolt
Bourrelet	m	Draught excluder
Calfeutrage	m	Draught-proofing
Calfeutrer	verb	Draught-proof (to)
Cantonnière	f	Pelmet
Carton dur / Isorel®	m	Hardboard
Chambranle	m	Door or window frame
Charnière	f	Hinge
Charpente	f	Framework
Charpenterie	f	Carpentry
Carreau	m	Window pane
Chanvre	m	Hemp (for insulation)
Châssis	m	Frame
Châssis de fenêtre	m	Window frame
Châssis de porte	m	Door frame
Châssis à guillotine	m	Sash window
Chatière	f	Cat flap
Cheville	f	Peg/plug/dowel
Chevron	m	Rafter
Chien-assis	m	Dormer window
Cloison	f	Partition
Cloisonner	verb	Partition (to)
Coffrage	m	Shuttering
Coffre d'enroulement	m	Roller shutter casing
Colle à bois	f	Wood glue
Colonne	f	Column
Comble	m	Roof structure (wood)
Combles	mpl	Loft, attic
Contrefiche	f	Brace or strut
Contremarche	f	Stair riser
Corniche	f	Cornice
Couche d'étanchéité	f	Damp-proof course

Glossary 143

Coulisse	f	Roller shutter tracking	Liteau/tasseau	m	Shelf bracket
Crémone	f	Shutter/window fastening	Loquet	m	Latch
			Loqueteau	m	Small catch
Crochet	m	Hook	Lucarne	f	Dormer window
Découper	verb	Cut out (to)	Madrier	m	Plank
Double vitrage	f	Double glazing	Main courante	f	Handrail
Echelle meunier	f	Open staircase	Marche	f	Step/stair
Ecrou	m	Nut	Meneau	m	Mullion
Escalier	m	Staircase	Menuiserie	f	Joinery
Escalier en colimaçon	m	Spiral staircase	Moisissure humide	f	Wet rot
Espagnolette	f	Window catch	Moulure	f	Moulding (ornamental)
Etagère	f	Shelf			
Etai	m	Prop/strut	Moulurer	verb	Cut a moulding (to)
Etai réglable	m	Adjustable/accro prop	Mur de cloison	f	Dividing wall
			Mur de refend	f	Partition wall
			Noyau	m	Newel
Etaiement/étayage	m	Shoring/propping up	Œil-de-bœuf	m	Bull's-eye window
			Oriel	f	Oriel window
Faîtage	m	Ridgepole	Panne	f	Purlin, side timber
Faux plafond	f	False ceiling	Panneau de particules	m	Chipboard
Fenêtre	f	Window	Paroi	f	Interior/partition wall
Fenêtre à battants	f	Casement window			
Fenêtre à coulisse	f	Sliding window	Parquet	m	Parquet flooring
Fenêtre à guillotine	f	Sash window	Pas	m	Step (stair)
Fenêtre de toit Velux®	f	Velux® window	Passe-plat	m	Service hatch
Fenêtre en mansarde	f	Dormer window	Percer	verb	Drill (to)
Fenêtre en saillie	f	Bay window	Pilastre	m	Newel post
Feuillure	f	Rabbet	Placard	m	Cupboard
Garde-corps	m	Balustrade	Planche	f	Plank/floorboard
Gerçure	f	Timber shake/flaw	Planchéiage	m	Boarding/planking
Giron	m	Stair tread	Plancher	m	Floor
Glisse-main	m	Handrail/banister	Planches à rainure et languette	fpl	Tongue-and-groove
Gond	m	Hinge			
Goujon	m	Dowel	Plan de travail	m	Work top
Gousset	m	Shelf bracket	Plastique	m	Plastic
Grincer	verb	Creak (to)	Plexiglas®	m	Perspex®
Hotte aspirante	f	Extractor hood	Pliant	adj	Folding
Huisserie	f	Door frame	Plinthe	f	Skirting board/plinth
Imposte	f	Fanlight			
Insonore	adj	Soundproof	Poignée	f	Handle
Jambage	m	Jamb	Poignée de porte	f	Door handle
Jambe de force	f	Prop/brace	Bouton	m	Door knob
Lambrequin	m	Pelmet	Porte	f	Door
Lambris	m	Wooden panelling	Porte à deux battants	f	Double door
Lasure	f	Wood stain	Porte à deux vantaux	f	Stable door
Latte	f	Batten	Porte à panneaux	f	Panelled door
Linteau	m	Lintel	Porte arrière	f	Back/rear door

144 Glossary

Porte battante	f	Swing door
Porte communicante	f	Inter-connecting door
Porte coulissante/ roulante	f	Sliding door
Porte d'entrée	f	Front door
Porte de garage	f	Garage door
Porte de garage motorisée	f	Motorized garage door
Porte de placard	f	Cupboard door
Portes pliantes	fpl	Folding doors
Porte-fenêtre	f	French window
Porte va-et-vient	f	Swing door
Porte vitrée	f	Glass door
Pourriture	f	Rot
Pourriture humide	f	Wet rot
Pourriture sèche	f	Dry rot
Poutre	f	Beam
Poutre de plancher	f	Ceiling joist
Poutre en fer	f	Iron girder (RSJ)
Poutres apparentes	fpl	Exposed beams
Poutrelle	f	Girder
Rampe	f	Banister/handrail
Rayonnage	m	Shelving
Rebord	m	Window sill
Recoin	m	Recess
Serre-joint	m	Clamp
Seuil	m	Doorway/threshold
Socle	m	Base/pedestal
Socle de lambris	m	Skirting board
Solin	m	Space between two rafters/joists
Solive	f	Joist
Solive en acier	f	Steel joist
Store	m	Blind
Store vénitien	m	Venetian blind
Support	m	Prop
Tablette	f	Shelf
Tablette de fenêtre	f	Windowsill
Tiroir	m	Drawer
Tourniquet	m	Shutter catch
Traverse	f	Transom
Trémie	f	Hearth cavity
Trou de sondage	m	Bore hole
Vantail	m	Single panel of a door, window or shutter

Vasistas	m	Fanlight
Velux®	m	Skylight window
Verre	m	Glass
Verre de sécurité	m	Safety glass
Vis	f	Screw
Visser	verb	Screw (to)
Vitrage	m	Glazing
Vitre	f	Window pane/glass
Vitrier	m	Glazier
Voilé	adj	Warped
Volet	m	Shutter
Volet penture	m	Shutter with strap hinges
Volet persienne	m	Louvred shutter
Volet roulant	m	Roller shutter
Volet roulant motorisé	m	Motorized roller shutter
Voûte	f	Arch
Vriller	verb	Bore (to)
Volige	f	Batten
Peintre	**m**	**Painter/ Decorator**
Acétate	m	Acetate
Acétone	f	Acetone
Agent de conservation	m	Preservative
Alcali	m	Alkali
Apprêt	m	Primer
Apprêter	verb	Prime (to)
Argenté	adj	Silver
Bac plastique	m	Roller tray
Badigeon	m	Colour wash
Balai à encoller	m	Pastebrush
Bande de masquage	f	Masking tape
Bitumineux	adj	Bituminous
Blanc	adj	White
Blanchir à la chaux	verb	Whitewash (to)
Bleu	adj	Blue
Boiserie	f	Woodwork
Boursoufflure	f	Blister/bubbling
Brillant	adj	Gloss (paint)
Brosse	f	Brush
Brosser	verb	Brush (to)
Brun/marron	adj	Brown
Camion à peinture	m	Paint bucket/ container
Cellulose	f	Cellulose

Glossary 145

Chaux	f	Lime	*Lasure*	f	Tint/stain
Ciseaux de tapissier	mpl	Paperhanger's scissors	*Lavable*	adj	Washable
			Lavage	m	Washing
Clair	adj	Light (colour)	*Lessivage*	m	Washing (wallpaper/walls, etc.)
Colle à tapisser	f	Wallpaper paste			
Couche	f	Coat			
Couche d'apprêt	f	Priming coat	*Liège*	m	Cork
Couche de fond	f	Undercoat	*Marbrure*	f	Marbling
Couleur	f	Colour	*Mastic*	m	Mastic/filler/putty
Couleurs chaudes	fpl	Warm colours	*Mat*	adj	Matt
Couleurs froides	fpl	Cold colours	*Monocouche*	f	Single coat
Couteau de peintre	m	Paint scraper/pallet knife	*Nettoyant*	m	Cleaning product
			Noir	adj	Black
Crépi	m	Roughcast/pebbledash	*Or*	adj	Gold
			Orange	adj	Orange
Décapage	m	Stripping/sanding down	*Papier de verre*	m	Glasspaper/sandpaper
Décapant	m	Paint stripper	*Papier peint*	m	Wallpaper
Décapeur thermique	m	Heat stripper	*Papier peint en tontisse*	m	Flock wallpaper
Décoller	verb	Strip wallpaper (to)			
Décolleuse (de papier peint)	f	Wallpaper steam stripper	*Papier peint préencollé*	m	Ready pasted wallpaper
Décorer	verb	Decorate (to)	*Papier peint sans raccords*	m	Wallpaper with no pattern match
Diluant	m	Thinner			
Dorer	verb	Gild (to)	*Peindre*	verb	Paint (to)
Email	m	Enamel	*Peinture*	f	Paint/paintwork
Encollage	m	Pasting/sizing	*Peinture acrylique*	f	Acrylic paint
Enduit	m	Coat/application	*Peinture à l'huile*	f	Oil paint
Enduit de lissage	m	Finishing plaster	*Peinture brillante*	f	Gloss paint
Enduit de rebouchage	m	Filler	*Peinture crépi*	f	Masonry paint
Eponge	f	Sponge	*Peinture en bombe*	f	Spray paint
Eponger	verb	Sponge (to)	*Peinture glycéro*	f	Oil-based (glyptal) paint
Essence de térébenthine	f	Turpentine			
			Peinture mat	f	Matt paint
Faire des raccords de peinture	verb	Touch up the paintwork (to)	*Peinture mate*	f	Emulsion paint
			Peinture métallisée	f	Metallic paint
Feutre	m	Felt	*Peinture murale*	f	Mural
Fil à plomb	m	Plumb-line	*Pinceau*	m	Paintbrush
Foncé	adj	Dark (colour)	*Polyuréthane*	m	Polyurethane
Fresque	f	Fresco	*Pointiller*	verb	Stipple (to)
Fresquiste	f	Fresco painter	*Ponçage*	m	Rubbing down/sanding down
Frise	f	Frieze/border			
Gaufré	adj	Embossed	*Poncer*	verb	Rub down/sandpaper (to)
Gris	adj	Grey			
Jaune	adj	Yellow	*Pot de peinture*	m	Paint pot
Lambris d'appui	m	Dado rail	*Raccord*	m	Join
Laque	f	Lacquer	*Racloir*	m	Scraper

Rayure	f	Stripe
Résine	f	Resin
Revêtement	m	Surface covering
Rose	adj	Pink
Rouge	adj	Red
Rouleau à peinture	m	Paint roller
Ruban adhésif	m	Masking tape
Sans odeur	f	Without odour
Satiné	adj	Satin
Séchage	m	Drying
Séchage rapide	m	Quick-drying
Soie	f	Silk
Solvant	m	Solvent
Sous-couche	f	Undercoat
Spatule	f	Spatula
Table à encoller	f	Pasting table
Taché	adj	Stained
Tampon de peinture	m	Paint pad
Tapisserie	f	Wallpaper
Toile de jute	f	Hessian
Ton	m	Tone
Tréteau	m	Trestle
Uni	adj	Plain, non-patterned
Velouté	adj	Velvety
Vernis	m	Varnish
Vernis à bois	m	Wood varnish
Vert	adj	Green
Vinylique	adj	Vinyl
Violet	adj	Purple
White spirit	m	White spirit

Plâtrier	**m**	**Plasterer**

SOS!

Une grande fissure est apparue au plafond — A large crack has appeared on the ceiling

Chape	f	Screed
Cloison	f	Partition (wall)
Cloison en treillis	f	Stud wall
Crépi	m	Roughcast (exterior)/stucco
Crépir	verb	Roughcast (to)
Efflorescence	f	Efflorescence
Enduit	m	Filler
Enduit de lissage	m	Easy-to-sand fine top coat plaster
Finition	f	Finishing
Isolation	f	Insulation
Isolation acoustique	f	Soundproofing
Isolation thermique	f	Thermal insulation
Lissage	m	Smoothing
Lisse	adj	Smooth
Lisser	verb	Smooth (to)
Placoplâtre®	m	Plasterboard
Plâtrage	m	Plastering
Plâtras	mpl	Rubble/lump of plaster
Plâtre	m	Plaster
Plâtrer	verb	Plaster (to)
Plâtres	m	Plasterwork
Plâtres colorés	m	Coloured plaster
Protection incendie	f	Fire-proofing
Ravalement	m	Repointing/roughcasting
Sécher	verb	Dry (to)
Stuc	m	Stucco
Taloche	f	Float
Truelle	f	Trowel

Plombier	**m**	**Plumber**

SOS!

Il n'y a pas d'eau (chaude/froide) — There isn't any (hot/cold) water

La chasse d'eau ne marche pas — The toilet won't flush

Les toilettes sont bouchées — The toilet is blocked

Le tuyau d'eau fuit et l'eau goutte par terre — The water pipe is dripping on to the floor

La cuisine/salle de bains est inondée — The kitchen/bathroom is flooded

Le tuyau d'eau est gelé — The water pipe is frozen

Où se trouve le robinet d'arrêt pour l'eau? — Where do I turn off the water supply?

Glossary

L'eau passe sous la porte de la douche		Water is leaking under the shower door

Adaptateur femelle	m	Female coupling
Adaptateur male	m	Male coupling
Adoucir	verb	Soften (to)
Adoucisseur	m	Water softener
Aération	f	Ventilation
Alimentation d'eau	f	Water supply
Anticalcaire	m	Scale preventer
Appareils sanitaires	mpl	Sanitary fittings
Assainissement	m	Drainage
Bac à douche	m	Shower tray
Bac pour évier	m	Kitchen sink
Bague du robinet	f	Tap washer
Baignoire	f	Bathtub
Baignoire balnéo	f	Whirlpool bath
Baignoire d'angle	f	Corner bath
Baignoire encastrée	f	Sunken bath
Baignoire sabot	f	Hip bath
Balnéothérapie	f	Balneotherapy
Bassine	f	Basin
Bonde	f	Plug (of basin, sink)
Bouché	adj	Blocked
Bouchon	m	Cap (tap, pipe, etc.)/plug (of basin, sink)
Broyeur d'ordures	m	Waste disposal unit
Cabine de douche	f	Shower cubicle
Cabinet de toilette	m	Cloakroom
Cabinets	mpl	Lavatory
Calcaire	adj	Chalky/hard (water)
Calcaire	m	Limestone
Canalisation	f	Piping
Caniveau	m	Conduit
Chalumeau	m	Blow lamp
Chasse d'eau	f	Flush mechanism (toilet)
Chéneau	m	Gutter
Cintrer	verb	Bend (to)
Citerne	f	Cistern
Clapet	m	Valve
Compteur	m	Meter
Compteur à gaz	m	Gas meter
Compteur d'eau	m	Water meter
Conduite d'eau	f	Water pipe
Conduite principale	f	Water main
Couche anticorrosion	f	Underseal
Coude	m	Bend (@ 25°, 45°, 90°, etc.)
Cuivre	m	Copper
Cuve (d'eau)	f	Cistern, tank
Cuvette	f	Toilet bowl
Déborder	verb	Overflow (to)
Déboucher	verb	Unblock (to)
Déboucheur	m	Drain cleaner
Débouchoir	m	Plunger
Descente	f	Downpipe/rainwater pipe
Déshumidificateur	m	Dehumidifier
Détendeur	m	Pressure relief valve
Douche	f	Shower
Douche à l'italienne	f	Walk-in shower
Douchette	f	Shower head
Eau	f	Water
Eau calcaire	f	Hard water
Eau d'égout	f	Sewage
Eau distillée	f	Distilled water
Eau de javel	f	Bleach
Eau de ville	f	Mains water
Eau froide/chaude	f	Cold/hot water
Eaux usées	fpl	Waste water
Ecoulement	m	Drainage
Egout	m	Sewer
Egout collecteur	m	Main sewer
Egouttement	m	Dripping
Egoutter	verb	Drain (to)
Egouttoir	m	Draining board
Envelopper	verb	Lag (to)
Etanche	adj	Watertight
Etanchéité	f	Watertightness
Etancher	verb	Make watertight (to)
Evacuation	f	Drainage
Evacuer	verb	Drain off (to)
Evier	m	Kitchen sink
Femelle	adj	Female (coupling)
Fer à souder	m	Soldering iron
Filet	m	Thread (screw/bolt)
Filtration	f	Filtration
Filtre	m	Filter
Filtre d'eau	m	Water filter

148 Glossary

Flexible	m	Hose, flexible tubing	*Plan de salle de bains*	m	Bathroom plan
Flotteur	m	Ballcock	*Plaque d'égout*	f	Manhole cover
Fosse d'aisance	f	Cesspool	*Plomb*	m	Lead
Fosse septique / Fosse toutes eaux	f	Septic tank	*Plomberie*	f	Plumbing
			Pomme de douche	f	Shower head
Fuite	m	Leak	*Pompe de surface*	f	Surface pump
Fuite d'eau	f	Water leak	*Porte-serviette*	m	Towel rail
Fuite de gaz	f	Gas leak	*Pression*	f	Pressure
Gazinière	f	Gas cooker	*Puisard*	m	Cesspool, soakaway
Gelé	adj	Frozen	*Puits*	m	Well
Geler	verb	Freeze (to)	*Puits artésien*	m	Artesian well
Gouttière	f	Gutter	*Puits de sondage*	m	Borehole
Gravité	f	Gravity	*Puits absorbant / perdu*	m	Soakaway
Humide	adj	Damp			
Humidité	f	Dampness	*Raccord*	m	Joint / connection
Humidité par capillarité	f	Rising damp	*Raccord coudé*	m	Elbow joint
			Raccordement	m	Connecting
Hydrofuge	adj	Water repellent	*Receveur de douche*	m	Shower tray
Hydrofuger	verb	Waterproof (to)	*Recuire*	verb	Anneal (to)
Hydrothérapie	f	Hydrotherapy	*Réseau d'assainissement*	m	Sewage system
Imperméable	adj	Waterproof			
Infiltration d'eau	f	Water infiltration	*Réservoir*	m	Cistern
Inox	m	Stainless steel	*Revêtement calorifuge*	m	Lagging
Installateur sanitaire	m	Plumber	*Revêtement de plomb*	f	Lead flashing
Jacuzzi®	m	Jacuzzi®	*Revêtement de zinc*	f	Zinc flashing
Lampe à souder	f	Blowlamp	*Robinet*	m	Tap
Lavabo / lave-mains	m	Hand basin	*Robinet à flotteur*	m	Ballcock
Lave-linge	m	Washing machine	*Robinet à tournant sphérique*	m	Ball / float valve
Lave-vaisselle	m	Dish washer			
Machine à laver	f	Washing machine	*Robinet d'arrêt*	m	Stopcock
Mâle	adj	Male (coupling)	*Robinet de purge*	m	Bleed tap
Manchon	m	Coupling sleeve	*Robinet du gaz*	m	Gas tap
Manomètre	m	Pressure gauge	*Robinet mélangeur*	m	Mixer tap (with separate hot / cold controls)
Mastic	m	Putty / sealant			
Masticage	m	Puttying / sealing			
Mécanisme de WC	m	Toilet mechanism	*Robinet orientable*	m	Swivel tap
Mitigeur	m	Mixer tap (with single control)	*Robinetterie*	f	Tap fittings
			Rondelle	f	Washer
Mitigeur thermostatique	m	Thermostatic mixer tap	*Ruban*	m	Sealant tape ('plumber's mate')
Obstruction	f	Blockage			
Orifice	m	Vent	*Salle de bain(s)*	f	Bathroom
Panneau de visite	m	Inspection panel	*Sans soudure*	f	Without solder
Papier d'émeri	m	Emery paper	*Sèche-linge*	m	Tumble drier
Percer	verb	Pierce / drill (to)	*Sèche-serviette*	m	Heated towel rail
Perforé	adj	Perforated	*Sel régénérant*	m	Water softener salt

Glossary 149

Siphon	m	U-bend
Soudage	m	Soldering
Souder	verb	Solder (to)
Soudure	f	Solder
Souterrain	adj	Underground
Tartre	m	Scale (deposit)
Thermostat	m	Thermostat
Tout à l'égout	m	Mains drainage
Trop-plein	m	Overflow pipe
Trou de visite	m	Manhole
Trou d'écoulement, trou de vidange	m	Plughole
Tube cuivre	m	Copper pipe
Tube en HTA2	m	Polythene pipe
Tuyau	m	Pipe
Tuyau d'écoulement	m	Overflow pipe/drain
Tuyau de descente	m	Downpipe
Tuyau d'égout	m	Soil pipe
Tuyauterie	m	Pipework
Valeur du pH	f	pH value
Vanne	f	Valve
Vasque	f	Basin
Vérifier l'étanchéité	verb	Check for leaks (to)
Vidange	f	Drain
Ventouse	f	Suction plunger/pad
Vriller	verb	Bore (to)
WC	m	Lavatory
Zinc	m	Zinc
Zinguerie	m	Zinc items
Zingueur	m	Zinc worker

Serrurier / Métallier	f	**Locksmith / Metal worker**

SOS!

Je suis à la porte de chez moi, et je me suis enfermé(e) dehors	I have locked myself out
J'ai perdu les clés de la maison	I have lost my house keys
La clé s'est coincée dans la serrure	The key is jammed in the lock
Je ne retrouve pas la clé qui ouvre la porte	I can't find the key to unlock the door
La serrure est coincée	The lock is jammed
Je n'arrive pas à arrêter la sonnerie de l'alarme antivol	I cannot turn my burglar alarm off

Acier	m	Steel
Acier à ressort	m	Spring steel
Acier au carbone	m	Carbon steel
Acier embouti	m	Pressed steel
Acier galvanisé	m	Galvanized steel
Acier inoxydable / inox	m	Stainless steel
Acier trempé	m	Tempered steel
Alarme	f	Alarm
Alarme antivol	f	Burglar alarm
Alarme à ultrasons	f	Ultrasonic alarm
Alarme incendie	f	Fire alarm
Alarme lumineuse	f	Warning light
Alarme périmétrique	f	Perimeter alarm
Alarme sonore	f	Beep
Alarme télécommandée	f	Remote-control alarm
Alliage métallique	m	Metal alloy
Aluminium / alu	m	Aluminium
Antirouille	m	Rust preventive
Antirouille	adj	Rustproof
Arrêt	m	Catch
Articles en fer-blanc	mpl	Tinware
Barre	f	Bar
Bouton de porte	m	Door knob
Brasure	f	Braze/brazing
Bronze	m	Bronze
Cadenas	m	Padlock
Cheville en fer	f	Bolt
Chrome	m	Chromium
Clé / clef	f	Key
Crochet de sécurité	m	Safety catch
Cuivre	m	Copper
Dégrippant	m	Penetrating oil
Ecusson	m	Key plate
Entrebâilleur	m	Door chain
Espagnolette	f	Window fastener
Fer	m	Iron
Fer-blanc	m	Tin(plate)
Fer coulé / de fonte	m	Cast iron
Ferronnerie / fer forgé	f	Wrought ironwork
Fonte	f	Casting/founding
Forge de serrurier	f	Locksmith's workshop

Glossary

Forger	verb	Forge (to)
Forgeron	m	Blacksmith
Galvanisé	adj	Galvanized
Galvaniser	verb	Galvanize (to)
Grille	f	Grill/metal gate
Grille de défense	f	Security grill
Grille en ferronnerie	f	Wrought-iron gate
Judas optique	m	Peephole
Interphone vidéo	m	Video entry-phone
Laiton	m	Brass
Maréchal-ferrant	m	Farrier
Penture	f	Strap hinge
Poignée de porte	f	Door handle
Profilé	adj	Shaped
Quincaillerie	f	Ironmongers
Rivet	m	Rivet
Rivetage	m	Riveting
Riveter	verb	Rivet (to)
Riveteuse	f	Riveting machine
Rouille	f	Rust
Serrure	f	Lock
Serrure à barillet	f	Cylinder lock
Serrure encastrée	f	Mortise lock
Sonnette d'alarme	f	Alarm bell
Sonnette de porte	f	Doorbell
Souder	verb	Weld (to)
Souder à l'arc	verb	Arc weld (to)
Soudure à l'arc	m	Arc welding
Soudeur	m	Welder
Soudure par points	m	Spot welding
Soudeuse	f	Welding machine
Tôle	f	Sheet metal
Tôle ondulée	f	Corrugated metal
Trou de la serrure	f	Keyhole
Verrou	m	Bolt

Administration	**f**	**Administration**
Abonnement	m	Subscription
Accueil	m	Reception
Achat	m	Purchase
Acheter	verb	Purchase (to)
Acheter au comptant	verb	Buy for cash (to)
Achèvement	m	Completion
Acompte	m	Deposit/instalment
Acquéreur	m	Purchaser/buyer
Acquérir	verb	Acquire/obtain (to)
Acte authentique	m	Deed executed by a notary
Acte de vente	m	Deed of sale
Actuel	adj	Current
Actuellement	adv	Currently
Administrateur judiciaire	m	Receiver (legal)
Administration communale/municipale	f	Local government
Administration des douanes	f	Customs and Excise
Administration fiscale	f	Tax authorities
Adresse	f	Address
Affaire	f	Business/transaction
Agence	f	Agency/bureau
Agence immobilière	f	Estate agency
Agent d'assurance(s)	f	Insurance agent
Agios	mpl	Bank charges
Agrandir	verb	Expand/enlarge (to)
Agrandissement	m	Extension
Alignement (de rue)	m	Building line
Architecte	m/f	Architect
Architecte d'intérieur	m/f	Interior designer
Arrêté municipal	m	By-law
Arrhes	f	Deposit
Arriéré	adj	In arrears/overdue
Artisan	m	Tradesman
Assistance téléphonique	f	Telephone assistance
Assurance	f	Insurance
Assurance décennale	f	Builders' ten-year insurance
Assurance décès	f	Life assurance
Assurance dommages-ouvrages	f	New building insurance
Assurance garantie constructeur	f	Manufacturer's guarantee insurance
Assurance incendie	f	Fire insurance
Assurance maintenance étendue	f	Extended maintenance insurance
Assurance responsabilité civile	f	Public liability insurance

Glossary 151

Assurance multirisques habitation	f	Comprehensive household insurance	
Astreinte	f	Penalty (paid daily) for non-completion of a contract	
Attenant	adj	Adjacent/adjoining	
Attestation	f	Certificate	
Attestation d'acquisition	f	Proof of purchase	
Attestation d'assurance	f	Certificate of insurance	
Attestation de conformité aux règles de sécurité	f	Certificate of conformity to safety standards	
Authentique	adj	Authentic	
Avocat	m	Barrister	
Bail	m	Lease	
Bail commercial	m	Commercial lease	
Bailleur	m	Landlord/lessor	
Bancaire	adj	Bank(ing)	
Banlieue	f	Suburbs	
Banque	f	Bank	
Biens consommables	mpl	Consumables	
Biens consommation	mpl	Consumer goods	
Biens immobiliers	m	Property/real estate	
Bilan	m	Balance sheet/evaluation	
Bon de commande	m	Order form	
Bordereau	m	Form/slip	
Bornage	m	Boundary marking	
Borne	f	Boundary marker	
Budget	m	Budget	
Bureau	m	Office, desk	
Bureau de poste	m	Post office	
Bureau de perception	m	Tax-collection office	
Cadastre	m	Land registry	
Carnet des chèques	m	Cheque book	
Carte bancaire	f	Cheque card/cash card	
Carte d'affaires	f	Business card	
Carte d'affichage	f	Display card	
Carte de commerce	f	Trading licence	
Carte de crédit	f	Credit card	
Carte d'identification	f	Identity card	
Caution	f	Financial guarantee/deposit	
Centre/bureau des impôts	m	Tax office	
Centre ville	m	Town centre	
Certificat	m	Certificate	
Certificat d'assurance	m	Insurance certificate	
Certificat de bonne vie et mœurs	m	Character reference	
Certificat de conformité	m	Certificate of conformity	
Certificat de garantie	m	Guarantee certificate	
Certificat d'essai	m	Test certificate	
Certificat de qualité	m	Certificate of quality	
Certificat d'urbanisme	m	Certificate detailing allowed land usage	
Chambre des métiers	f	Chamber of trade	
Charges	fpl	Expenses/outgoings	
Chef d'entreprise	m	Company head	
Chèque	m	Cheque	
Chèque bancaire	m	Bank cheque	
Chèque barré	m	Crossed cheque	
Chèque bloqué	m	Stopped cheque	
Chèque compensé	m	Cleared cheque	
Chèque de banque	m	Banker's draft	
Chèque d'entreprise	m	Company cheque	
Chèque emploi service universel	m	Cheque to pay 'odd job men'	
Chèque en blanc	m	Blank cheque	
Chèque ouvert	m	Open cheque	
Chèque postal	m	Post office cheque	
Chèque sans provision	m	Bad (bounced) cheque	
Chéquier	m	Cheque book	
Clause	f	Clause	
Clause additionnelle	f	Rider	
Clause d'annulation	f	Cancellation clause	
Clause d'arbitrage	f	Arbitration clause	
Clause de remboursement	f	Refunding clause	
Clause facultative	f	Optional clause	
Clause limitative	f	Limiting clause	
Clause particulière	f	Special condition clause	

152 Glossary

Clause pénale	f	Penalty clause
Clause suspensive	f	Let-out clause
Code assujetti TVA	m	VAT registration number
Code civil	m	Civil law
Code client	m	Customer reference number
Code de commerce	m	Commercial law
Code du travail	m	Employment law
Code postal	m	Postcode
Commande client	f	Customer order
Commune	f	Commune (smallest administrative division)
Compagnie d'assurances	f	Insurance company
Compris	adj	Included
Comptable	m	Accountant
Comptabilité	adj	Accounting
Comptant	m	Cash
Compte	m	Account
Compte à terme	m	Deposit account
Compte courant	m	Current account
Compte de banque	m	Bank account
Compte joint	m	Joint account
Conseil	m	Advice
Conseiller financier	m	Financial adviser
Conseiller fiscal	m	Tax adviser
Conseiller juridique	m	Legal adviser
Conseiller municipal	m	Local councillor
Conseiller technique	m	Technical adviser
Consommateur	m	Consumer
Constat	m	Certified report
Constat d'huissier	m	Process server's affidavit
Constructible (terrain)	adj	Land approved for building
Contrat	m	Contract
Contrat d'embauche	m	Employment contract
Contrat de location	m	Rental agreement
Contrat de service	m	Service contract
Contrôle	m	Inspection
Convention	f	Agreement
Copropriétaire	f	Co-owner
Copropriété	f	Co-ownership
Crédit	m	Credit
Crédit d'impôt	m	Tax rebate
Crédit gratuit	m	Interest-free credit
Croquis	m	Sketch
Date butoir / limite	f	Deadline
Date d'achèvement	f	Completion date
Date d'émission	f	Date of issue
Date d'exigibilité	f	Due date
Date d'expiration	f	Expiry date
Date de facturation	f	Invoice date
Date de livraison	f	Delivery date
Date de remise	f	Remittance date
Date limite de paiement	f	Deadline for payment
Date de validité	f	Expiry date
DDE (Direction départementale de l'équipement)	f	Local Ministry of Environment office
Débuter	verb	Begin (to)
Dédommagement	m	Compensation
Dédommager	verb	Compensate (to)
Délai	m	Time period
Délai de livraison	m	Delivery time
Délai de garantie	m	Guarantee period
Délai de paiement	m	Payment period
Délai de réflexion	m	Cooling-off period
Demande de permis de construire	f	Building / planning permission application
Demeure	f	Residence
Département	m	Department / administrative area
Dépense	f	Expenditure
Déroulement	m	Progress
Dessin	m	Drawing / sketch
Devis	m	Estimate
Dirigeant	m	Director, manager
Discuter	verb	Discuss (to)
Disponible	m	Available
Domicile	m	Residence / home
Domicile fiscal	m	Tax domicile
Dossier	m	File
Droit	m	Right / law
Droit civil	m	Civil law
Droit commercial	m	Commercial law

Glossary

Droit de la consommation	m	Consumer law
Droit de passage	m	Right of way
Droit de puisage	m	Right to draw water
Droit d'enregistrement	m	Registration fees
Droit des contrats	m	Contract law
Droit fiscal	m	Tax law
Ebauche	f	Rough sketch
Echantillon	m	Sample
Echéance	f	Payment date/expiry date
Effectuer un versement	verb	Make a payment (to)
Emoluments	mpl	Remuneration
Emprunt	m	Loan
Emprunter	verb	Borrow (to)
Entreprise	f	Company/firm
Enterprise artisanale	f	Small business
Enterprise générale de bâtiment	f	General building company
Entreprise industrielle	f	Manufacturing company
Entreprise privée	f	Private company
Entreprise publique	f	Public company
Entreprise unipersonnelle	f	One man business/sole trader
Entreprise unipersonnelle à responsabilité limitée	f	Sole trader with limited liability
Escompte	m	Discount
Etat des lieux	m	Inventory
Etranger	adj	Foreign
Etranger	m	Foreigner
Etude	f	Legal office
Expert	m	Expert/specialist
Expert-comptable	m	Chartered accountant
Expert-conseil	m	Consultant
Expertiser	verb	Value (to)
Facture	f	Invoice
Facultative	adj	Optional
Faire opposition à un chèque	verb	Stop payment on a cheque (to)
Faire un chèque	verb	Write a cheque (to)
Financement	m	Financing
Fixer un prix	verb	Set a price (to)
Foncier	adj	Of land
Fonds	m	Fund
Fonds commercial	m	Goodwill
Fonds de roulement	m	Working capital
Forfait	m	Fixed price contract
Fournir	verb	Supply (to)
Fournisseur	m	Supplier
Fournitures et services	fpl	Supplies and services
Frais	mpl	Expenses/costs
Frais accessoires	mpl	Incidental costs/expenses
Frais d'achat	mpl	Purchase costs
Frais d'administration	mpl	Administrative costs
Frais d'annulation	mpl	Cancellation charge
Frais d'entretien	mpl	Maintenance costs
Frais de livraison	mpl	Delivery charges
Frais de main-d'œuvre	mpl	Labour costs
Frais de port et d'emballage	mpl	Postage and packing
Frais en sus	mpl	Additional costs
Frais financiers	mpl	Interest charges
Frais généraux	mpl	Overheads
Garant	m	Guarantor
Garantie	f	Guarantee
Garantie décennale	f	Ten-year guarantee
Garantir	verb	Guarantee (to)
Géomètre-expert	m	Land surveyor
Greffe	m	Clerk to the court
Heures creuses	fpl	Off-peak hours
Heures pointes	fpl	Peak hours
Honoraires	mpl	Fees
HT (Hors Taxe)	f	Exclusive of tax
Huissier	m	Court officer/bailiff
Hypothèque	f	Mortgage
Immobilier	m	Property
Imposition	f	Taxation
Impôt	m	Tax
Impôt direct	m	Direct tax
Impôt foncier	m	Land/property tax
Impôt indirect	m	Indirect tax
Impôt locaux	mpl	Local taxes (council tax)
Impôt sur les grandes fortunes	m	Wealth tax

Glossary

Impôt sur les plus-values	m	Capital gains tax
Inclure	verb	Include (to)
Indivision	f	Joint ownership
Ingénieur	m	Engineer
Inhabité	adj	Uninhabited
Intérêt	m	Interest
Inventaire détaillé	m	Inventory of rented property
Juge de proximité	m	Magistrate
Juge des référés	m	Judge in chambers
Lettre recommandée	f	Recorded delivery
Lettre recommandée avec accusé/avis de réception	f	Recorded delivery with confirmation of receipt
Livraison	f	Delivery
Livre	f	Pound sterling (£)
Local	m	Premises
Locataire	m	Tenant
Location	f	Rental
Louer	verb	Rent/hire (to)
Loyer	m	Rental payment
Main-d'œuvre	f	Workforce
Maître	m	Lawyer/solicitor/bailiff's title
Maître artisan	m	Master tradesman
Maître d'œuvre	m	Project manager
Maître d'ouvrage	m	Contracting person/company
Maire	m	Mayor
Mairie/Hôtel de ville	f	Town Hall
Mandat	m	Mandate
Mandataire	m	Representative/agent
Mandat-poste	m	Postal order
Mensualité	f	Monthly payment
Métier	m	Trade/occupation
Mise en demeure	f	Formal demand/notice
Modalité (de paiement)	f	Method (of payment)
Montant	m	Amount/sum (payment)
Monument historique	m	Listed building
Négociable	adj	Negotiable
Négociation	f	Negotiation
Négocier	verb	Negotiate (to)
Noir (sur le)	m	Black economy (on the)
Non meublé	adj	Unfurnished
Notaire	m	Notary (solicitor)
Notarié	adj	Certified by a notary
Notice d'utilisation	f	Operating instructions
Occupant	m	Occupier
Occupation	f	Occupancy/possession
Offre	f	Offer
Offrir	verb	Offer (to)
Opérations bancaire	adj	Bank(ing) transactions
Ordre de prélèvement	m	Standing order
Origine	f	Origin
Ouvrage	m	Work
Ouvrier	m	Workman
Paiement	m	Payment
Paiement comptant	m	Payment in cash
Paiement d'avance	m	Payment in advance
Paiement échelonné	m	Payment by instalments
Paiement par chèque	m	Payment by cheque
Parcelle	f	Plot of land
Patrimoine	m	Wealth
Payer au comptant	verb	Pay in cash (to)
Période de pointe	f	Peak period
Permis	m	Permit
Permis de construire	m	Building permit/planning permission
Permis de démolir	m	Demolition permit
Plainte	f	Complaint
Plan	m	Plan/blueprint
Plan de construction	m	Construction plan
Plan de financement	m	Financing plan
Plan de maison	m	House plan
Plan d'étage	m	Floor plan
Plus-value	f	Increase in value/capital gain
Police d'assurance	f	Insurance policy
Poser	verb	Install (to)
Pour cent	m	Per cent
Pouvoir	m	Power/ability

Glossary

Préavis	m	Advance notice
Préfecture	f	Main departmental administrative office
Prélèvement	m	Deduction/charge
Prélèvement automatique	m	Direct debit
Prêt	m	Loan
Prêt à la construction	m	Building loan
Prêt bancaire	m	Bank loan
Prime d'assurance	f	Insurance premium
Prix	m	Price
Prix d'acquisition	m	Purchase price
Prix de la main-d'œuvre	m	Labour cost
Prix fixe	m	Fixed price
Procuration	f	Power of attorney/proxy
Promoteur immobilier	m	Property developer
Propriétaire	m	Owner
Propriétaire foncier	m	Landowner
Propriété	f	Ownership/property
Propriété à restaurer	f	Property for restoration
Propriété en ruines	f	Property in ruins
Proposition de prix	f	Estimate
Quittance	f	Receipt
Quote-part	f	Share/portion
Raison sociale	f	Company name
Rapport	m	Report
Rapport d'expertise	m	Valuation/expert's report
Réalisation	f	Completion
Récépissé	m	Official receipt
Réception définitive	f	Handover/final acceptance
Réceptionniste	m/f	Receptionist
Rechercher	verb	Look for/inquire into (to)
Reçu	m	Receipt
Redevance	f	TV licence fee
Référé	m	Summary proceedings
Référence cadastrale	f	Land registry reference
Référence commerciale	f	Trade reference
Relevé	m	Statement
Relevé de compte	m	Statement of account
Relevé du compteur	m	Meter reading
Rendez-vous	m	Meeting/appointment
Rentes	f	Private/unearned income
Responsabilité décennale	f	Builders' ten-year guarantee
Répertoire d'adresses	m	Address book
Répertoire des métiers	m	Trade directory
Réseau	m	Network
Résiliation	f	Cancellation
Résiliation d'un contrat	f	Cancellation of a contract
Saisie	f	Seizure/distraint
Saisine	f	Referral to a court
Salarié	m	Employee
Salle des ventes	f	Sales/auction room
SA (Société Anonyme)	f	Limited liability company (Plc)
SARL (Société Anonyme à Responsabilité Limitée)	f	Limited liability company (Ltd)
Schéma	m	Plan
Sécurité	f	Safety
Se plaindre	verb	Complain (to)
Séquestre	m	Sequestration
Séquestrer	verb	Sequestrate (to)
Service d'urbanisme	m	Town planning department
Servitude	f	Easement/right of way
Signature	f	Signature
Société	f	Company
Solde	m	Balance outstanding (of payment)
Soldes	mpl	Sales (at reduced prices)
Stipulations	fpl	Conditions
Stipulations d'un contrat	fpl	Contract conditions
Subvention	f	Grant/subsidy

Succession	f	Inheritance	*Virement bancaire*	m	Bank transfer
Surface habitable	f	Interior area	*Virement postal*	m	Post office transfer
Tarif	m	Price list/tariff			
Tarif réduit	m	Reduced tariff	**Divers**		**Miscellaneous**
Taux	m	Rate			
Taux d'intérêt	m	Interest rate	*Abîmer*	verb	Damage/spoil (to)
Taxe	f	Tax/duty	*Abouter*	verb	Join end to end/ abut (to)
Taxe d'habitation	f	Council tax			
Taxe d'urbanisme	f	Planning tax	*Absorbant*	adj	Absorbent
Taxes foncières	fpl	Property tax	*Absorber*	verb	Absorb/soak up (to)
Taxe supplémentaire	f	Surcharge	*Accessoire*	m	Accessory
Testament	m	Will	*Accolé*	adj	Adjoining
Timbre	m	Stamp	*Additif*	adj	Additive
Timbre/tampon dateur	m	Date stamp	*Affaissement*	m	Subsidence
			Ajuster	verb	Adjust (to)
Timbre de quittance	m	Receipt stamp	*Aligner*	verb	Align (to)
Timbre fiscal	m	Tax stamp	*Aménagé*	adj	Converted/fitted out
Tracer un plan	verb	Draw a plan (to)			
Traducteur	m	Translator	*Aménager*	verb	Fit out (to)
Traduction	f	Translation	*Aménagement*	m	Fitting out
Traduire	verb	Translate (to)	*Ameublement*	m	Furnishing
Travail manuel	m	Manual labour	*Amiante*	m	Asbestos
Tribunal	m	Court (of law)	*Ancien*	adj	Ancient/former
Tribunal administratif	m	Administrative tribunal	*Appareils*	mpl	Equipment/ apparatus
TTC (Toutes Taxes Comprises)	f	Inclusive of tax	*Apparent*	adj	Visible
			Appartement	m	Flat/apartment
TVA (Taxe sur la Valeur Ajoutée)	m	VAT	*Appui*	m	Support
			Are	m	100 square metres
Urbanisme	m	Town planning	*Arrière*	adj	Back/rear
Urbain	adj	Urban	*Ascenseur*	m	Lift/elevator
Urgence	m	Emergency	*Assemblage*	m	Assembling
URSSAF	f	Social security office	*Assembler*	verb	Assemble (to)
Usage	m	Use	*Assise*	f	Base
Vendeur	m	Salesman	*Atelier*	m	Workshop
Vendeuse	f	Saleswoman	*Bâche*	f	Tarpaulin
Vente	f	Sale/selling	*Bâcler*	verb	Botch (to)
Versement	m	Payment	*Bâtiment*	m	Building
Versement à la commande	m	Down payment	*Bâtir*	verb	Build (to)
			Benne	f	Skip (rubbish)
Versements échelonnés	m	Staggered payments	*Bibliothèque*	f	Library
Verser	verb	Pay (to)	*Bitume*	m	Bitumen/asphalt
Vice de construction	m	Building fault	*Boîte*	f	Box
Vice de forme	m	Legal technicality	*Bombé*	adj	Bulging
Virement	m	Transfer/credit transfer	*Bombement*	m	Bulge
			Bomber	verb	Bulge (to)
Virement automatique	m	Automatic transfer	*Bon état*	adj	Good condition

Glossary

Bord	m	Border
Bord de la mer	m	Seaside
Bord de la rivière	m	Riverside
Bordure	f	Edge
Boucher	verb	Fill (to)
Bourg	m	Large village/small town
Bricolage	m	DIY
Bricoleur	m	Handyman
Bruit	m	Noise
Bruyant	adj	Noisy
Cadre	m	Frame
Caillebotis	m	Duckboard
Cale	f	Wedge
Campagne	f	Countryside
Caoutchouc	m	Rubber
Caoutchouc synthétique	m	Synthetic rubber
Carré	adj	Square
Cavité	f	Cavity/hollow
Centre commercial	m	Shopping centre
Cercle	m	Circle
Circulaire	adj	Circular
Chantier	m	Building site/builder's yard
Champ	m	Field
Chape	f	Screed
Charnière	f	Hinge
Château	m	Castle/mansion/palace
Chaumière	f	Thatched cottage
Chemin	m	Path/lane
Chemin de campagne	m	Country lane
Clair	adj	Clear
Clôture	f	Fence
Clôturer	verb	Fence (to)
Clôture de bornage	f	Boundary fence
Coin	m	Wedge
Colombage	m	Half-timbering
Composant	m	Component
Cône	m	Cone
Conique	adj	Conical
Confort	m	Comfort
Constructeur	m	Builder
Construire	verb	Build/construct (to)
Contenance	f	Capacity
Corps de bâtiment	m	Main building
Cotes	fpl	Dimensions
Couleur	f	Colour
Cour de ferme	f	Farmyard
Couvert de	adj	Covered with
Cube	m	Cube
Cubique	adj	Cubic
Cylindre	m	Cylinder
Cylindrique	adj	Cylindrical
Dallage	m	Paving
Débit	m	Flow (water/electricity)
Déchetterie	f	Municipal recycling facility
Dégâts	mpl	Damage
Dégâts des eaux	mpl	Water damage
Dégâts causés par le feu	mpl	Fire damage
Dégâts causés par la tempête	mpl	Storm damage
Délabré	adj	Dilapidated
Déménagement	m	Removal
Démolir	verb	Demolish (to)
Démolition	f	Demolition
Démontage	m	Dismantling/taking apart
Démonter	verb	Dismantle/take apart (to)
Dépannage	m	Emergency repairs
Déposer	verb	Take down (to)
Dépôt d'ordures	m	Rubbish dump/tip
Détritus	m	Rubbish
Diamètre	m	Diameter
Domaine	m	Estate/property
Duplex	m	Split-level apartment
Eau de source	f	Spring water
Effondrement	m	Collapse
Effondrer	verb	Collapse (to)
Elagage	m	Tree surgery
Encadrer	verb	Frame (to)
Encastrer	verb	Build in (to)
Enlèvement	m	Removal
Ensoleillement	m	Sunshine, hours of
Entrepreneur	f	Contractor/businessman
Enterrer	verb	Bury pipes, cables, etc. (to)

158 Glossary

Entretenir	verb	Maintain (to)
Entretien	m	Maintenance
Epaisseur	f	Thickness
Equipement	m	Equipment
Espace	m	Space
Etage	m	Storey
Etang	m	Pond/pool
Etat	m	State/condition
Etayage	m	Shoring/propping up
Etayer	verb	Shore up (to)
Eviter	verb	Avoid/miss (to)
Extérieur	adj	Exterior
Extincteur	m	Fire extinguisher
Façonnage	m	Shaping/turning
Faux plafond	m	False ceiling
Ferme	f	Farm/farmhouse
Fermette	f	Small farm/small-holding
Fibre de verre	f	Glass fibre
Finition	f	Finish/finishing off
Fissure	f	Crack
Fixer	verb	Fix (to)
Foncé	adj	Dark
Fongicide	m	Fungicide
Forme	f	Shape
Fosse	f	Pit/hole
Fourniture	f	Supply/provision
Gabarit	m	Template
Gamme	f	Range (of products/services)
Gardien	m	Caretaker
Gazon	m	Lawn/grass
Gîte	m	Self-catering accommodation
Gonfler	verb	Inflate (to)
Goudron	m	Tar
Goudronner	verb	Tar (to)
Goulotte d'évacuation	f	Rubbish chute
Gradient	m	Gradient
Gradué	adj	Graduated
Graisse	f	Grease
Graisser	verb	Grease (to)
Graisseur	m	Grease nipple
Gravats	m	Rubble
Gravier	m	Gravel
Gravillon	m	Stone chippings
Grenaillé	adj	Sandblasted
Grillage	m	Wire mesh
Grincer	verb	Creak (to)
Gros œuvre	m	Construction of fabric/shell of building
Habitation	f	Dwelling/house
Habiter	verb	Live in (to)
Haie	f	Hedge
Hameau	m	Hamlet
Hauteur	f	Height
Hauteur sous plafond	f	Ceiling height
Hectare	m	10,000 square metres
Immeuble	m	Building/block of flats
Inclinaison	f	Slope
Inflammable	adj	Inflammable/flammable
Ingénieur	m	Engineer
Installation	f	Installation/fitting/putting in
Installations	fpl	Fixtures and fittings
Jardin	m	Garden
Jardin potager	m	Vegetable/kitchen garden
Jardinerie	f	Garden centre
Joint	m	Joint/seal
Kit	m	Home or self-assembly kit
Lac	m	Lake
Lame	f	Strip (metal/glass/wood, etc.)
Largeur	f	Width
Levier	m	Lever
Lézarde	f	Crack
Liant	m	Binding agent
Lier	verb	Bind/fasten/tie (to)
Limite	f	Boundary
Logement	m	Accommodation
Longueur	f	Length
Lotissement	m	Housing development/estate
Magasin	m	Shop

Glossary

Maison	f	House
Maison ancienne	f	Old house
Maison à toit de chaume	f	Thatched cottage
Maison d'amis / secondaire	f	Holiday/second home
Maison de campagne	f	Country house
Maison de commerce	f	Business firm
Maison de ferme / paysanne	f	Farmhouse
Maison en pierre	f	Stone house
Maison individuelle	f	Detached house
Maison mitoyenne	f	Terraced house
Maison mitoyenne (d'un côté) / jumelée	f	Semi-detached house
Maison neuve	f	New house
Maisonnette	f	Cottage/small house
Malfaçon	f	Defect
Manoir	m	Manor house
Marais	m	Marsh
Marché	m	Market
Mas	m	Farmhouse (in Provence)
Massif	adj	Massive/bulky
Mécanisme	m	Mechanism
Mètre carré	m	Square metre
Mini pelle	m	Mini digger (mechanical)
Mobilier	m	Furniture
Modifier	verb	Alter / change (to)
Moquette	f	Fitted carpet
Moulin	m	Mill
Moulin à eau	m	Water mill
Moulin à vent	m	Windmill
Mousse	f	Expanding foam filler/moss
Mur	m	Wall
Mur mitoyen	m	Party wall
Nettoyage	m	Cleaning
Nettoyant	adj	Cleaning
Nettoyant	m	Cleaning product
Nettoyer	verb	Clean (to)
Neuf	adj	New
Niveau	m	Level
Nivellement	m	Levelling
Orifice	m	Opening/aperture
Ossature	f	Frame
Ouverture	f	Opening
Ovale	adj	Oval
Pages Jaune	f	Yellow Pages
Paillasson	m	Door mat
Palier	m	Landing
Palissade	f	Fence
Palissader	verb	Fence (to)
Panneau	m	Panel
Parc	m	Park/grounds
Pavé	m	Paving stone
Pavillon	m	House/bungalow
Paysage	m	Landscape
Pelouse	f	Lawn
Percer	verb	Pierce/make a hole (to)
Perpendiculaire	adj	Perpendicular
Perron	m	Front steps/flight of steps
Plafond	m	Ceiling
Plancher	m	Floor
Portail	m	Entrance gate
Portillon	m	Side gate
Pose	f	Putting up/installing/hanging
Potager	m	Kitchen/vegetable garden
Poteau	m	Fence post
Poussière	f	Dust
Prairie / pré	f	Meadow
Premier étage	m	First floor
Profondeur	f	Depth
Quartier	m	Neighbourhood
Quincaillerie	f	Ironmongery/shop
Quincaillier	m	Ironmonger
Raccordement	m	Connection
Rainure	f	Groove
Rainuré	f	Grooved
Rainurer	verb	Groove (to)
Ramoneur	m	Chimney sweep
Reboucher	verb	Fill in again (to)
Rectangle	adj	Right-angled
Rectangle	m	Rectangle
Rectangulaire	adj	Rectangular
Récupération	f	Recovery (debt/tax, etc.)

Glossary

Récupérer	verb	Recover (to)
Refaire	verb	Repair/mend (to)
Réfection	f	Repair/restoration (extensive)
Réglable	adj	Adjustable
Réglage	m	Adjustment
Rehausser	verb	Heighten (to)
Remettre à neuf	verb	Renovate (to)
Remise en état	f	Restoration
Remontage	m	Reassembly
Remplacer	verb	Replace (to)
Renforcement	m	Strengthening
Rénovation	f	Renovation
Rénover	verb	Renovate/restore (to)
Réparation	f	Repair
Réparer	verb	Repair (to)
Résistant	adj	Hard-wearing
Restauration	f	Restoration
Restaurer	verb	Restore (to)
Revêtement	m	Surface coating
Rez de chaussée	m	Ground floor
Riverain	m	Resident
Rivière	f	River
Roche	f	Rock (stone)
Rouille	f	Rust
S'affaisser	verb	To subside
Sans amiante	adj	Asbestos free
Second œuvre	m	Fitting out of building
Serrage	m	Tightening/clamping
Site	m	Site
Sphère	f	Sphere
Sphérique	adj	Spherical
Sol	m	Ground/soil
Source	f	Spring (water)
Souris	f	Mouse
Souterrain	adj	Underground
Stère	m	One cubic metre (of wood)
Stratifié	adj	Laminated
Store	m	Blind/shade
Store vénitien	m	Venetian blind
Surface (habitable)	f	Floorspace
Surplomb	m	Overhang
Table à tréteaux	m	Trestle table
Tapis	m	Carpet
Tapette	f	Mouse trap
Tassement	m	Settling/sinking/subsidence
Terrain	m	Land
Terrain à bâtir	m	Building land
Terrassement	f	Earthwork/embankment
Terrassier	m	Labourer
Tissu	m	Cloth
Tondeuse à gazon	f	Lawn mower
Traçage	m	Drawing/lay out
Tracer	verb	Draw (to)
Traitement	m	Treatment
Tranchant	adj	Sharp
Tranchée	f	Trench
Treillage	m	Trellis/lattice work
Treillis	m	Trellis
Triangle	m	Triangle
Triangulaire	adj	Triangular
Trou	m	Hole
Tuyau d'arrosage	m	Hose-pipe
Verger	m	Orchard
Vice	m	Fault/defect
Vice apparent	m	Obvious defect
Vice caché	m	Hidden defect
Vice de construction	m	Structural fault
Vice de fabrication	m	Manufacturing defect
Village	m	Village
Ville	f	Town
Vigneron	m	Wine maker
Voie	f	Lane/track
Voisin	m	Neighbour
Voisin	adj	Neighbouring
Voisinage	m	Neighbourhood
Vue	f	View/outlook

Outils	**m**	**Tools**
Agrafe	f	Staple
Agrafeuse	f	Stapler
Alène	f	Awl
Aspirateur	m	Vacuum cleaner
Balai	m	Broom
Bêche	f	Spade
Bédane/Burin	m	Cold chisel

Glossary

Bétonnière	f	Cement mixer
Boulon	m	Bolt (for nut)
Boulon à écrou	m	Screw bolt
Boulon à œil	m	Eyebolt
Boulon à oreilles	m	Wing bolt
Brosse	f	Brush
Brosse métallique	f	Wire brush
Brouette	f	Wheelbarrow
Cale à poncer	f	Sanding block
Chalumeau	m	Blowtorch
Chasse-clous	m	Nail punch
Cheville	f	Rawlplug®
Cisailles	fpl	Shears
Cisailles pour câble	fpl	Wirecutters
Ciseau	m	Chisel
Ciseau à bois	m	Wood chisel
Clé/clef	f	Spanner
Clé/clef à douille	f	Box spanner
Clé/clef à molette	f	Adjustable spanner
Clé/clef allen	f	Allen key
Clé/clef anglaise	f	Monkey wrench
Clé/clef ouverte	f	Open-ended spanner
Clou	m	Nail/stud
Clou à crochet	m	Hook
Clou cavalier	m	Staple
Coffre à outils	m	Toolbox
Colle	f	Glue
Compas	m	Compasses (pair of)
Compas à pointes sèches	m	Dividers
Compresseur d'air	m	Air compressor
Coupe-boulons	m	Bolt cutters
Coupe-verre/diamant	f	Glass-cutter
Cutter	m	Stanley knife®
Diable	m	Two-wheeled trolley
Douille	f	Socket
Echafaudage	m	Scaffolding
Echelle	f	Ladder
Echelle coulissante	f	Extending ladder
Echelle double	f	Stepladder (high)
Ecrou	m	Nut (for bolt)
Ecrou à oreilles	m	Wing nut
Ecrou de réglage	m	Adjusting/adjuster nut
Equerre à coulisse	f	Calliper gauge
Equerre à dessin	f	Set-square
Escabeau	m	Stepladder
Etabli	m	Work bench
Etau	m	Vice
Etau d'établi	m	Bench vice
Fil à plomb	m	Plumb line
Filet de vis	m	Screw thread
Foret	m	Drill bit/drill
Gants	mpl	Gloves
Gants en caoutchouc	mpl	Rubber gloves
Genouillère	f	Kneepad
Goupille	f	Pin
Goupille fendue	f	Split pin
Grattoir	m	Scraper
Hache	f	Axe
Hachette	f	Hatchet
Laine d'acier	f	Steel wool
Laine de verre	f	Glass wool
Lame	f	Blade
Lame de scie	f	Saw blade
Lime	f	File
Lunettes de sécurité	fpl	Safety glasses
Maillet	m	Mallet
Marteau	m	Hammer
Marteau à panne fendue	m	Claw hammer
Marteau-perforateur	m	Hammer drill
Marteau-piqueur/marteau pneumatique	m	Pneumatic drill
Masque anti-poussières	m	Anti-dust mask
Masque protecteur pour la soudure	m	Welder's mask
Massette	f	Two-handed hammer
Mèche	m	Auger/gimlet
Mèche anglaise	m	Centre bit
Mèche hélicoïdale	m	Twist bit/drill
Mètre	m	Tape measure/rule
Meuleuse d'angle	f	Angle grinder
Nettoyeuse haute pression	f	High pressure cleaner
Niveau	m	Level
Niveau à bulle	m	Spirit level
Niveau laser	m	Laser level
Outil à moteur/électrique	m	Power tool

162 Glossary

Paille de fer	f	Wire/steel wool
Papier corindon	m	Carborundum® paper
Papier de verre	m	Sand/glass paper
Pelle	f	Shovel
Pelle mécanique	f	Mechanical shovel
Perceuse	f	Drill
Perceuse à main	f	Hand drill
Perceuse à percussion	f	Hammer drill
Perceuse électrique	f	Electric drill
Perceuse sans fil	f	Electric drill (cordless)
Perforatrice	f	Jack hammer
Perforatrice à air comprimé	f	Compressed-air drill
Pierre à aiguiser	f	Grindstone/whetstone
Pince	f	Pliers
Pince à becs pointus	f	Pointed nose pliers
Pince à circlip	f	Circlip pliers
Pince à dénuder	f	Stripping pliers (electricity)
Pince coupante	f	Cutting pliers/wire cutters
Pince multiprise	f	Combination pliers
Pioche	f	Pickaxe
Pistolet	m	Spray gun
Poinçon	m	Awl/bradawl
Poinçonneuse	f	Punch
Ponceuse	f	Sander
Ponceuse à bande	f	Belt sander
Ponceuse vibrante	f	Vibrating sander
Queue-de-rat	f	Rat-tail file
Rabot	m	Plane
Râpe à main	f	Rasp
Rateau	m	Rake
Règle	f	Ruler
Scie	f	Saw
Scie à bois	f	Wood saw
Scie à carrelage	f	Tile saw
Scie à chaîne	f	Chain saw
Scie à chantourner	f	Bow saw
Scie à guichet	f	Panel saw
Scie à main/égoïne	f	Hand saw
Scie à métaux	f	Hacksaw
Scie à ruban	f	Band saw
Scie à tenon	f	Tenon saw

Scie anglaise	f	Fret saw
Scie circulaire	f	Circular saw
Scie sauteuse	f	Jig saw
Seau	m	Bucket/pail
Serre-joint	m	Clamp
Spatule	f	Spatula
Tamis	m	Sieve
Tenailles	f	Pincers
Toile émeri	f	Emery cloth
Tournevis	m	Screwdriver
Tournevis à choc	m	Impact screwdriver
Tournevis à lame plate	m	Flat blade screwdriver
Tournevis cruciforme	m	Cross headed screwdriver
Tournevis d'électricien	m	Electrician's screwdriver
Tournevis électrique/testeur	m	Electric screwdriver
Tournevis isolé	m	Insulated screwdriver
Tréteau	m	Trestle
Tronçonneuse à chaine	f	Chain saw
Tronçonneuse circulaire	f	Circular saw
Trousse à outils	f	Tool kit
Truelle	f	Trowel
Vilebrequin (et sa mèche)	m	Brace (and bit)
Vis	f	Screw
Vis à bois	f	Wood screw
Vis à tête fraisée	f	Countersunk screw
Vis à tête ronde	f	Round headed screw
Vis auto taraudeuse	f	Self-tapping screw
La maison	**f**	**The house**
Abri	m	Shelter
Abri de jardin	m	Garden shed
Alcôve	f	Alcove
Annexe	f	Annexe
Appentis	m	Lean-to
Arrière-cuisine	f	Scullery/utility room/back kitchen

Atelier	m	Workshop	*Lingerie*	f	Linen room/laundry
Buanderie	f	Utility room	*Living*	m	Living room
Bûcher	m	Woodshed	*Loggia*	f	Covered terrace
Bureau	m	Study	*Mansarde*	f	Attic
Cabanon	m	Hut/cabin	*Palier*	m	Landing
Cabinet	m	Small room	*Patio*	m	Patio
Cabinet de toilette	m	Toilet/cloakroom	*Pavillon de jardin*	m	Summerhouse
Cave	f	Cellar	*Périmètre*	m	Perimeter
Cave voûtée	f	Vault/vaulted cellar	*Pièce*	f	Room
Cellier	m	Storeroom	*Pigeonnier/colombier*	m	Dovecote/pigeon loft
Chambre	f	Bedroom			
Chambre d'amis	f	Guest room	*Piscine*	f	Swimming pool
Coin-cuisine	m	Kitchenette	*Placard*	m	Cupboard
Combles aménageables	mpl	Attic suitable for conversion	*Placard chauffé*	m	Airing cupboard
			Porche	m	Porch
Couloir	m	Corridor/passage	*Rangement*	m	Storage area
Cour	f	Courtyard	*Remise*	f	Shed
Cuisine	f	Kitchen	*Rez-de-chaussée*	m	Ground floor
Cuisine américaine	f	Open-plan kitchen	*Rez-de-jardin*	m	Garden level
Cuisine équipée	f	Fitted kitchen	*Salle*	f	Room
Débarras	m	Box room	*Salle à manger*	f	Dining room
Dégagement	m	Hall/passageway	*Salle de bains*	f	Bathroom
Dépendances	fpl	Outbuildings	*Salle d'eau*	f	Shower room
Ecurie	f	Stable	*Salle de séjour*	f	Living room
Entrée	f	Entrance hall	*Salon*	m	Lounge/sitting room
Entresol/mezzanine	m	Mezzanine			
Escalier	m	Staircase	*Serre*	f	Greenhouse
Garage	m	Garage	*Sous-sol*	m	Basement
Grange	f	Barn	*Terrasse*	f	Terrace
Grenier	m	Attic/garret	*Véranda*	f	Conservatory
Grenier à foin	m	Hayloft	*Vestibule*	m	Entrance hall

French–English: Arranged Alphabetically

A

100 square metres	m	*Are*	Acetate	m	*Acétate*
10,000 square metres	m	*Hectare*	Acetone	f	*Acétone*
			Acquire/obtain (to)	verb	*Acquérir*
Absorb/soak up (to)	verb	*Absorber*	Acrylic paint	f	*Peinture acrylique*
Absorbent	adj	*Absorbant*	Additional costs	mpl	*Frais en sus*
Accessory	m	*Accessoire*	Additive	adj	*Additif*
Accommodation	m	*Logement*	Additive	m	*Adjuvant*
Account	m	*Compte*	Address	f	*Adresse*
Accountant	m	*Comptable*	Address book	m	*Répertoire d'adresses*
Accounting	adj	*Comptabilité*	Adhesive	m	*Adhésif*

164 Glossary

English		French
Adjacent/adjoining	adj	Attenant
Adjoining	adj	Accolé
Adjust (to)	verb	Ajuster
Adjustable	adj	Réglable
Adjustable spanner	f	Clé/clef à molette
Adjustable/accro prop	m	Etai réglable
Adjusting/adjuster nut	m	Ecrou de réglage
Adjustment	m	Réglage
Administrative costs	mpl	Frais d'administration
Administrative tribunal	m	Tribunal administratif
Advance notice	m	Préavis
Advice	m	Conseil
Aerial/antenna	f	Antenne
Against the grain	adj	A contre-fil
Agency/bureau	f	Agence
Aggregate	m	Agrégat/granulat
Agreement	f	Convention
Air brick	f	Brique perforée
Air compressor	m	Compresseur d'air
Air conditioner	m	Climatiseur
Air conditioning	f	Climatisation
Air vent	f/m	Bouche/conduit d'aération
Airing cupboard	m	Placard chauffé
Alarm	f	Alarme
Alarm bell	f	Sonnette d'alarme
Alcove	f	Alcôve
Align (to)	verb	Aligner
Alkali	m	Alcali
Allen key	f	Clé/clef allen
Alter/change (to)	verb	Modifier
Alternating current (AC)	m	Courant alternatif
Aluminium	m	Aluminium/alu
Ammeter	m	Ampèremètre
Amount/sum (payment)	m	Montant
Ancient/former	adj	Ancien
Angle grinder	f	Meuleuse d'angle
Anneal (to)	verb	Recuire
Annexe	f	Annexe
Anti-dust mask	m	Masque anti-poussières
Anti-humidity	adj	Anti-humidité
Antique	adj	Ancien
Antique	m	Antique
Arbitration clause	f	Clause d'arbitrage
Arc weld (to)	verb	Souder à l'arc
Arc welding	m	Soudure à l'arc
Arch	f	Voûte
Arch brick	f	Brique à couteau
Arch pillar/pier	m	Trumeau
Architect	m/f	Architecte
Architrave	f	Architrave
Artesian well	m	Puits artésien
Asbestos	m	Amiante
Asbestos free	adj	Sans amiante
Aspen	m	Peuplier tremble
Asphalt	m	Asphalte
Assemble (to)	verb	Assembler
Assembling	m	Assemblage
Attic/loft	mpl/f	Combles/mansarde
Attic suitable for conversion	mpl	Combles aménageables
Attic/garret	m	Grenier
Auger/gimlet	m	Mèche
Authentic	adj	Authentique
Automatic timer	m	Programmateur
Automatic transfer	m	Virement automatique
Available	m	Disponible
Avoid/miss (to)	verb	Eviter
Awl	f	Aléne
Awl/bradawl	m	Poinçon
Awning/canopy	f	Banne
Axe	f	Hache

B

English		French
Back-up heating	m	Chauffage d'appoint
Back/rear	adj	Arrière
Back/rear door	f	Porte arrière
Bad (bounced) cheque	m	Chèque sans provision
Bags for rubble	mpl	Sacs de gravats
Balance sheet/evaluation	m	Bilan
Balance outstanding (of payment)	m	Solde

Glossary 165

Balcony	m	*Balcon*	
Ball/float valve	m	*Robinet à tournant sphérique*	
Ballast	f	*Pierraille*	
Ballcock	m	*Robinet à flotteur*	
Balneotherapy	f	*Balnéothérapie*	
Balustrade	f/m	*Balustrade/ garde-corps*	
Bamboo	m	*Bambou*	
Band saw	f	*Scie à ruban*	
Banister/handrail	f	*Rampe*	
Bank	f	*Banque*	
Bank account	m	*Compte de banque*	
Bank charges	mpl	*Agios/frais*	
Bank cheque	m	*Chèque bancaire*	
Bank loan	m	*Prêt bancaire*	
Bank transfer	m	*Virement bancaire*	
Banker's draft	m	*Chèque de banque*	
Bank(ing)	adj	*Bancaire*	
Bank(ing) transactions	adj	*Opérations bancaire*	
Bar	f	*Barre*	
Barn	f	*Grange*	
Barrister	m	*Avocat*	
Base	f	*Assise*	
Base plate	m	*Socle*	
Base/sub-foundation	m	*Soubassement*	
Base/pedestal	m	*Socle*	
Basement	m	*Sous-sol*	
Basin	f	*Bassine/vasque*	
Bathroom	f	*Salle de bains*	
Bathroom plan	m	*Plan de salle de bains*	
Bathtub	f	*Baignoire*	
Batten	m	*Latte/tasseau/ volige*	
Battening/lathing	m	*Voligeage*	
Bay window	f	*Fenêtre en saillie*	
Bayonet fitting bulb	f	*Ampoule à baïonnette*	
Beading/moulding	f	*Baguette*	
Beam	f	*Poutre*	
Bearing (load)	f	*Portée*	
Bed of concrete	m	*Lit de béton*	
Bedroom	f	*Chambre*	
Beech	m	*Hêtre*	
Beep	f	*Alarme sonore*	
Begin (to)	verb	*Débuter*	
Belt sander	f	*Ponceuse à bande*	
Bench vice	m	*Etau d'établi*	
Bend (@ 25° 45° 90°, etc.)	m	*Coude*	
Bend (to)	verb	*Cintrer*	
Bevel/chamfer	m	*Biseau*	
Bevel/chamfer (to)	verb	*Biseauter*	
Bill/statement	m	*Relevé*	
Bind/fasten/tie (to)	verb	*Lier*	
Binding agent	m	*Liant*	
Birch	m	*Bouleau*	
Bird guard	f	*Grille anti-volatile*	
Bitumen/asphalt	m	*Bitume*	
Bituminous	adj	*Bitumineux*	
Black	adj	*Noir*	
Black economy (on the)	m	*Noir (sur le)*	
Blacksmith	m	*Forgeron*	
Blade	f	*Lame*	
Blank cheque	m	*Chèque en blanc*	
Bleach	f	*Eau de javel*	
Bleed screw	f	*Vis de purge*	
Bleed tap	m	*Robinet de purge*	
Bleed valve	m/f	*Purgeur/soupape de purge*	
Blind	m	*Store*	
Blind wall (no doors or windows)	m	*Mur aveugle*	
Blind/shade	m	*Store*	
Blister/bubbling	f	*Boursoufflure*	
Block/lump (stone)	m	*Bloc*	
Blockage	f	*Obstruction*	
Blocked	adj	*Bouché*	
Blocking up	m	*Murage*	
Blow – a fuse, light bulb, etc. (to)	verb	*Griller*	
Blowlamp	m/f	*Chalumeau/lampe à souder*	
Blue	adj	*Bleu*	
Boarding/planking	m	*Planchéiage*	
Boiler	f	*Chaudière*	
Boiler room	f	*Chaufferie*	

166 Glossary

English	Gender	French
Bolt (for door, etc.)	m/f/m	Boulon/cheville en fer/verrou
Bolt cutters	m	Coupe-boulons
Bolt (for nut)	m	Boulon
Bond (to)	verb	Liaisonner
Border	m	Bord
Border (decorative)	f	Frise
Bore (to)	verb	Vriller
Borehole	m	Puits de sondage/trou de sondage
Borrow (to)	verb	Emprunter
Botch (to)	verb	Bâcler
Bottled gas	m	Gaz en bouteille
Boundary	f	Limite
Boundary fence	f	Clôture de bornage
Boundary marker	f	Borne
Boundary marking	m	Bornage
Bow saw	f	Scie à chantourner
Box	f	Boîte
Box spanner	f	Clé/Clef à douille
Box room	m	Débarras
Brace or strut	f	Contrefiche
Brace (and bit)	m	Vilebrequin (et sa mèche)
Brass	m	Laiton
Braze/brazing	f	Brasure
Breeze block	m	Parpaing
Brick	f	Brique
Brick paving	m	Carrelage en brick
Brick (to)	verb	Briqueter
Bricklaying	m	Maçonnage
Brickwork/masonry	f	Maçonnerie
Brightness	f	Luminance
Bronze	m	Bronze
Broom	m	Balai
Brown	adj	Brun/marron
Brush	f	Brosse
Brush (to)	verb	Brosser
Bucket/pail	m	Seau
Budget	m	Budget
Buffer tank	m	Ballon tampon
Build/construct (to)	verb	Bâtir/construire/maçonner
Build in (to)	verb	Encastrer
Builder	m	Constructeur
Builder's ten-year guarantee insurance	f	Assurance responsabilité décennale
Building	m	Bâtiment
Building fault	m	Vice de construction
Building firm	f	Entreprise de maçonnerie
Building land	m	Terrain à bâtir
Building line	m	Alignement (de rue)
Building loan	m	Prêt à la construction
Building permit	m	Permis de construire
Building site/builder's yard	m	Chantier
Building stone	f	Pierre à bâtir
Building/block of flats	m	Immeuble
Building/planning permission application	f	Demande de permis de construire
Built-in	adj	Encastré
Bulge	m	Bombement
Bulge (to)	verb	Bomber
Bulging	adj	Bombé
Bull's-eye window	m	Œil-de-bœuf
Bungalow	m	Pavillon
Burglar alarm	f	Alarme antivol
Buried cable	m	Câble enterré
Burner	m	Brûleur
Bury pipes, cables, etc. (to)	verb	Enterrer
Business card	f	Carte d'affaires
Business firm	f	Maison de commerce
Business/transaction	f	Affaire
Buttress	m	Contrefort
Buy for cash (to)	verb	Acheter au comptant
By-law	m	Arrêté municipal

C

English	Gender	French
Cabinet	m	Meuble à tiroirs
Cable laying	f	Pose de câbles
Cable/lead	m	Câble
Cable sleeving	f	Gaine
Calliper gauge	f	Equerre à coulisse
Cancellation	f	Résiliation

Glossary 167

Cancellation charge	mpl	*Frais d'annulation*	
Cancellation clause	f	*Clause d'annulation*	
Cancellation of a contract	f	*Résiliation d'un contrat*	
Cap (tap, pipe, etc.)	m	*Bouchon*	
Capacity	f	*Contenance*	
Capital gain/ increase in value	f	*Plus-value*	
Capital gains tax	m	*Impôt sur les plus-values*	
Capricorn beetle	m	*Capricorne*	
Carbon dioxide	m	*Gaz carbonique*	
Carbon steel	m	*Acier au carbone*	
Carborundum® paper	m	*Papier corindon*	
Caretaker	m	*Gardien*	
Carpentry	f	*Charpenterie*	
Carpet	m	*Tapis*	
Casement window	f	*Fenêtre à battants*	
Cash	m	*Comptant*	
Cast iron	m	*Fer coulé/fer de fonte*	
Casting/founding	f	*Fonte*	
Castle/mansion/palace	m	*Château*	
Cat flap	f	*Chatière*	
Catch	m	*Arrêt*	
Cavity wall	m	*Mur creux*	
Cavity wall insulation	f	*Isolation en murs creux*	
Cavity/hollow	f	*Cavité*	
Cedar	m	*Cèdre*	
Ceiling	m	*Plafond*	
Ceiling height	f	*Hauteur sous plafond*	
Ceiling joist	f	*Poutre de plancher*	
Ceiling light	m	*Plafonnier*	
Ceiling rose	f	*Rosace de plafond*	
Ceiling tile	f	*Dalle pour plafond*	
Cellar	f	*Cave*	
Cellulose	f	*Cellulose*	
Cement	m	*Ciment*	
Cement mixer	f	*Bétonnière*	
Cement powder	f	*Poudre à ciment*	
Cement (to)	verb	*Cimenter*	
Central heating	m	*Chauffage central*	
Central heating boiler	f	*Chaudière de chauffage central*	
Centre bit	m	*Mèche anglaise*	
Ceramic	f	*Céramique*	
Ceramic wall tile	m	*Carreau de faïence*	
Certificate	f/m	*Attestation/certificat*	
Certificate detailing allowed land usage	m	*Certificat d'urbanisme*	
Certificate of conformity	m	*Certificat de conformité*	
Certificate of conformity to safety standards	f	*Attestation de conformité aux règles de sécurité*	
Certificate of insurance	f	*Attestation d'assurance*	
Certificate of quality	m	*Certificat de qualité*	
Certified by a notary	adj	*Notarié*	
Certified report	m	*Constat*	
Cesspool	f/m	*Fosse d'aisance/puisard*	
Chain saw	f	*Tronçonneuse*	
Chalky (hard water)	adj	*Calcaire*	
Chamber of trade	f	*Chambre des métiers*	
Channel in the wall (e.g., for electrical cable)	f	*Saignée*	
Character reference	m	*Certificat de bonne vie et mœurs*	
Charge a battery (to)	verb	*Charger une batterie*	
Chartered accountant	m	*Expert-comptable*	
Check for leaks (to)	verb	*Vérifier l'étanchéité*	
Cheque	m	*Chèque*	
Cheque book	m	*Chéquier/carnet des chèques*	
Cheque card/cash card	f	*Carte bancaire*	
Cheque to pay 'odd job men'	m	*Chèque emploi service universel*	
Chest of drawers	m	*Meuble à tiroirs*	
Chestnut	f	*Châtaigne*	

Chimney	f	Cheminée/conduit de fumée
Chimney cap	m	Chapeau de cheminée
Chimney cowl	f	Mitre
Chimney stack	f/m	Souche/tuyau de cheminée
Chimney sweep	m	Ramoneur
Chimney sweeping	m	Ramonage
Chimney/fireplace	f	Cheminée
Chimney/flue	m	Conduit de fumée
Chipboard	m	Aggloméré/panneau de particules
Chisel	m	Ciseau
Chromium	m	Chrome
Circle	m	Cercle
Circlip pliers	f	Pince à circlip
Circuit	m	Circuit
Circuit breaker	m	Disjoncteur/coupe-circuit
Circular	adj	Circulaire
Circular saw	f	Scie circulaire/tronçonneuse circulaire
Circulation pump	f/m	Circulateur
Cistern	f/f/m	Citerne/cuve (d'eau)/réservoir
Civil law	m	Code/droit civil
Clamp	m	Serre-joint
Clause	f	Clause
Claw hammer	m	Marteau à panne fendue
Clay	f	Glaise
Clean (to)	verb	Nettoyer
Cleaning	m	Nettoyage
Cleaning	adj	Nettoyant
Cleaning product	m	Nettoyant
Clear	adj	Clair
Cleared cheque	m	Chèque compensé
Clerk to the Court	m	Greffe
Cloakroom	m	Cabinet de toilette
Cloth	m	Tissu
Co-owner	f	Copropriétaire
Co-ownership	f	Copropriété
Coal	m	Charbon
Coal fired heating	m	Chauffage au charbon
Coal merchant	m	Marchand de charbon
Coarse aggregate	m	Gros agrégats
Coat (layer)	f	Couche
Coating (application)	m	Enduit
Cold	m	Froid
Cold chisel	m	Bédane/burin
Cold colours	fpl	Couleurs froides
Cold/hot water	f	Eau froide/chaude
Collapse	m	Effondrement
Collapse (to)	verb	Effondrer
Colour	f	Couleur
Colour wash	m	Badigeon
Coloured plaster	m	Plâtre coloré
Column	f	Colonne
Combination pliers	f	Pince multiprise
Comfort	m	Confort
Commercial law	m	Code de commerce/droit commercial
Commercial lease	m	Bail commercial
Commune (smallest administrative division)	f	Commune
Company	f	Société
Company cheque	m	Chèque d'entreprise
Company head	m	Chef d'entreprise
Company name	f	Raison sociale
Company/firm	f	Entreprise
Compasses (pair of)	m	Compas
Compensate (to)	verb	Dédommager
Compensation	m	Dédommagement
Complain (to)	verb	Se plaindre
Complaint	f	Plainte
Completion	m/f	Achèvement/réalisation
Completion date	f	Date d'achèvement
Component	m	Composant
Comprehensive household insurance	f	Assurance multirisques habitation
Compressed-air drill	f	Perforatrice à air comprimé
Concrete	m	Béton
Concrete (to)	verb	Bétonner

Glossary 169

Concrete/cement mixer	f	Bétonnière	
Concreting	m	Bétonnage	
Condensation	f	Condensation	
Condensing boiler	f	Chaudière à condensation	
Conditions	fpl	Stipulations	
Conductor	m	Conducteur	
Conduit	m	Caniveau	
Cone	m	Cône	
Conical	adj	Conique	
Connect/switch on (to)	verb	Mettre en circuit	
Connecting	m	Raccordement	
Connection	m	Branchement/raccordement	
Conservatory	f	Véranda	
Construction of fabric/shell of building	m	Gros œuvre	
Construction plan	m	Plan de construction	
Consultant	m	Expert-conseil	
Consumables	mpl	Biens consommables	
Consumer	m	Consommateur	
Consumer goods	mpl	Biens consommation	
Consumer law	m	Droit de la consommation	
Contract	m	Contrat	
Contract conditions	fpl	Stipulations d'un contrat	
Contract law	m	Droit des contrats	
Contracting person/company	m	Maître d'ouvrage	
Contractor/businessman	f	Entrepreneur	
Converted	adj	Aménagé	
Cooling off period	m	Délai de réflexion	
Copper	m	Cuivre	
Copper pipe	m	Tube cuivre	
Core (of cable)	f	Mèche	
Cork	m	Liège	
Cork tile	m	Carreau de liège	
Corner bath	f	Baignoire d'angle	
Cornerstone	f	Pierre angulaire	
Cornice	f	Corniche	
Corridor/passage	m	Couloir	
Corrugated metal	f	Tôle ondulée	

Cottage	m/f	Cottage/maisonnette	
Council tax	f	Taxe d'habitation	
Countersink	f	Fraise	
Countersunk screw	f	Vis à tête fraisée	
Counting	m	Comptage	
Country house	f	Maison de campagne	
Country lane	m	Chemin de campagne	
Countryside	f	Campagne	
Coupling sleeve	m	Manchon	
Course/layer	f	Assise	
Court officer/bailiff	m	Huissier	
Court (of law)	m	Tribunal	
Courtyard	f	Cour	
Cover	m	Capot	
Covered terrace	f	Loggia	
Covered with	adj	Couvert de	
Crack	f	Fissure/lézarde	
Cracks in the wall	fpl	Fissures du mur	
Creak (to)	verb	Grincer	
Credit	m	Crédit	
Credit card	f	Carte de crédit	
Creditors representative	m	Représentant des créanciers	
Cross-flow radiator	m	Radiateur transversal	
Crossed cheque	m	Chèque barré	
Cross-headed screwdriver	m	Tournevis cruciforme	
Cube	m	Cube	
Cubic	adj	Cubique	
Cupboard	m	Placard	
Cupboard door	f	Porte de placard	
Cupboard (large)	f	Armoire	
Current	adj	Actuel	
Current account	m	Compte courant	
Current (electric)	f	Courant (électrique)	
Currently	adv	Actuellement	
Custom made	adj	Fait sur commande	
Customer order	f	Commande client	
Customer reference number	m	Code client	
Customs and Excise	f	Administration des douanes	

170 *Glossary*

Cut a moulding (to)	verb	*Mouler*
Cut out (to)	verb	*Découper*
Cutting pliers/ wire cutters	f	*Pince coupante*
Cylinder	m	*Cylindre*
Cylinder lock	m	*Serrure à barillet*
Cylindrical	adj	*Cylindrique*

D

Dado rail	m	*Lambris d'appui*
Damage	mpl	*Dégâts*
Damage/spoil (to)	verb	*Abîmer*
Damp	adj	*Humide*
Damp-proof course	f	*Couche d'étanchéité*
Dampness	f	*Humidité*
Dark (colour)	adj	*Foncé*
Date of issue	f	*Date d'émission*
Date stamp	m	*Timbre/tampon dateur*
Daylight	f	*Lumière du jour*
Dehumidifier	m	*Déshumidificateur*
Deadline	f	*Date butoir/limite*
Deadline for payment	f	*Date limite de paiement*
Deal/whitewood	m	*Bois blanc*
Death-watch beetle	f	*Vrillette*
Decorate (to)	verb	*Décorer*
Deduction/charge	m	*Prélèvement*
Deed executed by a notary	m	*Acte authentique*
Deed of sale	m	*Acte de vente*
Defect	f	*Malfaçon*
Delivery	f	*Livraison*
Delivery charges	mpl	*Frais de livraison*
Delivery date	f	*Date de livraison*
Delivery time	m	*Délai de livraison*
Demolish (to)	verb	*Démolir*
Demolition	f	*Démolition*
Demolition permit	m	*Permis de démolir*
Department/ administrative area	m	*Département*
Deposit	f/f/m	*Arrhes/caution/ acompte*
Deposit account	m	*Compte à terme*
Deposit/instalment	m	*Acompte*
Depth	f	*Profondeur*
Desk	m	*Bureau*
Detached house	f	*Maison individuelle*
Diameter	m	*Diamètre*
Dilapidated	adj	*Délabré*
Dimensions	fpl	*Cotes*
Dimmer switch	m	*Variateur*
Dining room	f	*Salle à manger*
Direct current	m	*Courant continu*
Direct debit	m	*Prélèvement automatique*
Direct tax	m	*Impôt direct*
Director, manager	m	*Dirigeant*
Disconnect a lamp (to)	verb	*Mettre une lampe hors circuit*
Disconnection	f	*Interruption*
Discount	m	*Escompte*
Discuss (to)	verb	*Discuter*
Dish washer	m	*Lave-vaisselle*
Dismantle/take apart (to)	verb	*Démonter*
Dismantling/ taking apart	m	*Démontage*
Display card	f	*Carte d'affichage*
Distilled water	f	*Eau distillée*
Distribution board	m	*Tableau de distribution*
Dividers	m	*Compas à pointes sèches*
Dividing wall	f	*Mur de cloison/ séparation*
DIY	m	*Bricolage*
Domestic appliances	m	*Electroménager*
Door	f	*Porte*
Door chain	m	*Entrebâilleur*
Door frame	m/f	*Châssis de porte/ huisserie*
Door handle	f	*Poignée de porte*
Door knob	m	*Bouton de porte*
Door mat	m	*Paillasson*
Door or window jamb	m	*Chambranle*
Doorbell	f	*Sonnette de porte*
Doorway/threshold	m	*Seuil*
Dormer window	m/f/f	*Chien-assis/fenêtre en mansarde/ lucarne*

Glossary

Double door	f		Porte à deux battants
Double glazing	f		Double vitrage
Dovecote/pigeon loft	m		Colombier/pigeonnier
Dowel	m		Goujon
Down payment	m		Versement à la commande
Downpipe/rainwater pipe	m		Tuyau de descente
Drain	f		Vidange
Drain cleaner	m		Déboucheur
Drain off (to)	verb		Evacuer
Drain (to)	verb		Egoutter
Drainage	m/m/f		Assainissement/écoulement/évacuation
Draining board	m		Egouttoir
Draught-proof (to)	verb		Calfeutrer
Draught-proofing	m		Calfeutrage
Draught excluder	m		Bourrelet
Draw a plan (to)	verb		Tracer un plan
Draw (to)	verb		Tracer
Drawer	m		Tiroir
Drawing/lay out	m		Traçage
Drawing/sketch	m		Dessin/croquis
Dress stone (to)	verb		Dresser
Dressed stone	f		Pierre de taille
Drill	f		Perceuse
Drill bit	m		Foret
Drill (to)	verb		Percer
Dripping	m		Egouttement
Drop front	adj		Abattant
Dry rot	f		Pourriture sèche
Dry (to)	verb		Sécher
Drying	m		Séchage
Duckboard	m		Caillebotis
Due date	f		Date d'exigibilité
Dust	f		Poussière
Dwelling/house	f		Habitation

E

Earth (electrical)	f		Borne de masse/prise de terre
Earth cable	m		Câble de terre
Earth return circuit	m		Circuit de retour à la masse
Earthwork/embankment	f		Terrassement
Easement/right of way	f		Servitude
Easy-to-sand fine top coat plaster	m		Enduit de lissage
Eaves	m		Avant-toit
Ebony	f		Ebène
Edge	f		Bordure
Efflorescence	f		Efflorescence
Elbow joint	m		Raccord coudé
Electromechanical ventilation system	f		VMC (ventilation mécanique contrôlée)
Electric drill (cordless)	f		Perceuse sans fil
Electric drill	f		Perceuse électrique
Electric fire	m		Radiateur électrique
Electric heating	m		Chauffage électrique
Electric light	f		Lumière électrique
Electric screwdriver	m		Testeur/tournevis électrique
Electric shock	f		Décharge
Electric storage heating	m		Chauffage électrique par accumulation
Electrical equipment	m		Appareillage électrique
Electrical surge	f		Surtension
Electrician's screwdriver	m		Tournevis d'électricien
Electricity	f		Electricité
Electricity meter	m		Compteur d'électricité
Elm	m		Orme
Embossed	adj		Gaufré
Emergency	m		Urgence
Emergency repairs	m		Dépannage
Emery cloth	f		Toile émeri
Emery paper	m		Papier d'émeri
Employee	m		Salarié
Employment contract	m		Contrat d'embauche
Employment law	m		Code du travail
Emulsion paint	f		Peinture mate
Enamel	m		Email
Engineer	m		Ingénieur
Enlarge (to)	verb		Agrandir

172 Glossary

English	Gender	French
Entrance gate	m	Portail
Entrance hall	m	Entrée/vestibule
Equipment	m	Equipement
Equipment/apparatus	mpl	Appareils
Estate agent	f	Agence immobilière
Estate/property	m	Domaine
Estimate	m/f	Devis/proposition de prix
Exclusive of tax	f	HT (Hors Taxe)
Expand (to)	verb	Agrandir
Expanding foam filler	f	Mousse
Expansion tank	m	Vase d'expansion
Expenditure	f	Dépense
Expenses/costs	mpl/fpl	Frais/charges
Expert/specialist	m	Expert
Expiry date	f	Date d'expiration/date de validité
Exposed beams	fpl	Poutres apparentes
Exposed stonework	f	Pierre apparentes
Extended maintenance insurance	f	Assurance maintenance étendue
Extending ladder	f	Echelle coulissante
Extension	m	Agrandissement
Extension cable	m	Câble de raccordement
Extension lead	f	Rallonge
Exterior	adj	Extérieur
Extractor hood	f	Hotte
Eyebolt	m	Boulon à œil

F

English	Gender	French
False ceiling	m	Faux plafond
Fan heater	m	Radiateur soufflant
Fanlight	f/m	Imposte/vasistas
Farm	f	Ferme
Farmhouse	f/m	Maison de ferme/mas (en Provence)
Farmyard	f	Cour de ferme
Farrier	m	Maréchal-ferrant
Fault/defect	m	Vice
Fees	mpl	Honoraires
Felt	m	Feutre
Female coupling	m	Adaptateur femelle
Female (coupling)	adj	Femelle
Fence	f	Clôture/palissade
Fence post	m	Poteau
Fence (to)	verb	Clôturer, palissader
Fibre glass	f	Laine de verre
Field	m	Champ
File (office)	m	Dossier
File (tool)	f	Lime
Fill in again (to)	verb	Reboucher
Fill (to)	verb	Boucher
Filler	m	Enduit de rebouchage
Filter	f	Filtre
Filtration	f	Filtration
Finned radiator	m	Radiateur à ailettes
Financial adviser	m	Conseiller financier
Financing	m	Financement
Financing plan	m	Plan de financement
Fine aggregate	mpl	Granulats fins
Fine gravel/grit	m	Gravillon
Finish/finishing off	f	Finition
Fir	m	Sapin
Fire-proofing	f	Protection incendie
Fire alarm	f	Alarme incendie
Fire damage	mpl	Dégâts causés par le feu
Fire extinguisher	m	Extincteur
Fire insurance	f	Assurance incendie
Firebrick	f	Brique réfractaire
Fireplace	m	Foyer
First floor	m	Premier étage
Fit out (to)	verb	Aménager
Fitted carpet	f	Moquette
Fitted kitchen	f	Cuisine équipée
Fitting out	m	Aménagement
Fitting out of building	m	Second œuvre
Fix (to)	verb	Fixer
Fixed price	m	Prix fixe
Fixed price contract	m	Forfait
Fixtures and fittings	fpl	Installations
Flashing	f/m	Bande de plomb/revêtement
Flat blade screwdriver	m	Tournevis à lame plate

Flat roof	m	*Toit en terrasse*
Flat/apartment	m	*Appartement*
Flex	m	*Fil souple*
Float	f	*Taloche*
Flock wallpaper	m	*Papier peint en tontisse*
Flood light	m	*Projecteur*
Floor	m	*Plancher*
Floor plan	m	*Plan d'étage*
Floor tiles	m	*Carrelage de sol*
Floorspace	f	*Surface (habitable)*
Fluorescent strip-light	f	*Réglette fluorescent*
Flow (water/ electricity)	m	*Débit*
Flue/air vent	f	*Ventouse*
Fluorescent lighting	m	*Eclairage au néon*
Flush-fitting spotlight	m	*Spot encastré*
Flush (toilet)	f	*Chasse d'eau*
Folding	adj	*Pliant*
Folding doors	fpl	*Portes pliantes*
Foreign	adj	*Etranger*
Foreigner	m	*Etranger*
Forge (to)	verb	*Forger*
Form/slip	m	*Bordereau*
Formal demand/notice	f	*Mise en demeure*
Foundation pile	m	*Pieu*
Foundations	fpl	*Fondations*
Frame	m/m/f	*Cadre/châssis/ossature*
Frame (to)	verb	*Encadrer*
Framework	f	*Charpente/ossature*
Freeze (to)	verb	*Geler*
French-polish (to)	verb	*Vernir au tampon*
French window	f	*Porte-fenêtre*
Fresco	f	*Fresque*
Fresco painter	f	*Fresquiste*
Fret saw	f	*Scie anglaise*
Frieze	f	*Frise*
Front door	f	*Porte d'entrée*
Front steps/flight of steps	m	*Perron*
Frost	m	*Gel*
Frost stat	m	*Thermostat à gel*
Frozen	adj	*Gelé*
Fuel gauge	f	*Jauge*
Fuel oil	m	*Fioul*
Fund	m	*Fonds*
Fungicide	m	*Fongicide*
Furnish (to)	verb	*Meubler*
Furnishing	m	*Ameublement*
Furniture	mpl/m	*Meubles/mobilier*
Fuse-box	f	*Boîte à fusibles*
Fuse/fuse wire	m	*Fusible*

G

Gable/gable end	m	*Pignon*
Gable wall	m	*Mur pignon*
Galvanize (to)	verb	*Galvaniser*
Galvanized	adj	*Galvanisé*
Galvanized steel	m	*Acier galvanisé*
Garage	m	*Garage*
Garage door	f	*Porte de garage*
Garden	m	*Jardin*
Garden centre	f	*Jardinerie*
Garden level	m	*Rez-de-jardin*
Garden shed	m	*Abri de jardin*
Gas	m	*Gaz*
Gas boiler	f	*Chaudière à gaz*
Gas cooker	f	*Gazinière*
Gas leak	f	*Fuite de gaz*
Gas meter	m	*Compteur à gaz*
Gas pipe	m	*Tuyau de gaz*
Gas tank	f	*Citerne à gaz*
Gas tap	m	*Robinet du gaz*
General building company	f	*Entreprise générale de bâtiment*
Generator	f	*Génératrice*
Get an electric shock (to)	verb	*Recevoir une décharge*
Gild (to)	verb	*Dorer*
Girder	f	*Poutrelle*
Girder (RSJ)	f	*Poutre en fer*
Glass	m	*Verre*
Glass-cutter	f	*Coupe-verre/diamant*
Glass brick	f	*Brique de verre*
Glass door	f	*Porte vitrée*
Glass fibre	f	*Fibre de verre*

English	Gender	French
Glass wool	f	Laine de verre
Glasspaper/sandpaper	m	Papier de verre
Glazier	m	Vitrier
Glazing	m	Vitrage
Gloss paint	f	Peinture brillante
Gloss (paint)	adj	Brillant
Gloves	mpl	Gants
Glue	f	Colle
Gold	adj	Or
Good condition	adj	Bon état
Goodwill	m	Fonds commercial
Gradient	m	Gradient
Graduated	adj	Gradué
Grain	m	Grain
Granite	m	Granit
Grant/subsidy	f	Subvention
Gravel	m	Gravier
Gravity	f	Gravité
Grease	f	Graisse
Grease nipple	m	Graisseur
Grease (to)	verb	Graisser
Green	adj	Vert
Greenhouse	f	Serre
Grey	adj	Gris
Grill	f	Grille
Grindstone/whetstone	f	Pierre à aiguiser
Groove	f	Rainure
Groove (to)	verb	Rainurer
Grooved		Rainuré
Ground floor	m	Rez-de-chaussée
Ground/soil	m	Sol
Grout	m	Coulis
Grout (to)	verb	Jointoyer
Grout(ing)	m	Mortier clair/liquide
Guarantee	f	Garantie
Guarantee certificate	m	Certificat de garantie
Guarantee (financial)	f	Caution
Guarantee period	m	Délai de garantie
Guarantee (to)	verb	Garantir
Guarantor	m	Garant
Guest room	f	Chambre d'amis
Gutter	m/f	Chéneau/gouttière
Gutter tile	f	Noue

H

English	Gender	French
Hacksaw	f	Scie à métaux
Half-timbering	m	Colombage
Hall (entrance)	f	Entrée
Hall (passageway)	m	Dégagement
Halogen	m	Halogène
Hamlet	m	Hameau
Hammer	m	Marteau
Hammer drill	f/m	Perceuse à percussion/marteau-perforateur
Hand basin	m	Lavabo/lave-mains
Hand drill	f	Perceuse à main
Hand saw	f	Scie à main/égoïne
Handle	f	Poignée
Handover/final acceptance	f	Réception définitive
Handrail	f	Main courante/rampe
Handyman	m	Bricoleur
Hard-wearing	adj	Résistant
Hard water	f	Eau calcaire
Hardboard	m	Carton dur/Isorel®
Hardcore	m	Empierrement
Hardwood	m	Bois dur
Hardwood (tropical)	m	Bois exotique
Hatchet	f	Hachette
Hayloft	m	Grenier à foin
Hearth	m	Foyer
Hearth cavity	f	Trémie
Heat pump	f	Pompe à chaleur
Heat stripper	m	Décapeur thermique
Heated towel rail	m	Sèche-serviette
Heating	m	Chauffage
Heating oil	m	Mazout
Heating oil tank	m	Réservoir de fioul
Hedge	f	Haie
Height	f	Hauteur
Heighten (to)	verb	Rehausser
Hemp (for insulation)	m	Chanvre
Hessian	f	Toile de jute
Hidden defect	m	Vice caché
High-tension circuit	m	Circuit haute tension

Glossary

English	Gender	French
High-pressure cleaner	f	Nettoyeuse haute pression
Hinge	f/m	Charnière / gond
Hip bath	f	Baignoire sabot
Hole	m	Trou
Holiday / second home	f	Maison d'amis / secondaire
Hollow brick	f	Brique tubulaire / creuse
Home or self-assembly kit	m	Kit
Honeycomb radiator	m	Radiateur en nid d'abeilles
Hook	m	Clou à crochet / crochet
Hose	m	Flexible
Hose-pipe	m	Tuyau d'arrosage
Hot air heating	m	Chauffage à air chaud
Hot water cylinder	m	Ballon d'eau chaude
Hot water radiator	m	Radiateur à eau chaude
Hotplate	f	Plaque chauffante
House	f/m	Maison / pavillon
House plan	m	Plan de maison
Housing development / estate	m	Lotissement
Hut / cabin	m	Cabanon
Hydrotherapy	f	Hydrothérapie

I

English	Gender	French
Identity card	f	Carte d'identification
Immersion heater	m	Chauffe-eau à immersion
Impact screwdriver	m	Tournevis à choc
Impermeable	adj	Imperméable
Impregnated wood	m	Bois imprégné
In arrears / overdue	adj	Arriéré
Incidental costs / expenses	mpl	Frais accessoires
Include (to)	verb	Inclure
Included	adj	Compris
Inclusive of tax	f	TTC (Toutes Taxes Comprises)
Indirect tax	m	Impôt indirect
Inductive circuit	m	Circuit d'induction
Inflammable / flammable	adj	Inflammable
Inflate (to)	verb	Gonfler
Inheritance	f	Succession
Inlayer	m	Marqueteur
Inlet valve	f	Soupape d'admission
Inspection	m	Contrôle
Inspection panel	m	Panneau de visite
Install (to)	verb	Poser
Install electricity (to)	verb	Installer l'électricité
Installation / fitting / putting in	f	Installation / pose
Insulate (to)	verb	Isoler
Insulated	adj	Isolé
Insulated screwdriver	m	Tournevis isolé
Insulating	adj	Isolant
Insulating tape	m	Ruban isolant
Insulation	f	Isolation
Insulator	m	Isolateur
Insurance	f	Assurance
Insurance agent	f	Agent d'assurance(s)
Insurance certificate	m	Certificat d'assurance
Insurance company	f	Compagnie d'assurances
Insurance policy	f	Police d'assurance
Insurance premium	f	Prime d'assurance
Inter-connecting door	f	Porte communicante
Interest	m	Intérêt
Interest-free credit	m	Crédit gratuit
Interest charges	mpl	Frais financiers
Interest rate	m	Taux d'intérêt
Integrated circuit	m	Circuit intégré
Interior building work	f	Petite maçonnerie
Interior designer	m/f	Architecte d'intérieur
Interior area	f	Surface habitable
Interior / partition wall	f	Paroi
Inventory	m	Etat des lieux

Invoice	f	Facture
Invoice date	f	Date de facturation
Iron	m	Fer
Ironmonger	m	Quincaillier
Ironmongery/shop	f	Quincaillerie

J

Jack hammer	f	Perforatrice
Jacuzzi®	m	Jacuzzi®
Jamb	m	Jambage
Jig saw	f	Scie sauteuse
Join	m	Raccord
Join end to end/abut (to)	verb	Abouter
Joinery	f	Menuiserie
Joint account	m	Compte joint
Joint ownership	f	Indivision
Joint/connection	m	Raccord
Joint/seal	m	Joint
Joist	f	Solive
Judge in chambers	m	Juge des référés
Junction box	f	Boîte de dérivation

K

Key	f	Clé/Clef
Key plate	m	Ecusson
Keyhole	f	Trou de la serrure
Keystone	f	Clé/Clef de voûte
Kitchen	f	Cuisine
Kitchen sink	m	Evier
Kitchen/vegetable garden	m	Potager
Kitchenette	m	Coin-cuisine
Kneepad	f	Genouillère
Knot (in wood)	m	Nœud

L

Labour cost	m	Prix de la main-d'œuvre
Labour costs	mpl	Frais de main-d'œuvre
Labourer	m	Terrassier
Lacquer	f	Laque
Ladder	f	Echelle
Lag (to)	verb	Envelopper
Lagging	m	Revêtement calorifuge
Lake	m	Lac
Laminated	adj	Stratifié
Lamp, light	f/m	Lampe/luminaire
Lamp socket	f	Douille d'une ampoule électrique
Lampshade	m	Abat-jour
Land	m	Terrain
Land approved for building	adj	Constructible (terrain)
Land registry	m	Cadastre
Land registry reference	f	Référence cadastrale
Land surveyor	m	Géomètre-expert
Land/property tax	m	Impôt foncier
Landing	m	Palier
Landlord/lessor	m	Bailleur
Landowner	m	Propriétaire foncier
Landscape	m	Paysage
Lane/track	m/f	Chemin/voie
Larch	m	Mélèze
Large supporting beam	f	Sablière
Large village/small town	m	Bourg
Laser level	m	Niveau laser
Latch	m	Loquet
Lath	f	Latte/volige
Lath (to)	verb	Voliger
Lavatory	mpl	Cabinets/WC
Lawn	f/m	Pelouse/gazon
Lawn mower	f	Tondeuse à gazon
Lawyer/solicitor/bailiff's title	m	Maître
Lead	m	Plomb
Lead flashing	m	Revêtement de plomb
Leak	m	Fuite
Lean-to	m	Appentis
Lease	m	Bail

English	Gender	French
Legal adviser	m	Conseiller juridique
Legal office	f	Etude
Legal technicality	m	Vice de forme
Length	f	Longueur
Let-out clause	f	Clause suspensive
Letter box	f	Boîte aux lettres
Level	m	Niveau
Levelling	m	Nivellement
Lever	m	Levier
Library	f	Bibliothèque
Life assurance	f	Assurance décès
Lift/elevator	m	Ascenseur
Light (colour)	adj	Clair
Light	f	Lumière
Light bulb	f	Ampoule
Light fitting	m	Appareil d'éclairage
Lighting	m	Allumage/éclairage
Lime, lime render	f	Chaux
Limestone	m/f	Calcaire/pierre à chaux
Limited liability company (Ltd)	f	SARL (Société Anonyme à Responsabilité Limitée)
Limited liability company (Plc)	f	SA (Société Anonyme)
Limiting clause	f	Clause limitative
Linen room/laundry	f	Lingerie
Linseed oil	m	Huile de lin
Lintel	m	Linteau
Listed building	m	Monument historique
Live	f	Phase
Live conductor	m	Conducteur en charge
Live in (to)	verb	Habiter
Live wire	m	Fil sous tension
Living room	f/m	Salle de séjour/living
Load-bearing wall	m	Mur porteur/gros mur
Loan	m	Emprunt/prêt
Local councillor	m	Conseiller municipal
Local government	f	Administration communale/municipale
Local Ministry of Environment office	f	DDE (Direction départementale de l'équipement)
Local stone	f	Pierre du pays
Local taxes (council tax)	mpl	Impôt locaux
Lock	f	Serrure
Locksmith's workshop	f	Forge de serrurier
Log	f	Bûche
Look for/inquire into (to)	verb	Rechercher
Lounge/sitting room	m	Salon
Louvred shutter	m	Volet persienne
Low-tension circuit	m	Circuit basse tension
Low-temperature boiler	f	Chaudière à basse température
Low wall	m	Muret

M

English	Gender	French
Magistrate	m	Juge de proximité
Mahogany	m	Acajou
Main building	m	Corps de bâtiment
Main departmental administrative office	f	Préfecture
Main sewer	m	Egout collecteur
Mains water	f	Eau de ville
Mains (drainage)	m	Tout a l'égout
Maintain (to)	verb	Entretenir
Maintenance	m	Entretien
Maintenance costs	mpl	Frais d'entretien
Make a payment (to)	verb	Effectuer un versement
Make watertight (to)	verb	Etancher
Male coupling	m	Adaptateur mâle
Male (coupling)	adj	Mâle
Mallet	m	Maillet
Mandate	m	Mandat
Manhole	m	Trou de visite
Manhole cover	f	Plaque d'égout
Manor house	m	Manoir

178 *Glossary*

Manual labour	m	*Travail manuel*
Manufacturer's guarantee insurance	f	*Assurance garantie constructeur*
Manufacturing company	f	*Entreprise industrielle*
Manufacturing defect	m	*Vice de fabrication*
Maple	m	*Erable*
Marble	m	*Marbre*
Marbling	f	*Marbrure*
Market	m	*Marché*
Marquetry	f	*Marqueterie*
Marsh	m	*Marais*
Masking tape	f/m	*Bande de masquage/ ruban adhésif*
Masonry paint	f	*Peinture crépi*
Masonry partition	f	*Cloison maçonnée*
Massive/bulky	adj	*Massif*
Master tradesman	m	*Maître artisan*
Mastic/filler/putty	m	*Mastic*
Matt	adj	*Mat*
Matt paint	f	*Peinture mat*
Mayor	m	*Maire*
Meadow	f	*Prairie/pré*
Mechanical shovel	f	*Pelle mécanique*
Mechanism	m	*Mécanisme*
Meeting/ appointment	m	*Rendez-vous*
Metal alloy	m	*Alliage métallique*
Metal gate	f	*Grille*
Metallic paint	f	*Peinture métallisée*
Meter	m	*Compteur*
Meter reading	m	*Relevé du compteur*
Method (of payment)	f	*Modalité (de paiement)*
Mezzanine	m	*Entresol/mezzanine*
Mill	m	*Moulin*
Mini digger (mechanical)	f	*Mini pelle*
Mixer tap (with single control)	m	*Mitigeur*
Mixer tap (with separate hot/cold controls)	m	*Robinet mélangeur*
Mixing (mortar)	m	*Gâchage (de mortier)*

Monkey wrench	f	*Clé/clef anglaise*
Monthly payment	f	*Mensualité*
Mortar	m	*Mortier*
Mortgage	f	*Hypothèque*
Mortise lock	f	*Serrure encastrée*
Mosaic	f	*Mosaïque*
Moss	f	*Mousse*
Moss removal product	m	*Démoussant*
Moss treatment	m	*Démoussage*
Motorized garage door	f	*Porte de garage motorisée*
Motorized roller shutter	m	*Volet roulant motorisé*
Mould/mildew	f	*Moisissure*
Moulding (ornamental)	f	*Moulure*
Mouse	f	*Souris*
Mouse trap	f	*Tapette*
Mullion	m	*Meneau*
Municipal recycling facility	f	*Déchetterie*
Mural	f	*Peinture murale*

N

Nail	m	*Clou*
Nail punch	m	*Chasse-clous*
Natural gas	m	*Gaz naturel*
Negotiate (to)	verb	*Négocier*
Negotiable	adj	*Négociable*
Negotiation	f	*Négociation*
Neighbour	m	*Voisin*
Neighbourhood	m	*Quartier/voisinage*
Neighbouring	adj	*Voisin*
Neon light	f	*Lampe/lumière au néon*
Neon tube	m	*Tube fluorescent*
Network	m	*Réseau*
Neutral	adj	*Neutre*
New	adj	*Neuf*
New building insurance	f	*Assurance dommages-ouvrages*
New house	f	*Maison neuve*
Newel	m	*Noyau*
Newel post	m	*Pilastre*
Noise	m	*Bruit*

Glossary 179

Noisy	adj		Bruyant
Non-slip	adj		Antidérapant
Notary (solicitor)	m		Notaire
Notch/groove	f		Entaille
Nut (for bolt)	m		Ecrou

O

Oak	m		Chêne
Obvious defect	m		Vice apparent
Occupancy/possession	f		Occupation
Occupier	m		Occupant
Of land	adj		Foncier
Off-peak hours	fpl		Heures creuses
Offer	f		Offre
Offer (to)	verb		Offrir
Office	m		Bureau
Official receipt	m		Récépissé
Oil-based (glyptal) paint	f		Peinture glycéro
Oil-filled radiator	m		Radiateur à bain d'huile
Oil-fired boiler	f		Chaudière à fioul/mazout
Oil-fired heating	m		Chauffage au fioul
Oil paint	f		Peinture à l'huile
Oil pipe	m		Tuyau de fuel
Oil tank	f		Citerne/cuve à mazout
Old house	f		Maison ancienne
On-off switch	m		Interrupteur marche-arrêt
One cubic metre (of wood)	m		Stère
One-man business/sole trader	f		Entreprise unipersonnelle
Open-ended spanner	f		Clé/clef ouverte
Open cheque	m		Chèque ouvert
Open plan kitchen	f		Cuisine américaine
Open staircase	f		Echelle meunier
Open/closed circuit	m		Circuit ouvert/fermé
Opening/aperture	f/m		Ouverture/orifice
Operating instructions	f		Notice d'utilisation
Optional	adj		Facultative
Optional clause	f		Clause facultative
Orange	adj		Orange
Orchard	m		Verger
Order form	m		Bon de commande
Oriel window	f		Oriel
Origin	f		Origine
Outbuildings	fpl		Dépendances
Outgoings	fpl		Charges
Outlet valve	f		Soupape d'échappement
Output/yield	m		Rendement
Outside lighting	m		Eclairage extérieur
Oval	adj		Ovale
Overflow pipe/drain	m		Trop-plein/tuyau d'écoulement
Overflow (to)	verb		Déborder
Overhang	m		Surplomb, débord
Overheads	mpl		Frais généraux
Owner	m		Propriétaire
Ownership/property	f		Propriété

P

Padlock	m		Cadenas
Paint (to)	verb		Peindre
Paint/paintwork	f		Peinture
Paint bucket/container	m		Camion à peinture
Paint pad	m		Tampon de peinture
Paint pot	m		Pot de peinture
Paint roller	m		Rouleau à peinture
Paint scraper/pallet knife	m		Couteau de peintre
Paint stripper	m		Décapant
Paintbrush	m		Pinceau
Panel	m		Panneau
Panel saw	f		Scie à guichet
Panelled door	f		Porte à panneaux
Panelling	m		Panneaux
Paperhanger's scissors	mpl		Ciseaux de tapissier
Paraffin	m		Pétrole lampant
Parapet	m		Parapet
Park/grounds	m		Parc
Parquet flooring	m		Parquet

180 *Glossary*

Partition	f	*Cloison*	
Partition wall	f	*Mur de refend*	
Partition (to)	verb	*Cloisonner*	
Party wall	m	*Mur mitoyen*	
Paste	f	*Pâte*	
Pastebrush	m	*Balai à encoller*	
Pasting table	f	*Table à encoller*	
Pasting/sizing	m	*Encollage*	
Path	m	*Chemin*	
Patina	f	*Patine*	
Patio	m	*Patio*	
Pave (to)	verb	*Daller*	
Paving	m	*Dallage*	
Paving stone	f/m	*Dalle/pavé*	
Pay in cash (to)	verb	*Payer au comptant*	
Pay (to)	verb	*Verser*	
Payment	m	*Paiement/versement*	
Payment by cheque	m	*Paiement par chèque*	
Payment by instalments	m	*Paiement échelonné*	
Payment date/expiry date	f	*Echéance*	
Payment in advance	m	*Paiement d'avance*	
Payment in cash	m	*Paiement comptant*	
Payment period	m	*Délai de paiement*	
Peak hours	fpl	*Heures pointes*	
Peak period	f	*Période de pointe*	
Pebbledash	m	*Crépi*	
Pebbles	mpl	*Galets*	
Peephole	m	*Judas optique*	
Peg/plug/dowel	f	*Cheville*	
Pelmet	f/m	*Cantonnière/lambrequin*	
Penalty clause	f	*Clause pénale*	
Penalty for non-completion of a contract	f	*Astreinte*	
Penetrating oil	m	*Dégrippant*	
Per cent	m	*Pour cent*	
Perforated	adj	*Perforé*	
Perimeter	m	*Périmètre*	
Perimeter alarm	f	*Alarme périmétrique*	
Permit	m	*Permis*	
Perpendicular	adj	*Perpendiculaire*	
Perspex®	m	*Plexiglas®*	
pH value	f	*Valeur du pH*	
Pickaxe	f	*Pioche*	
Picture/bay window	f	*Baie vitrée*	
Pierce/make a hole (to)	verb	*Percer*	
Pigment	m	*Colorant*	
Pillar/column	m	*Pilier*	
Pin	f	*Goupille*	
Pincers	f	*Tenailles*	
Pine	m	*Pin*	
Pink	adj	*Rose*	
Pipe	m	*Tuyau*	
Pipework	f	*Tuyauterie*	
Pipe/duct	m	*Conduit*	
Piping	f	*Canalisation/tuyauterie*	
Pit/hole	f	*Fosse*	
Pitch of roof	f	*Chute/pente*	
Plain, non-patterned	adj	*Uni*	
Plan	m	*Schéma*	
Plan/blueprint	m	*Plan*	
Plane	m	*Rabot*	
Plank/floorboard	f/m	*Planche/madrier*	
Planning permission	m	*Permis de construire*	
Planning tax	f	*Taxe d'urbanisme*	
Plaster	m	*Plâtre*	
Plaster (to)	verb	*Plâtrer*	
Plasterboard	m	*Placoplâtre®*	
Plastering	m	*Plâtrage*	
Plasterwork	m	*Plâtres*	
Plastic	m	*Plastique*	
Pliers	f	*Pince*	
Plot of land	f	*Parcelle*	
Plug (of basin, sink)	m/f	*Bouchon/bonde*	
Plug (electrical)	f	*Fiche*	
Plughole	m	*Trou d'écoulement/trou de vidange*	
Plumb line	m	*Fil à plomb*	
Plumber	m	*Installateur sanitaire*	
Plumbing	f	*Plomberie*	
Plunger	m	*Déboucheur*	
Plywood	m	*Bois contreplaqué*	
Pneumatic drill	m	*Marteau-piqueur/marteau pneumatique*	

Glossary

English		French
Postage and packing	mpl	Frais de port et d'emballage
Point (to)	verb	Jointoyer
Pointed nose pliers	f	Pince à becs pointus
Pointing	m	Jointoiement
Pollutant	m	Polluant
Pollute (to)	verb	Polluer
Polythene pipe	m	Tube en HTA2
Polyurethane	m	Polyuréthane
Pond/pool	m	Etang
Poplar	m	Peuplier
Porch	m	Porche
Porch roof	m	Auvent
Post office	m	Bureau de poste
Post office cheque	m	Chèque postal
Post office transfer	m	Virement postal
Postal order	m	Mandat-poste
Postcode	m	Code postal
Pound sterling (£)	f	Livre
Powder	f	Poudre
Power (ability)	m	Pouvoir
Power (wattage)	f	Puissance
Power cut, failure	f	Panne d'électricité
Power line	f	Ligne alimentation
Power of attorney/proxy	f	Procuration
Power supply	f	Alimentation en électricité/bloc d'alimentation
Power tool	m	Outil à moteur/électrique
Premises	m	Local
Preservative	m	Agent de conservation
Pressed steel	m	Acier embouti
Pressure	f	Pression
Pressure gauge	m	Manomètre
Pressure relief valve	m	Détendeur
Price	m	Prix
Price list, tariff	m	Tarif
Prime (to)	verb	Apprêter
Primer	m	Apprêt
Priming coat	f	Couche d'apprêt
Principal rafter	m	Arbalétrier
Private company	f	Entreprise privée
Private unearned income	f	Rentes
Process server's affidavit	m	Constat d'huissier
Programmer	m	Programmateur
Progress	m	Déroulement
Project manager	m	Maître d'œuvre
Proof of purchase	f	Attestation d'acquisition
Prop	m	Etai/support
Prop/brace	f	Jambe de force
Propane gas	m	Gaz propane
Property	m	Immobilier/biens immobiliers
Property developer	m	Promoteur immobilier
Property for restoration	f	Propriété à restaurer
Property in ruins	f	Propriété en ruines
Property tax	fpl	Taxes foncières
Public company	f	Entreprise publique
Public liability insurance	f	Assurance responsabilité civile
Pull-out shelf	f	Tirette
Pump	f	Pompe
Punch	f	Poinçonneuse
Purchase	m	Achat
Purchase costs	mpl	Frais d'achat
Purchase price	m	Prix d'acquisition
Purchase (to)	verb	Acheter
Purchaser/buyer	m	Acquéreur
Purlin	f	Panne
Purple	adj	Violet
Putting up/hanging	f	Pose
Putty/sealant	m	Mastic
Puttying/sealing	m	Masticage
Pylon (electricity)	m	Pylône (de transformateur électrique)

Q

Quarry stone	m	Moellon
Quick-setting cement	m	Ciment à prise rapide

English	Gender	French
Quick drying	m	Séchage rapide
Quicklime	f	Chaux vive
Quote (to)	verb	Fixer un prix

R

English	Gender	French
Rabbet	f	Feuillure
Rack	m	Râtelier
Radiator	m	Radiateur
Radiator bleed key	f	Clé de purge
Rafter	m	Chevron
Rainwater pipe	f	Conduite d'eau pluviale
Rake	m	Râteau
Range (of products or services)	f	Gamme
Rasp	f	Râpe à main
Rat-tail file	f	Queue-de-rat
Rate (financial)	m	Taux
Rawlplug®	f	Cheville
Ready-mix concrete	m	Béton prêt à l'emploi
Ready-pasted wallpaper	m	Papier peint préencollé
Real estate	m	Biens immobiliers
Reassembly	m	Remontage
Receipt	f/m	Quittance / reçu
Receipt stamp	m	Timbre de quittance
Receiver (legal)	m	Administrateur judiciaire
Reception	m	Accueil
Receptionist	m/f	Réceptionniste
Recess	m	Recoin
Recorded delivery	f	Lettre recommandée
Recorded delivery with confirmation of receipt	f	Lettre recommandée avec accusé / avis de réception
Recover (to)	verb	Récupérer
Recovery	f	Récupération
Rectangle	m	Rectangle
Rectangular	adj	Rectangulaire
Red	adj	Rouge
Reduced tariff	m	Tarif réduit
Referral to a court	f	Saisine
Refunding clause	f	Clause de remboursement
Registration fees	m	Droit d'enregistrement
Regulator	m	Régulateur
Reinforced cement	m	Ciment armé
Reinforced concrete	m	Béton armé
Reinforcement	f	Armature
Relay	m	Relais
Remittance date	f	Date de remise
Remote-control alarm	f	Alarme télécommandée
Removal	m	Déménagement / enlèvement
Remuneration	mpl	Emoluments
Render	m	Enduit
Renewable energy	f	Energie renouvelable
Renovate / restore (to)	verb	Remettre à neuf / rénover
Renovation	f	Rénovation
Rent / hire (to)	verb	Louer
Rental	f	Location
Rental agreement	m	Contrat de location
Rental payment	m	Loyer
Repair	f	Réparation
Repair / mend (to)	verb	Réparer / refaire
Repair / restoration (extensive)	f	Réfection
Replace (to)	verb	Remplacer
Repointing / roughcasting	m	Ravalement
Report	m	Rapport
Representative / agent	m	Mandataire
Re-roof (to)	verb	Refaire le toit
Residence	f/m	Demeure / domicile
Resident	m	Résident / riverain
Resin	f	Résine
Resistance	f	Résistance
Restoration	f	Remise en état / restauration
Restore (to)	verb	Restaurer
Retaining wall	m	Mur de soutènement
Rewire (to)	verb	Refaire l'installation électrique

Glossary 183

Rheostat	m		Rhéostat
Rider	f		Clause additionnelle
Ridge	m		Faîte
Ridge tile	f		Faîtière / tuile faîtière
Ridge tiling	mpl		Faîtages (tuiles)
Ridgepole	m		Faîtage
Right-angled	adj		Rectangle
Right of way	m		Droit de passage
Right to draw water	m		Droit de puisage
Right / law	m		Droit
Rising damp	f		Humidité par capillarité
River	f		Rivière
Riverside	m		Bord de la rivière
Rivet	m		Rivet
Rivet (to)	verb		Riveter
Riveting	m		Rivetage
Riveting machine	f		Riveteuse
Rock (stone)	f		Roche
Roller shutter	m		Volet roulant
Roller shutter casing	m		Coffre d'enroulement
Roller shutter tracking	f		Coulisse
Roller tray	m		Bac plastique
Roof	m		Toit
Roof structure (wood)	m		Comble
Roof tiles	fpl		Tuiles
Roof truss	f		Armature à toit
Roofing	f		Couverture / toiture
Roofing felt	m		Feutre à toit
Room	f		Pièce / salle
Room temperature	f		Température ambiante
Rosewood	m		Bois de rose
Rot	f		Pourriture
Rotten wood	m		Bois pourri
Rough sketch	f		Ebauche / croquis
Roughcast (exterior)	m		Crépi
Roughcast (to)	verb		Crépir
Round headed screw	f		Vis à tête ronde
Rub down / sandpaper (to)	verb		Poncer
Rubber	m		Caoutchouc
Rubber gloves	mpl		Gants en caoutchouc
Rubbing down / sanding down	m		Ponçage
Rubbish	m		Détritus
Rubbish chute	f		Goulotte d'évacuation
Rubbish dump / tip	m		Dépôt d'ordures
Rubble	mpl/m		Gravats / déblais / plâtras
Ruler	f		Règle
Rust	f		Rouille
Rust preventive	m		Antirouille
Rustproof	adj		Antirouille

S

Safety	f		Sécurité
Safety catch	m		Crochet de sécurité
Safety glass	m		Verre de sécurité
Safety glasses	fpl		Lunettes de sécurité
Safety valve	f		Soupape de sûreté
Sale / selling	f		Vente
Sales (at reduced prices)	mpl		Soldes
Sales / auction room	f		Salle des ventes
Salesman	m		Vendeur
Saleswoman	f		Vendeuse
Sample	m		Echantillon
Sand	m		Sable
Sand / glass paper	m		Papier de verre
Sandblasted	adj		Grenaillé
Sandblasting	m		Sablage
Sander	f		Ponceuse
Sanding block	f		Cale à poncer
Sandstone	m		Grès
Sanitary fittings	mpl		Appareils sanitaires
Sash window	m/f		Châssis à guillotine / fenêtre à guillotine
Satellite dish	f		Antenne parabolique
Satin	adj		Satiné
Saw	f		Scie
Saw blade	f		Lame de scie
Scaffolding	m		Echafaudage

English	Gender	French
Scale (deposit)	m	Tartre
Scale preventer	m	Anticalcaire
Schist	f	Lauze
Scraper	m	Grattoir / racloir
Screed	f	Chape
Screw	f	Vis
Screw bolt	m	Boulon à écrou
Screw fitting bulb	f	Ampoule à vis
Screw thread	m	Filet de vis
Screw (to)	verb	Visser
Screwdriver	m	Tournevis
Scullery / utility room / back kitchen	f	Arrière-cuisine
Sealant tape ('plumber's mate')	m	Ruban
Seaside	m	Bord de la mer
Seasoning	m	Séchage
Security grill	f	Grille de défense
Seizure / distraint	f	Saisie
Self-catering accommodation	m	Gîte
Self-tapping screw	f	Vis auto taraudeuse
Semi-detached house	f	Maison mitoyenne (d'un côté) / jumelée
Sensor	f	Sonde
Sensor (smoke)	m	Détecteur (de fumée)
Septic tank	f	Fosse septique / fosse toutes eaux
Sequestrate (to)	verb	Séquestrer
Sequestration	m	Séquestre
Service contract	m	Contrat de service
Service hatch	m	Passe-plat
Set-square	f	Equerre à dessin
Settling / sinking / subsidence	m	Tassement
Sewage	f	Eau d'égout
Sewage system	m	Réseau d'assainissement
Sewer	m	Egout
Shape	f	Forme
Shaped	adj	Profilé
Shaping / turning	m	Façonnage
Share / portion	f	Quote-part
Sharp	adj	Tranchant
Shaver socket	f	Prise pour rasoir électrique
Shears	fpl	Cisailles
Shed	f	Remise
Sheet metal	f	Tôle
Shelf	f	Etagère / tablette
Shelf bracket	m	Liteau / gousset
Shelter	m	Abri
Shelving	m	Rayonnage
Shingle	m	Bardeau
Shop	m	Magasin
Shopping centre	m	Centre commercial
Shore up (to)	verb	Etayer
Shoring / propping up	m	Etaiement / étayage
Short circuit	m	Court-circuit
Shovel	f	Pelle
Shower	f	Douche
Shower cubicle	f	Cabine de douche
Shower head	f	Douchette / pomme de douche
Shower room	f	Salle d'eau
Shower tray	m	Bac à douche / receveur de douche
Shutter	m	Volet
Shutter catch	m	Tourniquet
Shutter with strap hinges	m	Volet penture
Shutter / window fastening	f	Crémone / espagnolette
Shuttering	m	Coffrage
Side gate	m	Portillon
Sieve	m	Tamis
Signature	f	Signature
Silk	f	Soie
Silver	adj	Argenté
Single-phase current	m	Courant monophasé
Single coat	f	Monocouche
Single panel of a door, window or shutter	m	Vantail
Site	m	Site
Skip (rubbish)	f	Benne
Skirting board	f/m	Plinthe / socle de lambris

English	Gender	French
Skylight	f	Lucarne
Skylight window	m	Velux®
Slate	f	Ardoise
Slate roof	m	Toit d'ardoises
Sledgehammer	f	Massette
Sliding door	f	Porte coulissante/roulante
Sliding window	f	Fenêtre à coulisse
Slimline radiator	m	Radiateur extraplat
Slope	f	Inclinaison
Sloping roof	m	Toit en auvent
Small business	f	Entreprise artisanale
Small catch	m	Loqueteau
Small farm/smallholding	f	Fermette
Small room	m	Cabinet
Smooth	adj	Lisse
Smooth (to)	verb	Lisser
Smoothing	m	Lissage
Soakaway	m	Puisard/puits absorbant/puits perdu
Social security office	f	URSSAF
Socket (of a lamp)	f	Douille
Socket/power point	f	Prise
Socket adaptor	f	Multiprise
Soft light	f	Lumière tamisée
Soften (to)	verb	Adoucir
Softwood	m	Bois tendre
Soil pipe	m	Tuyau d'égout
Solar heating	m	Chauffage solaire
Solar panel	m	Panneau solaire
Solar power	f	Energie solaire
Solar-powered water heater	m	Chauffe-eau solaire
Solder	f	Soudure
Solder (to)	verb	Souder
Soldering	m	Soudage
Soldering iron	m	Fer à souder
Sole trader with limited liability	f	Entreprise unipersonnelle à responsabilité limitée
Solid brick	f	Brique pleine
Solid (wood)	adj	Massif
Solvent	m	Solvant
Soot	f	Suie
Soundproof	adj	Insonore
Soundproofing	f	Isolation acoustique
Space	m	Espace
Space between two rafters/joists	m	Solin
Spade	f	Bêche
Span	f	Portée
Spanner	f	Clé/clef
Spatula	f	Spatule
Special condition clause	f	Clause particulière
Sphere	f	Sphère
Spherical	adj	Sphérique
Spiral staircase	m	Escalier en colimaçon
Spirit level	m	Niveau à bulle
Split-level apartment	m	Duplex
Split pin	f	Goupille fendue
Sponge	f	Eponge
Sponge (to)	verb	Eponger
Spot welding	m	Soudure par points
Spotlight	m	Spot
Spray gun	m	Pistolet
Spray paint	f	Peinture en bombe
Spring steel	m	Acier à ressort
Spring water	f	Eau de source
Spring (water)	f	Source
Spruce	m	Epicéa
Square	adj	Carré
Square metre	m	Mètre carré
Stable	f	Ecurie
Stable door	f	Porte à deux vantaux
Stained	adj	Taché
Stainless steel	m	Acier inoxydable/inox
Stair riser	f	Contremarche
Stair tread	m	Giron
Staircase	m	Escalier
Stamp	m	Timbre
Standing order	m	Ordre de prélèvement
Stanley knife®	m	Cutter
Staple	f/m	Agrafe/clou cavalier
Staple (to)	verb	Agrafer
Stapler	f	Agrafeuse

State/condition	m	Etat	
Statement (of account)	m	Relevé (de compte)	
Steel	m	Acier	
Steel joist	f	Solive en acier	
Steel wool	f	Laine d'acier/paille de fer	
Step (stair)	m/f	Pas/marche	
Stepladder	m	Escabeau	
Stepladder (high)	f	Echelle double	
Stick/adhere (to)	verb	Adhérer	
Sticking (up)	m	Collage	
Sticking/adhesion	f	Adhésion	
Stipple (to)	verb	Pointiller	
Stone	f	Pierre	
Stone chippings	m	Gravillon	
Stone house	f	Maison en pierre	
Stonemason's knife/chisel	m	Couteau à pierre	
Stop payment on a cheque (to)	verb	Faire opposition à un chèque	
Stopcock	m	Robinet d'arrêt	
Stopped cheque	m	Chèque bloqué	
Stop end (of a gutter)	m	Talon gouttière	
Storage area	m	Rangement	
Storage heater	m	Radiateur à accumulation	
Storage tank	f	Cuve de stockage	
Storeroom	m	Cellier	
Storey	m	Etage	
Storm damage	mpl	Dégâts causés par la tempête	
Strap hinge	f	Penture	
Strengthening	m	Renforcement	
Strip wallpaper (to)	verb	Décoller	
Strip (metal/glass/wood, etc.)	f	Lame	
Stripe	f	Rayure	
Stripping pliers (electricity)	f	Pince à dénuder	
Stripping/sanding down	m	Décapage	
Structural fault	m	Vice de construction	
Stucco	m	Stuc/Crépi	
Stud	m	Clou	
Stud wall	f	Cloison en treillis	
Study	m	Bureau	
Subdued lighting	f	Lumière d'ambiance	
Subscription	m	Abonnement	
Subside (to)	verb	S'affaisser	
Subsidence	m	Affaissement	
Suburbs	f	Banlieue	
Suction pad or plunger	f	Ventouse	
Summary proceedings	m	Référé	
Summerhouse	m	Pavillon de jardin	
Sunken bath	f	Baignoire encastrée	
Sunlight	f	Lumière du soleil	
Sunshine, hours of	m	Ensoleillement	
Supplier	m	Fournisseur	
Supplies and services	fpl	Fournitures et services	
Supply valve	f	Vanne d'alimentation	
Supply (to)	verb	Fournir	
Supply/provision	f	Fourniture	
Support	m	Appui	
Surcharge	f	Taxe supplémentaire	
Surface coating/covering	m	Revêtement	
Surface pump	f	Pompe de surface	
Supporting wall	m	Mur d'appui	
Surrounding wall	m	Mur de clôture	
Sweep the chimney (to)	verb	Ramoner	
Swimming pool	f	Piscine	
Swing door	f	Porte battante/porte va-et-vient	
Switch	m	Bouton	
Switch off (to)	verb	Couper le circuit	
Switch on the current again (to)	verb	Rétablir	
Switch (one way)	m	Interrupteur	
Switch (two way)	m	Interrupteur va-et-vient	
Swivel tap	m	Robinet orientable	
Synthetic rubber	m	Caoutchouc synthétique	

T

Take down (to)	verb	Déposer	
Tamp (to)	verb	Damer	

English	Gender	French
Tap	m	Robinet
Tap fittings	f	Robinetterie
Tap washer	f	Bague du robinet
Tape measure/rule	m	Mètre
Tar	m	Goudron
Tar (to)	verb	Goudronner
Tarpaulin	f	Bâche
Tax	m	Impôt
Tax adviser	m	Conseiller fiscal
Tax authorities	f	Administration fiscale
Tax domicile	m	Domicile fiscal
Tax law	m	Droit fiscal
Tax collection office	m	Bureau de perception
Tax office	m	Centre/bureau des impôts
Tax rebate	m	Crédit d'impôt
Tax stamp	m	Timbre fiscal
Tax/duty	f	Taxe
Taxation	f	Imposition
Teak	m	Teck
Technical adviser	m	Conseiller technique
Telephone assistance	f	Assistance téléphonique
Telephone wire	m	Fil téléphonique
Television aerial	f	Antenne de télévision
Temperature	f	Température
Temperature drop	f	Chute de température
Tempered steel	m	Acier trempé
Template	m	Gabarit
Ten-year guarantee	f	Garantie décennale
Tenant	m	Locataire
Tenon saw	f	Scie à tenon
Terminal	f	Borne
Terminal/pole	m	Pôle
Termite	m	Termite
Terrace	f	Terrasse
Terraced house	f	Maison mitoyenne
Terracotta	f	Terre cuite
Terracotta tile	f	Tuile terre cuite
Test certificate	m	Certificat d'essai
Thatch	m	Chaume
Thatched cottage	f	Chaumière/maison à toit de chaume
Thatched roof	m	Toit de chaume
Thermal	adj	Thermique
Thermal insulation	f	Isolation thermique
Thermal energy	f	Energie thermique
Thermostat	m	Thermostat
Thermostatic mixer tap	m	Mitigeur thermostatique
Thermostatic radiator valve/tap	m	Robinet thermostatique
Thickness	f	Epaisseur
Thinner	m	Diluant
Thread (screw/bolt)	m	Filet
Three-phase current	m	Courant triphasé
Three-way adaptor	f	Prise triple
Tightening/clamping	m	Serrage
Tile	m	Carreau
Tile adhesive	f/m	Colle à carreaux/mortier-colle
Tile cutters	m/f	Coupe-carreaux/carrelette
Tile saw	f	Scie à carrelage
Tile scorer	f	Griffe
Tile spacer	m	Croisillon
Tile (to)	verb	Carreler
Tiled roof	m	Toit de tuiles
Tiling	m	Carrelage
Timber	m	Bois
Timber framework	f	Bois de charpente
Timber shake/flaw	f	Gerçure
Timber yard	m	Chantier de bois
Time period	m	Délai
Timer/time switch	f	Minuterie
Tinware	mpl	Articles en fer-blanc
Tin (plate)	m	Fer-blanc
Toggle switch	m	Interrupteur à bascule
Toilet bowl	f	Cuvette
Toilet mechanism	m	Mécanisme de WC
Toilet/cloakroom	m	Cabinet de toilette
Tone	m	Ton
Tongue-and-groove	fpl	Planches à rainure et languette
Tool	m	Outil
Tool kit	f	Trousse à outils
Toolbox	m	Coffre à outils
Touch up the paintwork (to)	verb	Faire des raccords de peinture

Glossary

English		French
Towel radiator	m	Sèche-serviette
Towel rail	m	Porte-serviette
Town	f	Ville
Town centre	m	Centre ville
Town gas	m	Gaz de ville
Town gas heating	m	Chauffage au gaz de ville
Town hall	f	Mairie/hôtel de ville
Town planning	m	Urbanisme
Town planning department	m	Service d'urbanisme
Trade directory	m	Répertoire des métiers
Trade reference	f	Référence commerciale
Trade/occupation	m	Métier
Tradesman	m	Artisan
Trading licence	f	Carte de commerce
Transfer/credit transfer	m	Virement
Transformer	m	Transformateur
Translate (to)	verb	Traduire
Translation	f	Traduction
Translator	m	Traducteur
Transom	f	Traverse
Treated wood	m	Bois traité
Treatment	m	Traitement
Tree surgery	m	Elagage
Trellis	m	Treillis
Trellis/lattice work	m	Treillage
Trench	f	Tranchée
Trestle	m	Tréteau
Trestle table	m	Table à tréteaux
Triangle	m	Triangle
Triangular	adj	Triangulaire
Trowel	f	Truelle
Tumble drier	m	Sèche-linge
Turpentine	f	Essence de térébenthine
TV licence fee	f	Redevance
Twist bit/drill	m	Mèche hélicoïdale
Two-phase current	m	Courant diphasé
Two-handed hammer	f	Massette
Two-wheeled trolley	m	Diable

U

English		French
U-bend	m	Siphon
Ultrasonic alarm	f	Alarme à ultrasons
Unblock (to)	verb	Déboucher
Under-floor heating	m	Chauffage sous-sol
Under roof covering	f	Sous-toiture
Undercoat	f	Couche de fond/sous-couche
Underfloor heating	m	Plancher chauffant/chauffage par le sol
Underground	adj	Souterrain
Underseal	f	Couche anticorrosion
Unfurnished	adj	Non meublé
Uninhabited	adj	Inhabité
Unseasoned/green timber	m	Bois vert
Urban	adj	Urbain
Use	m	Usage
Utility room	f	Buanderie

V

English		French
Vacuum cleaner	m	Aspirateur
Valuation/expert's report	m	Rapport d'expertise
Value (to)	verb	Expertiser
Valve	m/f/f	Clapet/soupape/vanne
Varnish	m	Vernis
Varnish (to)	verb	Vernir
VAT	m	TVA (Taxe sur la Valeur Ajoutée)
VAT registration number	m	Code assujetti TVA
Vault/vaulted cellar	f	Cave voûtée
Vegetable/kitchen garden	m	Jardin potager
Velux® window	f	Fenêtre de toit Velux®
Velvety	adj	Velouté
Veneer	m	Placage
Veneered	m	Plaqué
Venetian blind	m	Store vénitien

English		French
Vent	m	Orifice
Ventilation	f	Aération / ventilation
Ventilation brick	f	Brique de ventilation
Ventilation shaft	m	Conduit de ventilation
Ventilator	m	Aérateur / ventilateur
Vertical-flow radiator	m	Radiateur vertical
Vibrating sander	f	Ponceuse vibrante
Vice	m	Etau
Video entry-phone	m	Interphone vidéo
View / outlook	f	Vue
Village	m	Village
Vinyl	adj	Vinylique
Visible	adj	Apparent
Voltage (low/high)	f	Tension (basse/haute)
Voltmeter	m	Voltmètre

W

English		French
Walk-in shower	f	Douche à l'italienne
Wall	m	Mur
Wall in (to)	verb	Murer
Wall lamp	f	Applique
Wall light	f	Lampe murale
Wallpaper	m/f	Papier peint / tapisserie
Wallpaper paste	f	Colle à tapisser
Wallpaper steam stripper	f	Décolleuse (de papier peint)
Wallpaper with no pattern match	m	Papier peint sans raccords
Wall tiles / tiling	f	Faïence
Walnut	m	Noyer
Wardrobe	f	Armoire / penderie
Warm air heating	m	Chauffage à air pulsé
Warm colours	fpl	Couleurs chaudes
Warning indicator	f	Lampe témoin
Warning light	f	Alarme lumineuse
Warped	adj	Voilé
Washable	adj	Lavable
Washable (wallpaper, etc.)	adj	Lessivage
Washer	f	Rondelle
Washing	m	Lavage
Washing machine	m/f	Lave-linge / machine à laver
Waste disposal unit	m	Broyeur d'ordures
Waste water	fpl	Eaux usées
Water	f	Eau
Water damage	mpl	Dégâts des eaux
Water filter	m	Filtre d'eau
Water heater	m	Chauffe-eau / chauffe-bain
Water infiltration	f	Infiltration d'eau
Water leak	f	Fuite d'eau
Water main	f	Conduite principale
Water meter	m	Compteur d'eau
Water mill	m	Moulin à eau
Water pipe	f	Conduite d'eau
Water pressure gauge	m	Manomètre de pression d'eau
Water return valve	f	Vanne de retour d'eau
Water softener	m	Adoucisseur
Water softener salt	m	Sel régénérant
Water supply	f	Alimentation d'eau
Waterproof	adj	Hydrofuge / imperméable
Waterproof (to)	verb	Hydrofuger
Waterproofing	f	Imperméabilisation
Watertight	adj	Etanche
Watertightness	f	Etanchéité
Watertight strip-light	f	Réglette étanche
Wax polish	f	Cire
Wealth	m	Patrimoine
Wealth tax	m	Impôt sur les grandes fortunes
Weather-boarding	m	Bardage
Weather vane	f	Girouette
Wedge	f/m	Cale / coin
Weld (to)	verb	Souder
Welder	m	Soudeur
Welder's mask	m	Masque protecteur pour la soudure
Welding machine	f	Soudeuse
Well	m	Puits
Wet rot	f	Moisissure / pourriture humide
Wheelbarrow	f	Brouette
Whirlpool bath	f	Baignoire balnéo
White	adj	Blanc
White spirit	m	White spirit

Whitewash (to)	verb	Blanchir à la chaux	Wood saw	f	Scie à bois
Width	f	Largeur	Wood screw	f	Vis à bois
Will	m	Testament	Wood varnish	m	Vernis à bois
Wind turbine	f	Eolienne	Wooden furniture	m	Meubles en bois
Windmill	m	Moulin à vent	Wooden panelling	m	Lambris
Window	f	Fenêtre	Wood preservative	m	Xylophène®
Window catch	f	Espagnolette	Wood stain	f	Lasure
Window frame	m	Châssis de fenêtre	Woodshed	m	Bûcher
Window ledge	m	Appui de fenêtre	Woodwork	f/m	Boiserie/travail du bois
Window pane/glass	m/f	Carreau/vitre			
Window sill	m	Rebord/tablette de fenêtre	Woodworm	m	Ver du bois
			Work	m	Ouvrage
Wine maker	m	Vigneron	Work bench	m	Etabli
Wing bolt	m	Boulon à oreilles	Work top	m	Plan de travail
Wing nut	m	Ecrou à oreilles	Worker in mosaic	f	Mosaïste
Wire	m	Fil	Workforce	f	Main-d'œuvre
Wire brush	f	Brosse métallique	Working capital	m	Fonds de roulement
Wire mesh	m	Grillage	Workman	m	Ouvrier
Wire (to)	verb	Faire l'installation électrique	Workshop	m	Atelier
			Worm eaten	adj	Vermoulu
Wire wool	f	Paille de fer	Write a cheque (to)	verb	Faire un chèque
Wirecutters	fpl	Cisailles pour câble	Wrought-iron gate	f	Grille en ferronnerie
Without odour	f	Sans odeur	Wrought ironwork	f	Ferronnerie/fer forgé
Without solder	f	Sans soudure			
Wood	m	Bois			
Wood (species)	f	Essence	**Y**		
Wood-burning boiler	f	Chaudière au bois	Yellow	adj	Jaune
			Yellow Pages	fpl	*Pages Jaune*
Wood-burning stove	m	Poêle à bois	**Z**		
Wood-burning stove (built-in)	m	Insert de cheminée	Zero voltage	f	Tension nulle
Wood chisel	m	Ciseau à bois	Zinc	m	Zinc
Wood glue	f	Colle à bois	Zinc flashing	m	Revêtement de zinc
Wood panel	m	Panneau à bois	Zinc items	m	Zinguerie
Wood preservative	m	Xylophène®	Zinc worker	m	Zingueur

Index

after-sales service 46, 84
ANAH (Agence Nationale de
    l'Habitat) 97, 125
ANIL (Agence Nationale pour
    l'Information sur le
    Logement) 98, 113, 125
apartments 88–89
APE (Activité Principale
    Exercée) 56–58
apprenticeship 13
architect 23, 31
    Architecte des Bâtiments de
        France (ABF) 77
    employing 23
    planning permission 76
    professional association 31
artisan 12–34, 51–60
    bankruptcy/receivership 103
    contacting 39–40
    definition 12
    failure to carry out the work
        101–113
    finding the right one 125–130
        CAPEB 28
        cold calling 30
        DIY stores 28
        EDF & GDF 28
        equipment suppliers 28
        exhibitions 28
        FFB 28
        Internet 28
        local press 28
        other artisans 26
        outdoor advertising 27
        Qualibat 29
        using an intermediary 29
        word-of-mouth 25
        Yellow Pages (Pages
            Jaunes) 29
    legal registration 52
    maître artisan 12
    meeting 41–42
    points to check 45–47
    taking delivery of the work
        103–104
bankruptcy of artisan 103
black economy 52
    penalties for using 52
    reporting illegal working
        59–60

boiler maintenance 46, 83
bricklayer 19
    glossary, SOS phrases 140
builder 13, 19
    British builders 25, 59
building industry statistics 23
cabinet maker 16
    glossary 138
capital gains tax 99
carpenter 19
    glossary, SOS phrases 142
carreleur 14
    glossary 135
CAUE (Conseils d'Architecture,
    d'Urbanisme et de
    l'Environnement) 24
certificat d'urbanisme 69
CESU (Chèque emploi service
    universel) 66
Chamber of Trade (Chambre des
    Métiers) 12, 26
    carte d'identification 52,
        54–55, 59
    directory 12, 26
charpentier 19
    glossary, SOS phrases 142
chauffagiste 15
    glossary, SOS phrases 135
cheque
    paying by 62
    receipt of payment 64
    stopping 63
chimney sweeping 15, 84
consumer rights 109
contrat d'entreprise 39
    retenue de garantie 39
conversion tables 130–133
    area 130
    capacity 131
    length 130
    metric prefixes 133
    nail sizes 132–133
    paint brushes 132
    sheet glass 132
    temperature 132
    volume 131
    weight 130–131
co-ownership properties 88–89
couvreur 15
    glossary, SOS phrases 137

dates 122–123
déclaration préalable 70–71
deposits 62
devis 35–50, 61–66
    accepting 37
    after acceptance 64
    cooling-off period 39, 47
    language 39
    legalities 35
    penalties 39, 48
    selecting an estimate 61
    understanding 47
directions to your house in
    French 40, 118–119
ébéniste 16
    glossary 138
EDF (Electricité de France) 17, 98
electrician (électricien) 16
    glossary, SOS phrases 138
energy saving measures 83,
    93–94
entreprise artisanale 13
entreprise générale de bâtiment
    23, 39, 59
estimate see devis
ex-directory options 30
GDF (Gaz de France) 21, 98
general building company 23,
    39, 59
gros œuvre 92
guarantees 36
guarantees, contractual 107
guarantees, legal 56, 104–108
    assurance dommages-
        ouvrages 108
    making a claim 106–108
    public liability (responsabilité
        civile) 107
    ten-year guarantee (assurance
        décennale) 104–105
heating engineer 15
    glossary, SOS phrases 135
home improvement grants 97–99
    gîtes & chambres d'hôtes 98
    historic properties 97
home improvement loans 98
Internet 28
    caution when using 10
    planning permission forms 73
    use of email 40

192 Index

invoice
  paying 62
  contesting 63
joiner 20
  glossary, SOS phrases 142
larger building projects 39
legal system 109–114
  avocat 111
  courts 110
  huissier 111–113
  independent advice 114
  legal aid 113
  notaire 110–111
  taking action 112–114
letters
  contesting an invoice 63
  contesting planning refusal 79, 80
  requesting access to neighbour's land 87
  requesting artisan to complete the work 102
  requesting artisan to repair faults 108
  writing a letter in French 119
local taxes 82
locksmith 22
  glossary, SOS phrases 149
maçon (bricklayer) 19
  glossary, SOS phrases 140
maintenance contracts 36, 46, 84
maître d'œuvre/maître d'ouvrage 24
menuisier 19
  glossary, SOS phrases 142
metal worker (métallier) 22
  glossary, SOS phrases 149
NAF see APE
neighbours 86–88
  access to property 86
  neighbours' rights 86
numbers (nombres) 120–122
painter/decorator (peintre) 20
  glossary 144
permis de construire 71–72
permis de démolir 73
planning permission 67–82
  certificat d'urbanisme 69
  completion of the project 82
  COS (coefficient d'occupation des sols) 69

DDE (Direction départementale de l'équipement) 67
déclaration préalable 70–71
local planning department 67
local regulations 67
  carte communale 67
  PLU/POS 67, 69
making an application 73–77
  bordereau de dépôt des pièces jointes 76
  land registry reference 76
  plans required 77
  receipt (récépissé) 77
  summary of planning application forms 78
permis de construire 71–72
permis de démolir 73
planning approval 79
  contesting the decision 79–80
  modifications to the plans 81
  starting the work 81
  what happens next 80
planning tax 78
property in conservation areas 77
summary of requirements 74
transfer 82
work not requiring authorization 69–70
plasterer (plâtrier) 21
  glossary, SOS phrases 146
plumber (plombier) 21
  glossary, SOS phrases 146
product liability 109
professional accreditations 31
  AB5 31
  CAPEB 31
  PG (Professionnel du Gaz) 32
  PMG (Professionnel Maintenance Gaz) 32
  Quali'bois 33
  Quali'Eau 34
  Quali'Pv 33
  Quali'sol 33
  Qualibat 31
  Qualifelec 31
  Qualifioul 32
pronunciation of French 116

properties on estates 89
proposition de prix see devis
Qualigaz 21
ramonage 15, 84
RCS (Registre du Commerce et des Sociétés) 13, 53
receivership of artisan 103
réception des travaux 103–104
rental property 90
Répertoire des Métiers 12, 26, 52–53
roofer 15
  glossary, SOS phrases 137
second œuvre 92
septic tanks 85–86
serrurier 22
  glossary, SOS phrases 149
SIREN / SIRET 53–56
smaller projects 66
stage payments 62
surface area, SHOB & SHON 68
swimming pools
  planning permission 71, 72, 74
  regulations 84–85
tax credits 66, 92–97
  energy conservation 93–94
  health & safety measures 96
  making a claim 96–97
telephoning in French 40, 116–118
tiler 14
  glossary 135
time (l'heure) 123–124
useful words & phrases 124
VAT 91–93
vocational qualifications 13
websites
  checking SIRET numbers 53, 56, 127
  DIY & other chain stores 128
  finding an artisan 28, 126
  French language 128
  French life 128
  government & other official information 125
  home improvement 127
  miscellaneous 129
  trade associations 126
writing a letter in French 119–125